Popperfoto

Helicopters at War

Hamlyn

LONDON · NEW YORK · SYDNEY · TORONTO

in association with Phoebus

Written by Bill Gunston
Illustrated by John Batchelor
Edited by Christy Campbell
Designed by Jeff Gurney and David Harper

Published 1977 by
The Hamlyn Publishing Group Limited
London · New York · Sydney · Toronto
Astronaut House, Feltham, Middlesex,
England

ISBN 0 600 34530 0

Made and printed in Great Britain by
Waterlow (Dunstable) Limited

Bill Gunston is an aviation historian who has spent many years flying and writing about all types of aircraft. With the experience of a flying instructor behind him, he joined the editorial staff of Flight International in 1951 and was appointed Technical Editor in April 1955. In 1964 he moved on to become the Technology Editor of Science Journal until in December 1970 he became a freelance writer and editor. As well as countless articles he has written 27 books for aerospace publishers throughout the English-speaking world. He is Assistant Compiler of Jane's All the World's Aircraft, and European Editor of the Australian journal Aircraft.

John Batchelor, after serving in the RAF, worked in the technical publications departments of several British aircraft firms, and went on to contribute on a freelance basis to many technical magazines. Since then his work for Purnell's History of the World Wars Specials has established him as one of the most outstanding artists in his field.

Westland/Aérospatiale Puma flies over the Atlantic shores of Belize

MOD

ABOUT THIS BOOK

Compared with the conventional aeroplane, the helicopter as we know it today is a modern invention. Although Leonardo da Vinci had sketched a man-carrying 'air gyroscope' around 1500, it was not until after the Second World War that this most versatile aircraft came into general use throughout the world.

The long delay in realising Leonardo's dream was not for want of trying. In fact a successful model helicopter was first made in 1784 by two Frenchmen, and after over a century of experimentation it was in France that the first man-carrying rotorcraft rose some two feet off the ground in 1907. The autogyro was a dead end, although a fascinating one; however designers in Germany and the United States had almost perfected practical true helicopters by the outbreak of the Second World War.

After the war, development was rapid in the West and in Russia, producing models that have since enjoyed tremendous commercial and military success. In size, too, modern helicopters range from the tiny Westland Wisp to the enormous Russian Mi-12, capable of lifting up to 40 tons.

This readable history is illustrated throughout by John Batchelor, whose excellent drawings combine with a lavish use of photographs to show all the major rotorcraft, from the first frail and primitive designs to the most advanced combat machines of today.

CONTENTS

A Scout helicopter of 655 Squadron AAC firing an SS.11 anti-tank missile at Suffield, Canada.

MOD

Two Thousand Years of Vertical Takeoff

GETTING OFF THE GROUND

Watching a sycamore seed spiralling earthwards, man was presented with an alternative means of achieving flight other than by slavish copying of the birds. Just as a whirling aerofoil could break a seed's descent, so power would reverse the process – a machine could be made which would rise vertically from the ground.

Since the Chinese first played with simple rotary wing toys 2000 years ago the principle of vertical takeoff was understood. Then, in the early years of the twentieth century a lightweight power source appeared in the shape of the internal combustion engine. The primitive machines which hopped spasmodically from the ground were virtually uncontrollable – but once these problems were overcome, with the helicopter man could at last outdo the birds in their own element . . .

By the beginning of the twentieth century everyone was familiar with the concept of the flying machine. The term could mean almost anything, but almost always it referred to what today we call an aeroplane, or airplane. Nearly all modern 'flying machines' are of this type. They are the most efficient way of flying from A to B, but they suffer from the fact that they cannot slow down and hover. Even to get into the air at all they have to accelerate forward along the ground, until the airflow over their wings is moving past fast enough to bear their weight.

Thousands of years ago men could only dream of flight. It is unlikely that a single one of those dreamers ever thought of anything like today's aeroplanes, because not many 'fixed-wing' animals exist in nature. On the contrary, most early dreams of flight were of men flapping wings like birds. If wings are flapped hard enough, and if they are sufficiently light and efficient, they can generate enough lift for flying with no forward run at all. They can also allow some birds to hover.

It so happens that not one of man's many attempts to build an ornithopter – a flapping-wing aircraft – has ever succeeded. But man has gone one better than the birds with another class of machine whose only counterpart in nature is certain seeds: the rotorcraft, or rotary-wing machine. There are several species in this big category, but the most important is the helicopter.

Before outlining the long and varied history of these devices, it is important to stand back for a moment, and compare them with the fixed-wing aeroplane. There is one obvious way in which rotorcraft are better: most of them can take off straight up, hover motionless, move sideways or backwards and land straight down again. Such machines are today often classed as VTOL (Vertical TakeOff and Landing) aircraft. There are several kinds of mission where VTOL capability is absolutely essential, and many more where it is extremely useful. However, it is invariably attained at the price of increased costs or reduced flight performance.

Leonardo da Vinci's design for an 'air gyroscope' with a rim made of iron wire and the linen lifting surfaces made 'airtight with starch'

Lift systems

One of the fundamental factors affecting the flight efficiency of all aircraft other than balloons and airships is the amount of airflow acted upon by its lift system. The most efficient aircraft act on a very large airflow but deflect it downwards only very gently. Examples of which are the high-performance sailplane and man-powered aircraft, with very large, very slender wings. Ordinary aeroplanes come next, with long-span machines being generally more efficient than stubby-winged fighters (whose shape is dictated by considerations of speed and strength). Then come the helicopters and other rotary-winged machines, whose long rotor blades behave literally as wings that whirl round a central axis. Less efficient still are the VTOL aircraft supported by fans and jets – though if these also have fixed wings then they are much more efficient in translational flight, or flying from one place to another. Least efficient of all are ballistic missiles and space rockets that rise on a violently accelerated column of hot gas, though they come into their own at hypersonic speeds outside the atmosphere.

This means that to carry goods or passengers from one place to another a helicopter has to burn more fuel than an aeroplane. Nor can it fly very fast, though today's helicopters cruising at 150 to 200 mph are as fast as equivalent lightplanes and many business and executive aeroplanes. In carrying people and cargo a helicopter can actually make better time than an aeroplane over short distances, especially if it can fly a direct route instead of having to go to inconvenient airports. But when it comes to carrying hundreds of people for thousands of miles the helicopter has no chance of competing with the speed and economy of the aeroplane. In the military field, again, the helicopter cannot quite equal the sheer speed and other capabilities of the latest aeroplanes. But that still leaves a vast range of tasks that, for all its noise, inefficiency and high costs, the helicopter can do better than anything else.

A second important species of rotorcraft is the autogyro, which became a practical proposition earlier than the helicopter, though there are not many flying today. The basic difference between the two categories is that a helicopter has its engine geared to the main lifting rotor (or rotors). The rotor blades are driven round and beat the air downwards, lifting the helicopter and pulling it in the direction it needs to go.

Leonardo da Vinci c. 1500
Drawing based on Leonardo's sketch (opposite). Although obsessed with the flapping flight of birds, Leonardo got near the airscrew and modern flight with this design powered by a hand windlass. He experimented with rulers 'whirling most rapidly through the air so that you will find your arm borne in the same direction and along the same axis as the plane of the ruler'

The autogyro, on the other hand, has a power-driven propeller that pulls it along, just as in an aeroplane, while the lifting rotor freewheels and is driven round by the action of the air flowing back and up past the blades. An autogyro is something of a cross between a helicopter and an aeroplane.

Modern rotorcraft, both autogyros and helicopters, are far more complicated than they may appear. They are based upon extremely complex aerodynamics, with airflows that almost defy exact description. And their mechanical design is also complicated, with long blades that bend and twist and which in most designs are arranged to hinge to and fro, flap up and down and twist in their sockets. In contrast the very earliest helicopter-like devices were simple toys. They were probably inspired by the whirling seeds of such plants and trees as the sycamore and zenobia, whose 'rotary wings' enable them to be carried on the breeze far from the original parent.

At least 2000 years ago the Chinese were playing with simple rotary-wing toys, with two twisted blades sliding freely on a vertical rod. In one version the rod itself forms a twisted helix, and the rotor is swiftly catapulted up, spinning as it goes. In another form the rotor blades are mounted on a small drum on which thread is wound. Pulling the thread spins the rotor, which climbs away by itself. By 1800 such toys were common in Western Europe, and Sir George Cayley – the so-called 'father of aeronautics' – made some that soared to at least 90 ft above the ground.

Long before Sir George Cayley, visionaries of the Renaissance had begun to dream of mechanical flight in ways other than mere slavish copying of birds, and one of them – Leonardo da Vinci – has left detailed sketches of an 'aerial screw' flying machine. In 1784 the French naturalist Launoy, and his mechanically skilled assistant Bienvenu, constructed an outstanding 'Chinese top' with feathered wings 28 ft across, which delighted and impressed the august Académie des Sciences by swooping and soaring all round their great meeting-chamber. Like many of the best of such devices it had two screws, one at the top of the shaft and the other at the bottom, driven round in opposite directions by a helically wound-up crossbow. By 1828 Vittorio Sarti, an Italian, and Englishman R Mayer were building large machines, and Mayer even tried to fly with himself on board.

A major step forward was accomplished by W H Phillips in 1842. He actually flew a

Launoy and Bienvenu, 1784
This outsize Chinese top consisted of two contra-rotating feathered propellers, one at each end of a shaft. Power was provided by a whalebone bow, tensioned as its string was wound helically around the shaft

Sir George Cayley, 1843
The great aeronautical pioneer, Sir George Cayley, published plans for this 'Aerial Carriage' in 1843. Two contra-rotating propellers placed either side of a boat-like body were for takeoff and hover, with two pusher propellers for forward flight. All it lacked was an adequate lightweight power source

steam-driven model, the first mechanically propelled rotary-wing aircraft ever to fly, other than toys using stored energy. A feature of the Phillips design was that the rotor blades contained pipes from which the steam issued from ejector nozzles at the tips. Such tip-drive rotors have many advantages, and came back into prominence after the Second World War.

In the 1860s vertical-rising rotorcraft became a craze. Every well-to-do child had at least one, and countless adults tried to build improved models, some of which reached the proportions of a modern airliner. Some even got off the ground, driven by bows, coiled springs, stretched rubber, steam, compressed air or groups of watch-springs.

One of the more scientific designers was Alphonse Pénaud, who also worked on fixed-wing aeroplanes. At about the time (1870–72) that he was working, the name helicopter at last came into general use for such devices, from the Greek *helix* (a spiral) and *pteron* (a wing). The name stuck, even though everyone soon gave up trying to build spiral wings; long radial ones worked much better.

In 1900 the German, Karl Zenker, completed building his *Bremen I*, a complicated device with eight lifting rotors and two propellers. It failed to get off the ground. A rival, George Davidson, spent more than 30 years trying to build a vast flying machine with a fixed wing and VTOL lifting rotors, his final Gyropter form of 1911 having 26·83-ft rotors on each side of a double-deck hull containing the steam powerplant. Though almost completed, at Taplow,

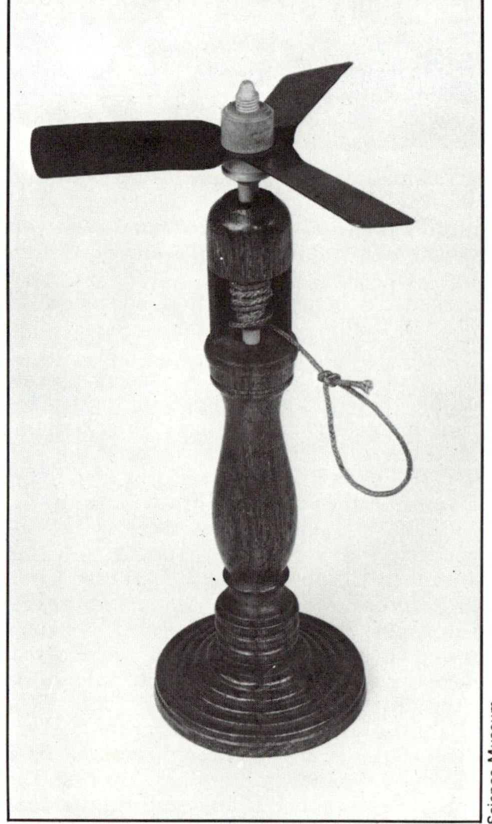

Science Museum

Sir George Cayley made this 'Aerial Top' in 1854, right at the end of his career. The blades are made of tinfoil, the stand of rosewood

Buckinghamshire, the Gyropter never flew either.

More practical advances were being made, however. In 1904 Frenchman Charles Renard described ways of articulating rotor blades to the hub, so that they could pivot in any desired direction. Two years later an Italian, G A Crocco – who was also a pioneer of the hydrofoil boat – patented cyclic pitch control. This is a basic feature of modern helicopters. The lift of a rotor blade depends, within certain limits, on its angular setting to the air. If it is tilted in its socket so that the leading edge rises, it deflects the air down more sharply and gives increased lift; edge-on it may give no lift at all, and if the pitch is made negative it can actually give a downward force.

Crocco saw that if a helicopter was to work properly, with a lifting rotor moving bodily along through the air, the pitch would have to be varied up and down all the time. The 'advancing blade' on one side of the rotor disc would meet the air at its own velocity plus the speed of the helicopter, so it would need a shallow pitch setting. The 'retreating blade' on the other side would have a much lower relative airspeed; in fact, if the speed due to rotation at one point was the same as the forward speed of the helicopter, the net airspeed would be zero. So it would need a very coarse pitch setting. Modern helicopters have cyclic pitch control made variable to enable the rotor to be tilted in the direction the pilot wishes to go. They also have 'collective pitch', which alters the pitch of all blades simultaneously, for rising and descending.

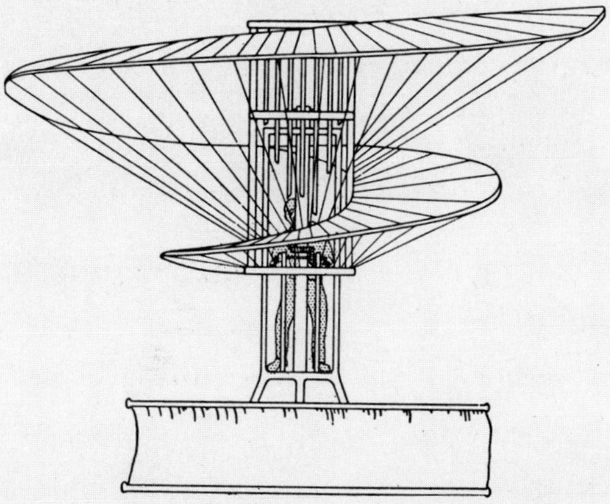

Count Lambertgye, 1818

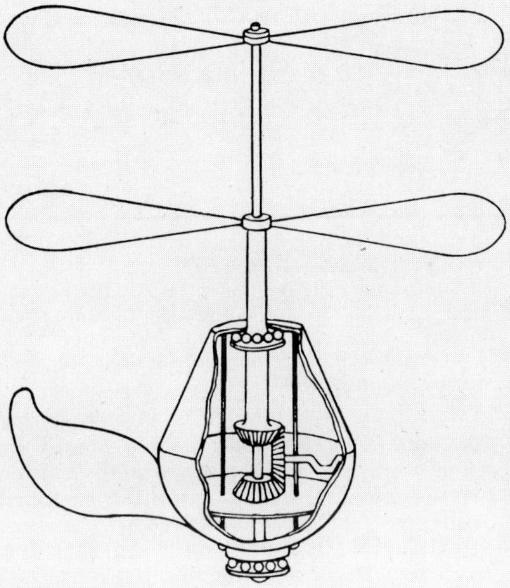

Henry Bright, 1859

Inventor Unknown, 1860

V Sarti, 1828

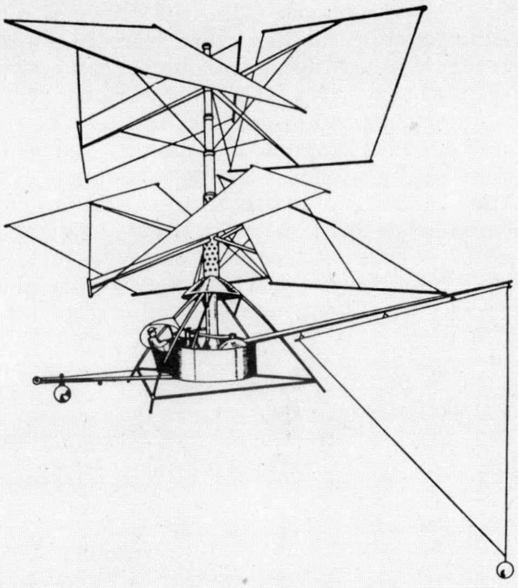

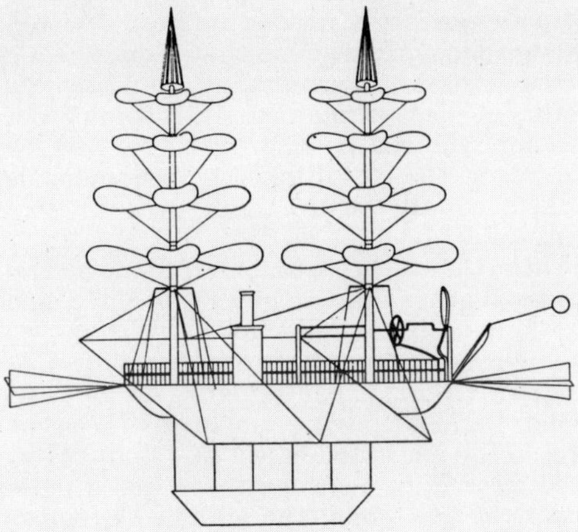

Gabriel de la Laundelle, 1861

Chinese Tops and Flying Galleons

R G Owen, 1885

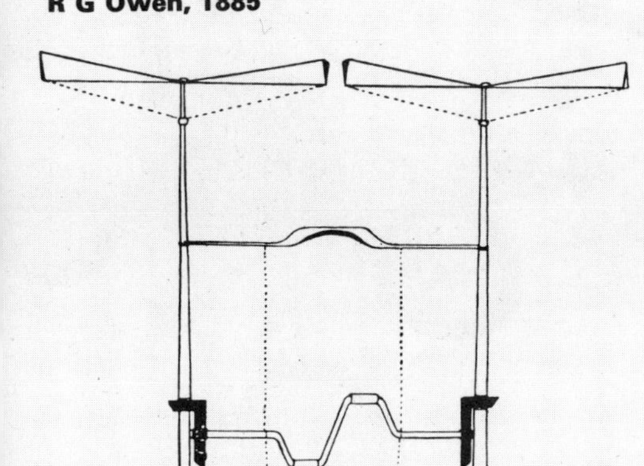

B R Beenen, 1897

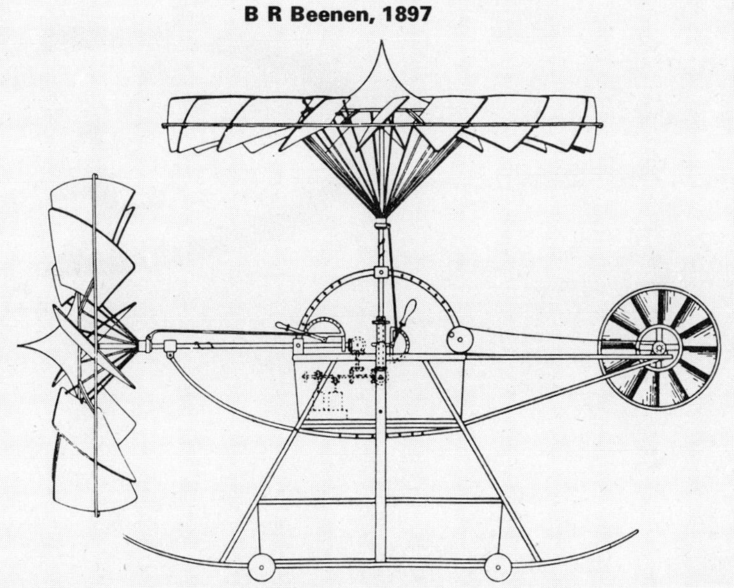

The First To Fly

HOPPERS AND HOVERERS

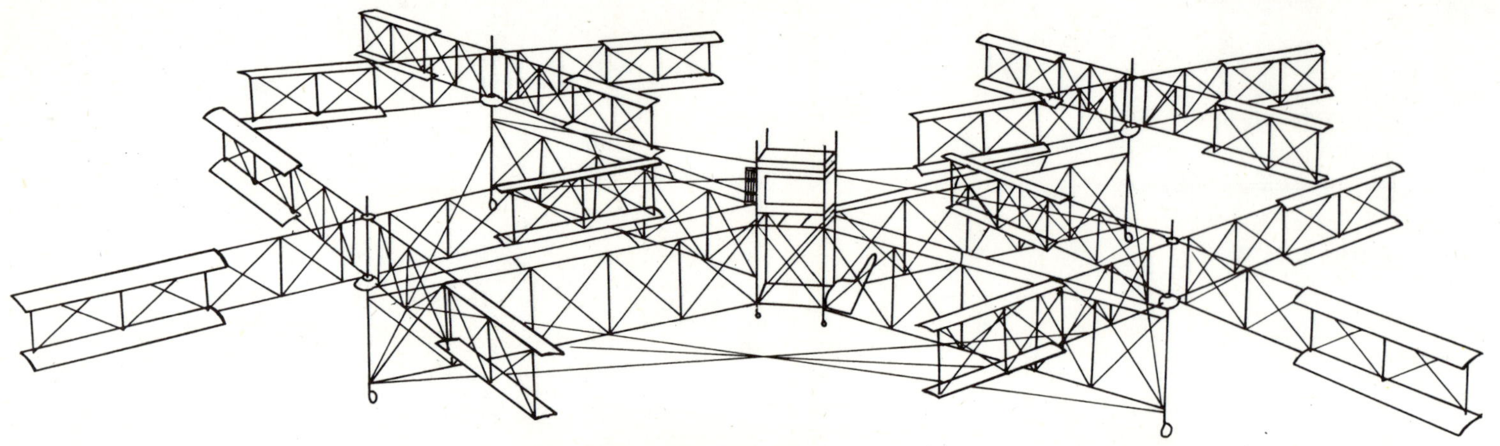

Breguet-Richet No 1, 1907
In September 1907 this machine was the first to raise itself and its pilot in a vertical takeoff using rotating wings. But four helpers had to hold it at arm height, without letting go, so it did not qualify as a free flyer

The first two full-size helicopters ever to fly took to the air in France in the second half of 1907. It was a time of general excitement: automobiles, flying machines, airships and a host of other inventions such as the phonograph, radio and telephone were all new developments. All over Europe and America hopeful inventors were building rotary-winged flying machines, and two showed they knew what they were about.

One team comprised the brothers Louis and Jacques Breguet. Their family had been first in the world of clocks in Louis XVI's time, and with wealth and good technical knowledge behind them they began the story of Breguet aircraft – a story which is still being written. Their first Gyroplane looked like a confused assemblage of ladders, but actually comprised a steel-tube frame carrying a 40-hp Antoinette engine driving four biplane rotors which provided 32 lifting surfaces. Louis preceded the work by exhaustive tests of blade (wing) sections, control methods and the whole mechanical design and contemporary aerodynamic theory of the helicopter. In this respect he followed the methodical approach of the Wright Brothers – not then generally known in Europe – and, like them, he achieved his objective.

With helper Volumard at the controls, Gyroplane No 1 was first flown at Douai on 19 September 1907 (many reports claim it was on 24 August, but the later date is the accepted one). Despite its laden weight of 578 kg (about 1275 lb) the great device lifted smoothly off the ground to a height of 2 ft, held steady by an assistant on each of the four arms. On 29 September the flying height was increased to 5 ft. The four helpers were still needed to keep control, though most of the time they were pulling downwards so there was no doubting the ability of the Gyroplane to fly. It was a great accomplishment by the brothers, and by Professor Charles Richet whose name is linked equally with their own in this venture.

Unfortunately this first Gyroplane had no controls other than an engine throttle, and the four assistants did not dare let go. So the helicopter flown by loner Paul Cornu, at Coquainvilliers, near Lisieux, on 13 November 1907, can fairly claim to have been the first in the world to make a free flight. Powered by a 24-hp Antoinette, it was a more practical job than the clumsy Breguet-Richet, but Cornu soon had to give up. Like his rivals, he had preceded his big machine with careful research and model flights, and used front and rear belt-driven rotors fitted with broad fabric-skinned blades. He added front and rear control planes, but these were not very effective and he knew it would be beyond his means to try to go further. It was his bad luck that his efforts came just as the attention of the public had become focused on fixed-wing aeroplanes and the French visit of Wilbur Wright; otherwise he might have been able to gain support for a more controllable machine.

In 1908 J Robertson Porter patented his 'turbine machine', which combined features of the helicopter and hovercraft. In the United States Wilbur R Kimball tried to fly a machine with a 40-hp engine. The following year a young Russian began flight attempts with a helicopter handicapped by having only 25 hp. In many ways it looked promising, and its contra-rotating rotors were outstandingly good, but it just failed to rise. An improved example built in 1910 rose off the ground with its creator standing beside it working the throttle, but it could not lift him as well. Discouraged, he turned his attention to aeroplanes, and within a year was building by far the biggest and most powerful aeroplane the world had then seen. It was to be nearly 30 years before his name would be publicly linked with helicopters, yet today he is generally regarded as the man who made the modern helicopter possible: Igor Sikorsky.

He was not the only bright young would-be rotorcraft aviator in Czarist Russia. K A Antonov built a rather similar co-axial helicopter, the Helikoplan of 1910, and in 1911 an absolutely outstanding machine was built by Boris N Yuriev. To an incredible degree Yuriev's helicopter showed what a modern helicopter engineer would do if he were to be transported 65 years back into the past, and it is a pity so little is known of how this obviously brilliant Russian accomplished his design.

The fundamental feature that distinguished it from all its contemporaries was that it had a single lifting rotor belt-driven by a 70-hp Gnome rotary. The engine

Pescara No 4, 1925
The most successful helicopter built by the Spanish pioneer Marquis Raul Pateras de Pescara had 16 lifting surfaces on two rotors with a pusher propeller that could be engaged as desired – all powered by a 40 hp Salmson engine

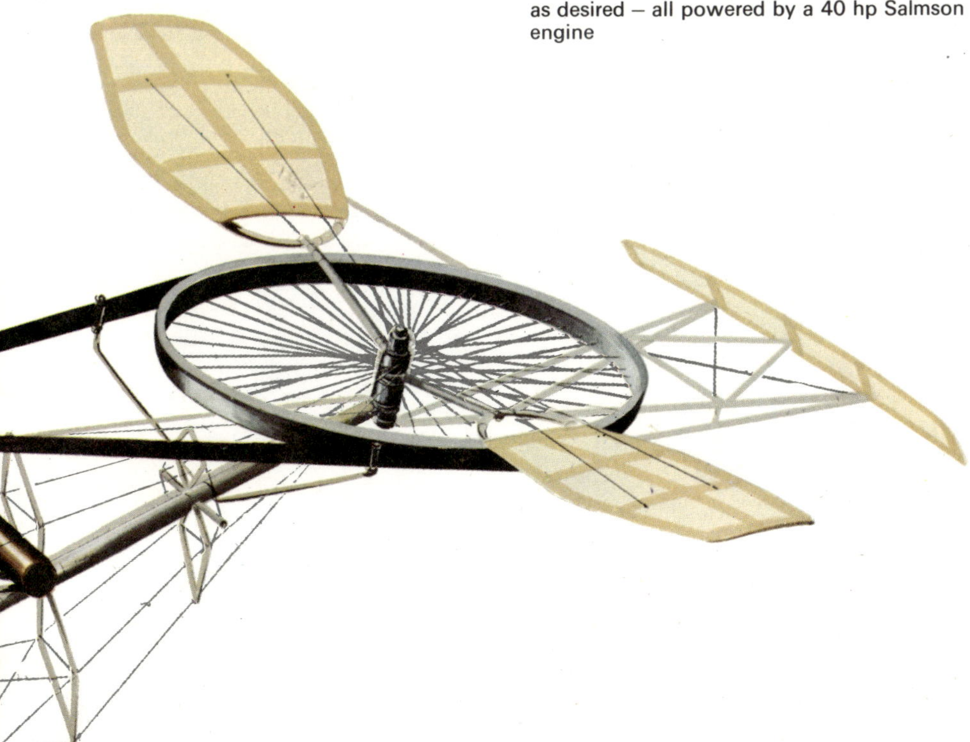

Cornu, 1907
On 13 November 1907, this machine with its inventor as pilot, rose to a height of one foot and remained airborne for about 20 seconds in free flight
Engine: 24 hp Antoinette *Weight fully loaded:* 573 lb

Oemichen, 1924
'Helicopter No 2' had 4 rotors and 8 stabilising propellers powered by a single 120 hp Le Rhône

was mounted with crankshaft vertical and connected by a second belt to the anti-torque tail rotor. This layout has many faults, but is used in about nine out of every ten modern helicopters. Moreover, Yuriev's helicopter was a neat job, and weighed only 860 lb. We do not know if this commendable machine ever flew.

In the following year, 1912, the Dane J C Ellehammer followed up his decade of immense success with various aeroplanes by flying a very significant helicopter. Powered by one of his own 36-hp air-cooled radials, Ellehammer's rotor system comprised two 20-ft rings, the lower one covered with fabric, rotating in opposite directions. Around the outer periphery of each ring were six 'wings', extending out about 5 ft. The significant feature was their ability to vary their pitch, and the pilot could control both the gross lift and the direction in which it acted by means of a cyclic pitch control. On 12 September 1912 Crown Prince Axel himself certified that the 'screw plane' had flown entirely under its own power, but financial problems eventually forced Ellehammer to give up, the last straw being a takeoff crash which wrecked the machine in 1916.

This was tough on the Dane, because workers elsewhere were continuing to build bigger and better helicopters. In the United States Henry Berliner, subsequently to become one of the best-known builders of light planes, helped his father construct reasonably successful helicopters from 1922 to 1926. In Spain the Marquis de Pescara built his first coaxial machine in 1919, flew a second in 1921 and finally achieved flights of up to ten minutes' duration with No 3, completed in late 1923. Though massive and ungainly, Pescara No 3 is the first helicopter that actually went where it was told, and it did so at speeds of up to 8 mph. Unlike most previous machines it had a modern articulated rotor, with both cyclic and collective pitch control. The pilot steered the aircraft by tilting the rotor disc by the cyclic control, and Pescara even made provision for autorotative descent in the event of engine failure. In this, the free-wheeling machine falls, keeping the rotor spinning. Near the ground the pilot suddenly increases pitch with the collective control, using the stored energy in the rotor to arrest the descent and allow a gentle landing.

Pescara's later helicopter work was done in France, where he had as direct rival Etienne Oehmichen of the Peugeot car

Etienne Oemichen's helicopter gets off the ground. On 11 November 1922, the Peugeot engineer's machine succeeded in flying 60 metres. Finally in May 1924 he completed the first 1 kilometre closed-circuit flight by a helicopter in 7 minutes 40 seconds. On this flight Oemichen was airborne for about 14 minutes

Davidson Gyropter
George Louis Outram Davidson spent thousands of pounds, published hundreds of pamphlets and patents, and the years 1896–1912 trying to get this VTOL airliner to fly. Two 27 ft 8 in fans enclosed in biplane wings provided lift, and they would tilt for forward flight. Power was provided by two 50 hp Stanley steam engines buried in the 60 ft-long body. On 6 May 1908, at Denver, Colorado, the Gyropter staggered into the air but fell in ruins when the engine blew up

company. Oehmichen caused a few smiles by adding a small balloon to his first machine in 1920, though this was a sensible way of adding lift and stability to an underpowered helicopter. His No 2, powered first by a 120-hp Le Rhône and then by a 180-hp Gnome rotary engine, looked grotesque and almost ridiculous with its four great rotors and eight small propellers, scattered about over its girder frame and facing in seemingly arbitrary directions. But in fact it was well thought out, and each propeller had a definite role to play in stabilizing the machine or moving it along. By 1924 Oehmichen was making quite good flights, and he accomplished the world's first helicopter closed-circuit flight of one kilometre in May 1924 during a 14-minute flight covering about twice this distance.

Another worker who tried to build a useful helicopter just after the First World War was Professor George de Bothezat. He was one of the many Russians who decided to leave after the October Revolution of 1917 and seek a new life in the West. Among these men were many Russian scientists and teachers, including three of the greatest pioneers of the helicopter. De Bothezat was a caricature of the Russian emigré scientists, huge and with a mighty beard and spectacles, wildly excitable and constantly bad-tempered. So continually did he harangue the US Army Air Service that they gave him $20,000 and let him build a helicopter at McCook Field. He had made fantastically extravagant claims, and nobody quite believed he could make good on them, but day and night his team hammered away under the most intense security, de Bothezat rushing out and screaming at any pilot who tried to fly over the site.

Eventually the screens were removed, to reveal a colossal machine with four rotors disposed as in the helicopters of Breguet and Oehmichen – but even bigger. It measured roughly 65 ft each way, and the pilot sat in the centre near the 180-hp engine. In December 1922 Major Bane began trials, and before long was hovering clear of the ground. Eventually he was threshing about, apparently under control, at a height of 10 ft. In April 1923 the monster hovered well off the ground while carrying the pilot and three men hanging on to its extremities. Though this was all it could accomplish, no other rotorcraft did as much for nearly 20 more years, apart from autogyros.

Davidson Gyropter, plan

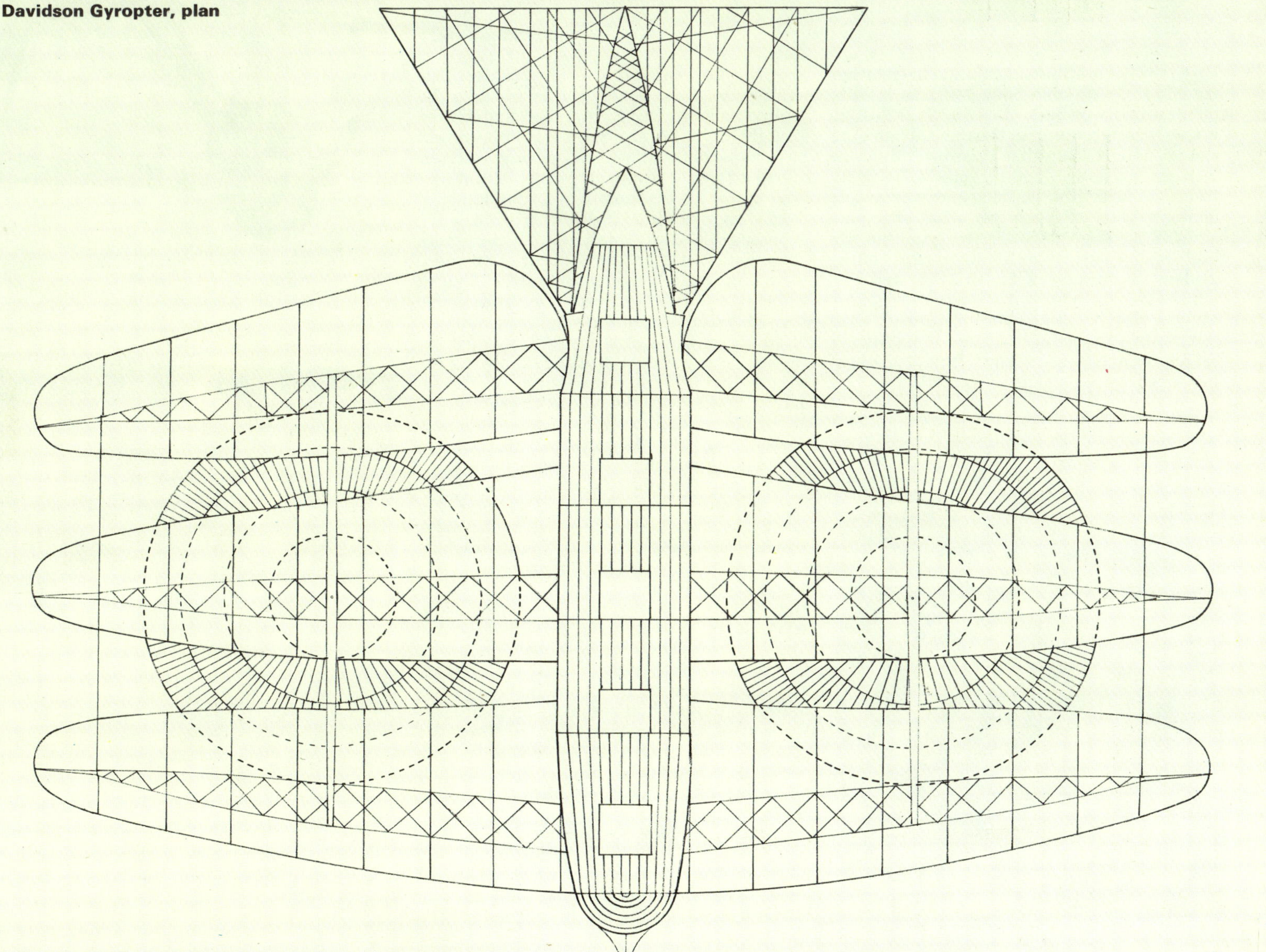

Cierva and the Autogyros

Up to this time all rotorcraft had been either unable to fly or such poor performers as to be practically useless. Clearly, their designers were still groping in the dark. Then onto the scene came another Spaniard, Juan de la Cierva. He was young, handsome, well-to-do, technically skilled and absolutely dedicated to overcoming what he considered the fatal flaw of the aeroplane. He had made surprisingly successful hang-gliders at the age of 14, in 1910, and two years later he rebuilt a wrecked aeroplane and turned it into a better aircraft than before. In 1919 he built a huge 14-passenger transport aeroplane with 80-ft wings, which he hoped would go into production for the Spanish government, but a reckless ex-fighter pilot made a violent turn too near the ground and wrecked it. It stalled and flicked straight into the ground, as anyone might have expected; but why? Cierva was determined to see if rotating wings might not offer a way of overcoming the tendency of fixed-wing machines to stall and spin.

Whereas previous helicopter designers had all started with the concept of powered lifting rotors, or 'vertical propellers', Cierva adopted a totally different approach. He started with an aeroplane, and simply fitted a new style of wing that was free to rotate. To avoid ever stalling, the wing (or wings) had to keep revolving. Then, no matter how slowly the whole aircraft might go, there would always be adequate air-speed over the wing surfaces. Cierva believed he could build what he called an Autogiro (he registered the name of the first and most common form of autogyro): a safe flying machine in which the lifting rotor was kept spinning by air flowing through it.

Juan de la Cierva, the Spanish rotorcraft pioneer and inventor of the Autogiro, at the controls of one of his later machines

The Flapping Hinge

His first two prototypes, converted from wartime fixed-wing machines, would not fly. No 3 flew but was dangerously unstable. Cierva was bright and perceptive, however, and the Spanish government supported him with money and research facilities. By the end of 1921 he had tracked down the problem and solved it by designing an articulated rotor with hinged blades. Each blade had a drag hinge, enabling it to swing slightly ahead or to the rear. Even more important, it had a flapping hinge, and could hinge slightly up, though it was normally kept spread out by centrifugal force. The flapping hinges enabled the blades to even out the lift on each side of the aircraft, the advancing blade being allowed to rise and the retreating blade to fall. Thus, the rotor disc appeared to lean backwards, the tips of the blades being highest in front and lowest at the rear.

Cierva's early rotors often had blades of a distinctive form. The inner part was a plain spar and the blade then increased in chord to a short parallel portion and finally tapered off to the rounded tip. The covering was of fabric, and rotor speed was quite slow – it was easy to watch any particular blade in flight (he tried rotors with three, four and five blades). Metal ties linked the blades just short of the mid-span point, and the complete assembly weighed about three-quarters as much as an equivalent fixed wing. The rotor was freely pivoted on a strong pylon carried on the fuselage.

Cierva's first prototypes were all modified aeroplanes, to save money. No 4, designated C 4, was based on a wartime Hanriot, but several of the subsequent machines were converted Avro 504s, and eventually Avro constructed Cierva Autogiros under licence and undertook their own development. Cierva also formed a British company, as well as negotiating licence agreements for the manufacture of his machines in other countries.

These were the first practical rotorcraft, and the first to be built and used in appreciable numbers. Many had a small wing, to bear some of the weight in cruising flight and ease the load on the rotor and pylon. One of the first fully developed models was the C 8L (L for Lynx engine), one of which made history by taking Cierva and a passenger from Croydon airport across the Channel to Paris on 18 September 1928.

In all these early Autogiros the engine spun only the propeller: when the engine had warmed up, a team of helpers spun the rotor by hauling on a rope wound round a drum beneath it. But from 1930 this was unnecessary: the C 19 and later models had a drive from the engine to spin the rotor. As soon as the rotor was running at full speed, the engine was de-clutched. To take off the pilot just opened the throttle. The propeller pulled the machine forward, and before it had gone more than a few yards it lifted off and climbed steeply away.

Cierva C-6, 1924
Built on the fuselage of an Avro 504K, the 110-hp Le Rhône rotary pulled the four-bladed rotor through the air windmilling in the slipstream at 140 rpm

Cierva C8L Mk II
The machine which made the first rotorcraft crossing of the Channel on 18 September 1928. *Engine:* 200 hp Armstrong Siddeley Lynx IVc radial *Max speed:* 100 mph *Weight fully loaded:* 2470 lb *Range:* 255 miles

Autogyro principle
Powered tractor or pusher propeller gives forward thrust. Auto-rotation of the lifting surfaces in the slipstream gives upward thrust

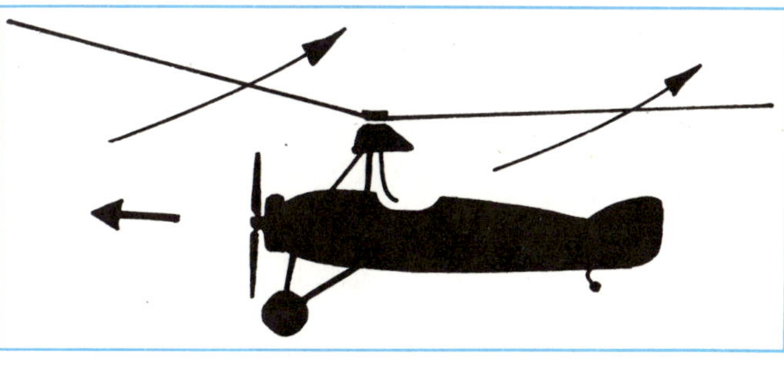

Buhl, 1931
Designed specifically for observation and photographic work, the US Buhl autogyro adopted the pusher layout
Engine: 165 hp Continental *Number of seats:* 2

Cierva-type machines were designed and built by Avro, Parnall, Westland and de Havilland in Britain, Kellett and Pitcairn in the United States, Lioré et Olivier (Le Père design) in France, Heinrich Focke in Germany and by a company in Japan. Buhl in the United States developed a version with a pusher propeller. Quite large numbers of these machines were built, and one model, the American Kellett KD-1B, made history by being the first rotorcraft of any kind ever to go into regular commercial operation. The date was 6 July 1939, the operator was Eastern Air Lines and the route was a mail run from the roof of the main Philadelphia post office to nearby Camden Airport. Kellett contined to develop the basic design throughout the 1930s, and in turn licensed Kayaba Industrial Co in Japan to build a version called the Ka-1, with a German Argus engine. About 240 of these Japanese machines were built during the Second World War – the largest quantity of any single design of piloted Autogiro and the biggest production of any rotorcraft up to that time.

Cierva's final major development took place in Britain, which was the centre of his activity during the 1930s. With the Cierva C 30A he introduced a direct-drive rotor with a neat tilting head under the direct control of the pilot, who could bodily tilt the rotor in the desired direction by means of a long control column extending downwards and to the rear from the hub. This greatly improved manoeuvrability, and especially the speed of response to pilot commands.

From the C 30A it was but a small step to the jump-start Autogiro, in which it was possible to spin-up the rotor, increase the pitch of the blades and leap vertically into the air, keeping the engine connected. As the machine accelerated away forwards the rotor was disengaged. The first jump-start demonstration took place at Hounslow, near London, in 1936. This was the first really practical, high-performance VTOL aircraft, and at takeoff it was to all intents and purposes a helicopter. During the Second World War various wingless Cierva designs, mainly of the C 30A or C 40 type, served with the RAF under the name Rota. They did many duties, one being to serve as targets at exact heights and distances for

Pitcairn PA 34
Harold Pitcairn, the founder of Eastern Airlines, began experimenting with autogyros in the 1930s. The PA 34 was an experimental military version, with the US Navy designation XOP-2
Engine: 420 hp Wright R-975-EQ radial
Cruising speed: 115 mph *Number of seats:* 2

Kellett KG-1A
Military version of the KD-1, developed both for the Army and city-centre airmail services, the KG-1A was tested by the US Army Air Corps in 1935
Engine: 165 hp Jacobs L4 *Number of seats:* 2

TsAGI A-4. Model in the Soviet Museum of Aviation. The A-4, first flown in 1934, was the first Soviet rotorcraft to enter series production. The engine was an M-26 radial delivering 300 hp, giving a max speed of 109 mph

Kellett K-3
Two-seater side-by-side autogyro with stub-wings, taken on Rear-Admiral R E Byrd's Antarctic expedition of 1934
Engine: 165 hp Continental *Weight fully loaded:* 2205 lb *Max speed:* 93 mph *Number of seats:* 2

Civil Cierva C30A G-ACWF. This machine made the first vertical takeoff by autogyro at Heston in 1936, gearing the engine to the rotor for a jump start

Flight

the calibration of ground radar stations.

Long before the success of Cierva's Autogiros was generally known, the Soviet Union began to look closely at rotary-wing craft. Still in turmoil after the revolution of 1917–23, the central government nevertheless paid early attention to the need to build an aviation industry, and set up the Central Aero and Hydrodynamics Institute (TsAGI) in Moscow to train designers.

In 1925 it formed a rotorcraft department, one of the first members being Yuriev who had built the remarkable helicopter of 1911. The first successful machine was not a helicopter but a Cierva-type autogyro, though it was developed at the TsAGI without external assistance. The design was by Nikolai Kamov and N K Skrzhinskii, the machine accordingly being designated KaSkr-1. At first it was underpowered, with a 110-hp Le Rhône rotary, but after making a number of flights it was rebuilt with a 230-hp Gnome-Rhône Titan (five-cylinder version of the Bristol Jupiter) and in this KaSkr-2 form it was very successful.

This was the start of a remarkable series of Soviet rotorcraft which today includes by far the biggest and most powerful helicopters in the world – and many of the latest Soviet machines are of Kamov design. The KaSkr was soon followed by more powerful autogyros, designed and built entirely at TsAGI, with performance that in many respects surpassed typical aeroplanes of the day. They were numbered in two series, A for true autogyros and EA for helicopters or autogyros with powered rotor. Among the designers were some who after the Second World War were to become famous for much better and more powerful rotorcraft, including not only Kamov but also Mikhail Mil and I P Bratukhin. There is no need for a detailed catalogue of the early TsAGI designs, but it is worth noting that some of V A Kuznetsov's autogyros had engines of up to 700 hp and reached speeds up to 176 mph, far in advance of anything achieved elsewhere until long after the war.

Avro Rota (Cierva C. 30A)
RAF Rotas were mainly employed during the Second World War as controllable targets for radar calibration
Engine: 140 hp Armstrong Siddeley Genet Major radial *Max speed:* 110 mph *Range:* 250 miles

The First True Helicopters

GOING STRAIGHT UP

Fw 186V1
Focke-Wulf main factory entry in competition for STOL battlefield liaison aircraft won by the Fi 156 Storch
Engine: 240 hp Argus As 10

As far as true helicopters were concerned the only thing that seems to apply to all of them before the war was that nobody knew how to build one. The basic idea of engine, speed-reducing gearbox, articulated hub and rotating blades could hardly be avoided; but the best way to arrange these for good performance, stable flight and positive control response was simply unknown. Several designers adopted configurations with two or more lifting rotors, either one above the other in the co-axial contra-rotating arrangement or side-by-side or in tandem.

In each case some way had to be found to cancel out the drive torque and keep the main body stationary. The common modern method, adopted by Yuriev in 1911, was seldom seen. The co-axials cancelled out automatically, and the multi-rotor machines did so if the rotors turned in opposite directions. Some twin-rotor designs had tilted rotors whose thrust axes cancelled out any turning moment. Other designers tried tip drive, either with steam jets (as in 1843) or with rockets. Isacco, in France, built a Hélicogyre in 1926 with a small piston engine and propeller near the tip of each blade, and it worked quite well. But the sheer difficulty of the helicopter is shown by the fact that nobody had been able to build one that was of any use. Performance was invariably pathetic.

Best performer of its day was a little helicopter built by d'Ascanio in Italy in 1929. He made a determined attack on the problem and came up with co-axial rotors, the blades of which had trailing control surfaces, rather like ailerons on an aeroplane wing, for direct pilot control of pitch. He also added small rotors to the fuselage, one at the side on an outrigger frame to prevent roll and the other at the tail to govern pitch attitude of the whole machine (climb and dive). He also fitted a small upright tail rotor to govern direction and cancel out any torque from the main rotors. In 1930 d'Ascanio set up world records of 1·078 km (3589 ft) for distance, 17·4 m (57 ft) for altitude and 8 minutes 45·2 seconds for duration. Not very impressive!

During the early 1930s additional workers came on to the scene. One was another expatriate Russian, Nicolas Florine, who during the 1920s had settled in Belgium and gained national research funding in that country. On 25 October 1933 his most successful full-scale prototype remained in the air nearly ten minutes, setting a world record, but in other respects it was not very encouraging. Asboth, a Hungarian, did not even manage ten minutes with his machine, despite its exceptionally sound design.

Another newcomer was a German, Anton Flettner, who after lengthy research decided in 1930 to build a small helicopter with the rotor driven by engine/propeller units mounted on the blades. His arrangement was strongly reminiscent of Isacco's of four years earlier, the two engines being 30-hp Anzanis. Tethered hovering began very well, but in 1933 a gust of wind blew the machine over and it was damaged beyond repair. Flettner then built a good-looking autogyro, the Navy-sponsored Fi 184, but in 1936 this caught fire in flight and was destroyed.

Away from the Autogyro

Before returning to Flettner, the centre of attention must shift west to France, and back to Louis Breguet. Since giving up the helicopter in 1909 he had built up a business producing aeroplanes which became one of the most important in the world, including the most advanced combat aircraft and airliners. Despite this his mind kept returning to the problem of the helicopter. Why would it not work properly? In 1929 he patented ideas for improving rotorcraft stability, and two years later he and his technical director René Dorand began to build the Gyroplane Laboratoire. This is generally regarded as the first really successful helicopter in history.

Rightly, Breguet and Dorand did not attempt to make their device look pretty. It had a steel-tube girder frame, with a 350-hp Hispano-Suiza 9Q radial engine in the nose, very widely spaced wheels on side outriggers, a seat in the rear and a rather clumsy plywood tail. Dominating all the fixed portions were the huge co-axial rotors, each having two tapered blades provided with cyclic and collective pitch control.

Without any publicity, test pilot Maurice Claisse made the first flight at Villacoublay on 26 June 1935, after having spent at least 18 months in tethered trials and short hovering hops. By November 1936 the unprepossessing Gyroplane Laboratoire had set world records with a speed of 61 mph, a height of 518 feet, a distance of 27·34 miles and duration of over 62 minutes. Later it also became the second rotorcraft to make a safe autorotative landing. Though Breguet's work was halted by the Second World War – during which the Gyroplane was bombed and in any case made obsolete – his last machine deserves fame which it never received as the first helicopter to be capable of positive, controllable flight for useful distances and speeds.

Exactly a year after the Gyroplane Laboratoire's first flight an all-German helicopter took to the air for the first time, and this was even better. Professor Heinrich Focke had become interested in rotary-wing aircraft in 1930, forming the Focke Achgelis company a year later to conduct research. Practical experience was gained by building Cierva Autogiros under licence, and to improve on these Focke built a neat little machine, the Fw 186, in 1936. Achgelis did not participate in this, which was a Focke-Wulf main factory product intended to compete with the fixed-wing Fieseler Storch for military STOL (Short Take-Off and Landing) liaison orders. The Fw 186 did not gain notoriety, but the first product of the Focke Achgelis company received world-wide publicity. It was designated Fa 61.

D'Ascanio in flight. This large helicopter of 1930 had two massive contra-rotating rotors. Three small propellers provided lateral, longitudinal and yaw control

At first glance it looked like a Cierva Autogiro with a nosewheel landing gear as well as a tailwheel and two rotors side-by-side. In fact, it was a true helicopter, though its structure was based on the fuselage of a regular Fw 44 biplane trainer. The 160-hp Bramo (Siemens) Sh 14A radial engine was retained in the nose, the tailplane was placed on top of the fin, and on each side was added a huge tubular outrigger carrying a remarkable rotor of small diameter. Each had three tapered blades, with cyclic pitch for longitudinal and directional control, and with differential collective pitch giving powerful lateral control. The rotors were driven by gears and torque shafts, the small propeller on the front of the engine being solely for cooling.

Nazi Gathering

The first flight was made by Edwald Rohlfs, who handled the bulk of developmental flying. The day before its first anniversary, on 25 June 1937, Rohlfs set an altitude record of 8002 ft and duration record of 80 minutes 49 seconds. On the following day he set a straight-line distance record of 10·18 miles, a closed-circuit distance record of 50·09 miles and a speed record of 76·15 mph over 20 km.

However, the event that put the Fa 61 on the front page of almost every newspaper in the world was its flying indoors. It was that incredible aviatrix Flugkapitän Hanna Reitsch – who survived countless amazing adventures and now lives in Frankfurt – who, in February 1938, flew the Fa 61 all around the Deutschlandhalle, in Berlin, during a great Nazi gathering, demonstrating that the new helicopter was totally docile and responsive. Reitsch had previously flown the helicopter from Bremen to Berlin, and by the time work had to cease with the outbreak of war the two Fa 61 prototypes had set a distance record of 143 miles and an altitude record of 11,243·5 ft. These were to stand for some years.

Though he never rivalled Focke in notoriety, Flettner made at least as great a contribution to rotorcraft, and followed his Fl 184 with a succession of increasingly superior designs. In 1936 he flew the Fl 185, an extremely neat machine with an Sh 14A radial engine in the nose driving a cooling fan, a three-blade main rotor, and two propellers on the tips of slender struts projecting far out on each side of the body.

Flettner Fl 185
A gearbox transmitted power to the main rotor and to two outrigger propellers to give the Fl 185 forward or reverse thrust. For vertical takeoff the propellers turned in opposite directions to counteract rotor torque. For forward flight they acted in unison as pusher propellers
Engine: 140 hp Siemens-Halske *Weight fully loaded:* 1980 lb

The arrangement seemed ideal. To take off as a helicopter the engine was geared to the rotor, while the pitch of the blades of the propellers was adjusted so that their thrust just cancelled out the torque needed to drive the rotor. In forward flight however, it was Flettner's intention that the rotor should be allowed to autorotate, the propellers then both being driven in forward pitch to provide propulsion. Flight trials showed that there were problems in making the scheme work, and Flettner's subsequent work concentrated on true helicopters. In designing these he broke new ground by using intermeshing rotors.

His first such design was the Fl 265, tested in ground rigs in 1937, ordered by the Kriegsmarine (German navy) in 1938 and flown for the first time in May 1939. Flettner believed that by using two rotor hubs close together, each tilted slightly outwards and rotating in opposite directions, it would be possible to build an efficient, light and stable helicopter without the need for an anti-torque tail rotor or outrigger propeller. The basic machine was very like the Fl 185, but the engine drove a gearbox from which extended two slightly diverging shafts each carrying one two-blade rotor. Later this arrangement was to be called the flying egg-whisk, or eggbeater, because the blades continually pass between those of the opposite rotor in the same way as the paddles of an eggbeater. In theory they should never touch, but unfortunately, owing to a gear stripping its teeth, the blades eventually did touch in the first Fl 265 after it had done a lot of very successful flying.

After exhaustive operational trials with both German naval and army forces, the Fl 265 was ordered into quantity production in 1940, the first production order for any helicopter. It is worth noting that, as one of the final tests before deciding on mass procurement, an Fl 265 was subject to simulated air-to-air attack by expert Luftwaffe fighter pilots. When their ciné films were processed it was found that they had been unable to get the nimble rotorcraft in their sights even once.

The Weir W2 with a 50 hp motor typified the 'flying motorcycle' idea in the 1930s

In the late 1930s many neat rotorcraft were built, nearly all of them autogyros. British workers were especially prominent, with the Kay Gyroplane and the rather similar machines of Raoul Hafner proving the superiority of cyclic control over the Cierva tilting head. The Weir autogyros likewise improved on the Cierva designs, and aimed at selling a 'motorcycle of the air' for £300. But after successfully flying the W-2 to W-4 in 1933–36, the designer C G Pullin turned to helicopters with the W-5 of 1938. This flew quite well, despite having only 50 hp from a Weir flat-twin, driving left and right rotors on outriggers. In October 1939 the bigger W-6 made its maiden flight, powered by a 200-hp Gipsy Six. Pullin had by this time done bench tests on a jet-tip-drive rotor, and patented it, but unfortunately the whole enterprise was halted by the outbreak of war.

In February 1938 Professor Focke's Fa 61 astonished a gathering of Nazi potentates when, flown by Hanna Reitsch, it performed the stunts only possible with a true helicopter inside the enormous Deutschlandhalle in Berlin. For the service officers present the military potential of the helicopter was made obvious

The First Convertiplane

Baynes Heliplane
(Estimated performance) *Max speed:* 365 mph
Range: 1000 miles *Bombload:* 500 lb

Another, even bolder, scheme that failed to get off the ground was the tilting-rotor VTOL combat aircraft designed in 1937–39 by L E Baynes. At the time it was unpublished, and it failed to get official backing – as did virtually every unorthodox project that had not been designed to an official specification. In fact it was fundamentally sound, and remarkably well thought out. But it was to be almost 40 years before similar machines finally took to the air, and the Baynes Heliplane paid the penalty for being ahead of its time.

Baynes disliked the term 'convertiplane', but that is what he planned. A convertiplane is generally taken to be a rotary-wing VTOL machine which can change to wing-borne aeroplane flight and then return to the rotor-supported mode. Baynes designed a basically conventional high-speed combat aircraft, with a crew of three in the glazed nose and equipment for bombing, reconnaissance or other missions. The wings were unusually small, having a span of less than 20 ft. On their tips were long but slender nacelles which could be swivelled to point vertically upwards. These contained extremely advanced gas-turbine drive units supplied with hot high-pressure gas from Pescara gas generators in the fuselage.

The Heliplane did not have to be powered by such an advanced propulsion system, but the free-piston Pescara gas generator was an extremely attractive scheme which would certainly have become very important had the gas turbine not come to fruition. One advantage was that the connection between the fuselage gas generators and the drive units on the wing tips took the form of thin-walled stainless steel tubing, much lighter and less troublesome than mechanical drive shafts. The scheme promised to be light, smooth and powerful and to provide a degree of twin-engine safety.

Key to the Heliplane was the large diameter (15 ft) of its two propellers. This was big enough for the two rotors to lift the machine when the axes were vertical. The main drawback was that the propellers were rather too big as propellers and rather too small as rotors, but the same can be said of almost all tilt-rotor or tilt-wing convertiplanes of today. The penalty was excessive propeller tip speed at high forward speeds, so that the rotational speed would need to be reduced by high-ratio reduction gearing, and excessive power demand, noise and fuel consumption while VTOL rotor-supported.

But there was nothing that could not have been solved, and the Baynes Heliplane could, if pressed forward with vigour, have made a notable contribution to the Second World War. One of its many novel features was that it was designed to be amphibious. In the VTOL mode it could sink gently on to the water, becoming supported by its sealed and buoyant fuselage (which, as it sank vertically, did not need any chines, steps or planing bottom of the kind usually found on flying boats). Lateral stability was to be provided by the wing-tip propeller nacelles. Baynes estimated that the complete machine could have weighed only 6000 lb, and would have reached a speed of 365 mph. It was to be more than 20 years before any VTOL aircraft other than the V-2 ballistic missile would reach this speed.

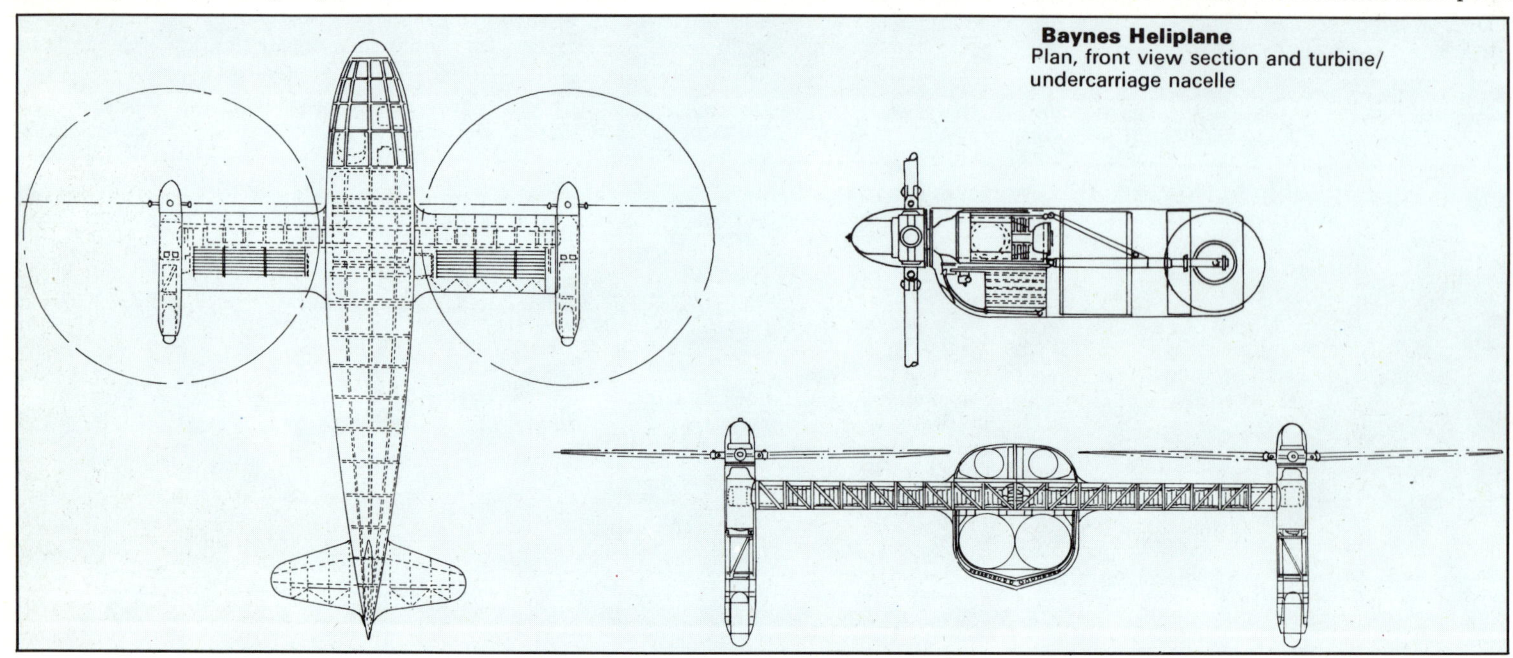

Baynes Heliplane
Plan, front view section and turbine/undercarriage nacelle

Founding The Industry

THE SIKORSKY STORY

Sikorsky VS-300
In pontoon configuration, April 1941, after two years trying to tame the beast. Already Sikorsky was working with the US Army and Navy on possible production versions
Engine: 150 hp Franklin *Max speed:* 50 mph *Range:* 75 miles

In the United States inventors enjoyed a less austere environment, and many would-be helicopter inventors were flourishing by the time of Pearl Harbor in December 1941. Ahead of them all was the expatriate Russian, Igor Sikorsky. For many years he had been a leader in the American aircraft industry, being especially noted for his large flying boats for Pan American. But he never stopped thinking about helicopters. In 1931, after years of study, he patented a helicopter design which incorporated almost all the features he later carried into metal.

Successful Prototype
During the early 1930s he never had time to build his design – or even the authority, because his firm had merged with that of Chance Vought, and the resulting Vought-Sikorsky Aircraft had become a division of the giant United Aircraft Corporation. But in 1938 the UAC board gave formal approval for Sikorsky to conduct research into helicopters. They had little idea they were giving permission for the work that was ultimately to lead to the useful modern helicopter, and to bring massive new business to UAC.

Today the name of Sikorsky is the first that comes to mind when the question arises: 'Who invented the helicopter?' But the helicopter was already a quite well-developed animal when Sikorsky built his own successful prototype. Moreover, the Sikorsky product went through years of difficult and often heartbreaking development before it was turned into anything that could be described as successful. And during these years Sikorsky's creation was not a patch on the contemporary Flettner and Focke Achgelis helicopters that were flying in Germany. Why, then, is Sikorsky's the preeminent name among helicopter engineers? It is partly a matter of luck – Sikorsky's side won the war and the two German programmes were halted. But the underlying reason is that gradually, through all the years of patient toil, it was Sikorsky who did most to unlock the riddles of helicopter design, and it was his line of development that has survived. After the war there was no need for any reappraisal of Allied helicopters; Sikorsky's work has continued unbroken to this day, though it was soon joined by rivals with different arrangements.

Suppose the Axis powers had won the war. Then the Flettner and Focke Achgelis programmes would have continued, and the American work would have stopped. Perhaps the helicopter would today be in very much its present state, especially in view of the tremendous capability of the Soviet Union in the rotorcraft field. But careful study of the technology of helicopters in the latter part of the Second World War leaves no doubt that the Americans, led by Sikorsky, were drawing ahead. So, even discounting his luck in being on the winning side, Igor Sikorsky is justly ranked as greatest of all the many pioneers of the helicopter. Before Sikorsky, the helicopter was always an uphill struggle which might or might not work. After Sikorsky, though particular helicopter programmes might very well still run into terrible trouble, there was always a known certain way of making a good helicopter.

Yet Sikorsky did not really do anything dramatic or revolutionary. He did not introduce anything completely new. He adopted the 'penny farthing' configuration, with one large lifting rotor and a small anti-torque tail rotor, just as many had done before. He used an articulated hub with drag and coning hinges, flapping hinges and cyclic and collective pitch control, as many had done before. Gearboxes and transmissions were already known quantities, and so were control systems. It just happened that he knew better than anyone else how to combine all the known ideas and devices, and how best to turn rough experimental hardware into polished production hardware. Of course he did have the giant advantage of being a top man in a vast company in the most advanced and powerful industrial society in the world. He also happened to begin his work just prior to a great international conflict which loosed all the purse-strings and poured unprecedented funds and talents into any new technology that had a bearing on winning the war. So by the end of the war ten years of normal development had been packed into only five.

Bucking Test Rig
Probably no single aircraft in history has gone through more metamorphoses than Sikorsky's first American helicopter, designated VS-300 to give it a number far above those of Vought-Sikorsky aeroplanes. Igor himself, then about 59, did all the early 'flying', though for the first year the job was little more than sitting in a seat in a bucking groundborne test rig.

Sikorsky R-4 Construction Breakdown

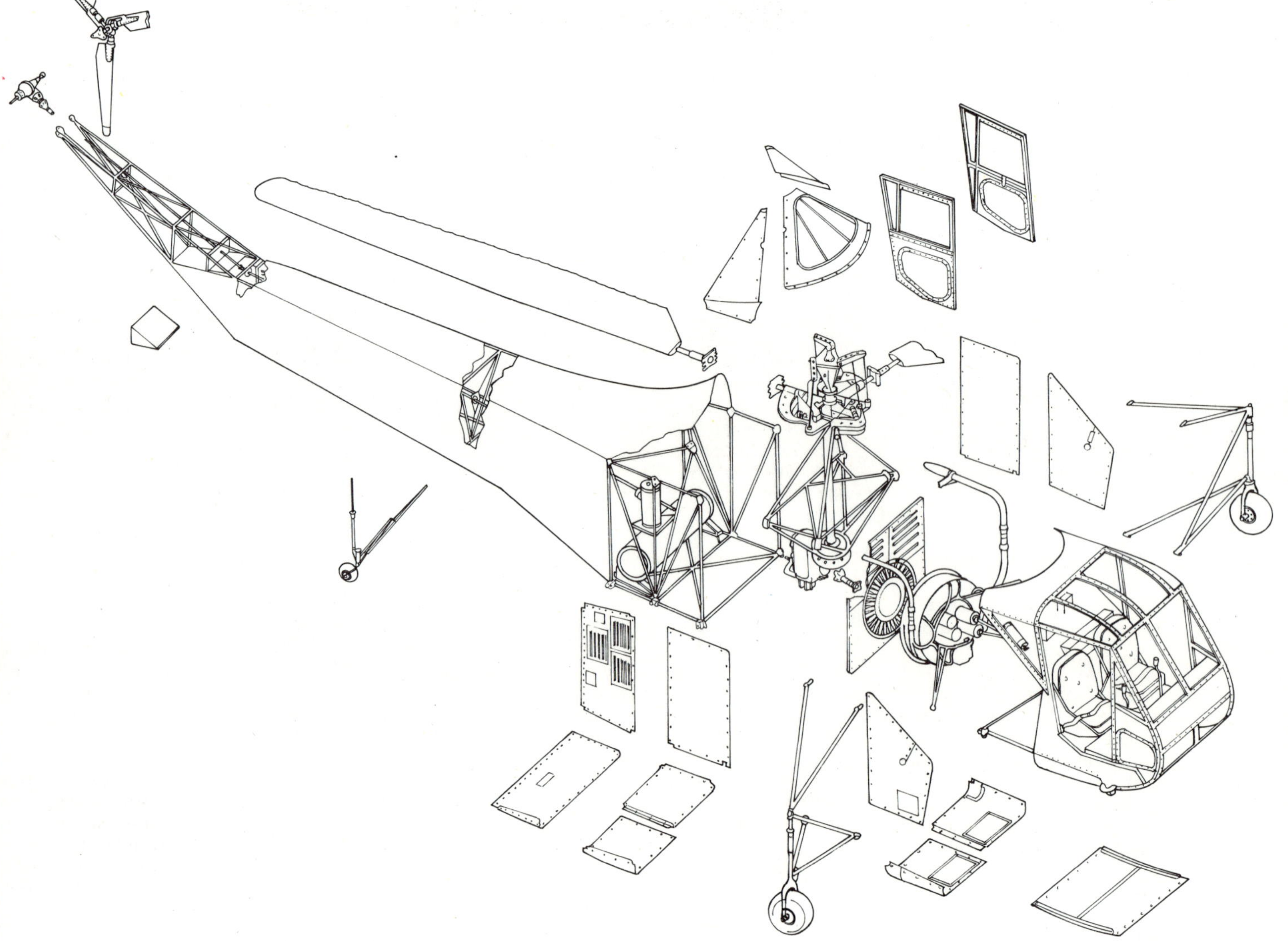

Sikorsky R-4B (RAF Hoverfly I)
Based on the successful VS-300, the R-4 was the world's first series-production helicopter and served with the US Navy and USAAF as well as the RAF and Royal Navy under combat conditions
Engine: 180 hp Warner Super Scarab R-550-1
Max speed: 75 mph *Weight fully loaded:* 2540 lb
Range: 200 miles *Number of seats:* 2

The VS-300 began with a framework of welded steel tube, on top of which was the three-blade rotor. Inside the frame was a fuel tank and a 75-hp Lycoming flat-four engine. On each side was a wide triangulated spaceframe carrying a landing wheel, while from the bottom there projected a forward extension carrying the seat, flight controls and nosewheel. From the top a similar extension to the rear carried a large fin and the anti-torque tail rotor. The pilot sat completely in the open. He had no instrument panel, but did need tight harness because before long the device showed signs of extreme irritability.

Taming the Beast

Sikorsky and a small team built it during the spring of 1939, at the main plant at Stratford, Connecticut. After many problems it was ready for testing on 14 September 1939, tethered to a heavy flat plate out on the airfield runway. At times it was actually tethered to the ground, and it invariably had weights hung underneath to improve stability. After endless attempts to make the cyclic control work it was abandoned temporarily. The engine was changed for a Franklin of 90 hp, and instead of a tail boom a complete braced-truss rear fuselage was added, much longer than the stubby boom. On each side at the tail grew a long braced outrigger carrying a small rotor (really a 6·66-ft horizontal propeller). Thus there was now a 28-ft three-blade main rotor (with no cyclic), an anti-torque tail rotor and two outrigger propellers to ensure positive lateral control. Sikorsky never expected to need the outriggers; he just had to have them while he made the beast better.

Sikorsky made the first free flight on 13 May 1940. By July he was making useful 15-minute free flights, and on 6 May 1941 the further-revised craft, now called VS-300A, beat the helicopter endurance record by staying aloft 1 hour 32 minutes 26·1 seconds. By this time the cyclic pitch had been perfected and made operative, and the A was added to the designation when Sikorsky felt he had reached a suitable configuration.

In all, there were 18 visibly different configurations of the VS-300. At one time, in mid-1940, it had no nosewheel, but only a curved skid under each end. In April 1941 Sikorsky fitted two large rubber-fabric flotation bags and carried out successful flights from water. Another important change was a further increase in power, the 90-hp Franklin being exchanged for a flat-six of the same make rated at 150 hp. Sikorsky and other pilots continued to improve this historic machine throughout 1942, and the following year it was placed on view in the Henry Ford Museum at Dearborn, Michigan, where it remained.

By 1941 Sikorsky's company was working with the US Army and US Navy on possible production helicopters, and the first Service pilots came to Stratford to inspect the VS-300. A few even flew it, and one – Capt Frank Gregory, from Wright Field – later recalled what the experience was like: 'More than anything else the VS-300 reminded me of a bucking bronco. She tried to throw me when she leaped into the air right at the start. When I wanted her to go down, she went up. When I tried to back her up, she persisted in going forward. About the only thing she was agreeable to was getting down again, and that was probably because she wanted to get fed and pampered by the mechanics and her maker.'

Harder to Fly

Part of Gregory's trouble was that the VS-300 was still crude and under-developed. Part, however, stemmed from the basic fact that a helicopter is harder to fly than an aeroplane. It has taken 30 years of development, and the perfection of autopilots and stability augmentation systems, to produce today's helicopters which can be flown effortlessly with forefinger and thumb, or even 'hands off', despite the presence of gusting winds and turbulent air.

Unlike an aeroplane, a rotary-wing machine visibly and audibly threshes about in the sky in order to stay up, and in all but the very latest machines the threshing can also be felt. This basic fact leads to many problems. One of the deepest difficulties is that the rotorcraft hangs from a rotor hub of very highly stressed metal with various parts which beat round and round and, at the same time, constantly oscillate to and fro and up and down. The cyclic pitch, for example, is working up and down all the time the helicopter is moving along through the air, twisting the blades to higher and lower pitch twice on each revolution of the rotor. This means that all these highly stressed parts must be made resistant to fatigue; if anything jammed or broke the result would be catastrophic. It also means that the pilot, in early helicopters at least, had a throbbing, churning, vibrating ride, rather like a cross between a small boat in a rough sea and a combine

Successful experiments with float versions of the R-4 proved the potential of the shipborne helicopter. Here a pontoon-equipped R-4 (Navy designation HNS-1) makes its first landing at sea aboard the tanker Bunker Hill, *May 1943*

Imperial War Museum

harvester. Unlike his colleague in a smooth aeroplane he constantly had to 'fly' his cavorting mount; and the controls were, and remain, by no means simple.

Consider just one manoeuvre that comes early in the basic textbooks of helicopter flight: the low-level square. In this the helicopter is flown round a large square, preferably marked out on the ground, whilst facing the same way the whole time. The pupil may lift off facing into wind, by rotating the twist-grip throttle (like that of a motorcycle) on the end of the collective lever and simultaneously pulling the lever slowly upwards to increase blade pitch and thus the lift of the rotor. To fly the first side of the square, into wind, he pushes forward on the cyclic lever, which corresponds to an aeroplane control column. He uses lateral movements of cyclic to correct drift and keep going exactly along the line, and rudder pedals work the tail rotor to keep the exact heading. Near the end he must slow to a hover, pulling back on cyclic and adjusting throttle and collective simultaneously. The problem is that each control affects the others; anyone but an experienced pilot finds he can correct one thing, such as forward speed, but fails to notice the helicopter has soared up 50 ft or landed on the ground.

The next leg of the square needs firm sideways movement of the cyclic lever, but the wind blows the helicopter back; so the cyclic goes into the front corner, and more throttle and collective is needed. Too much throttle and the sensitive beast climbs, and any adjustment of engine power also changes the side-thrust of the tail rotor, necessitating some rudder action. When all this has to be done at once it is easy to see why helicopter pilots need at least three hands – and concentrate so hard they hardly notice the threshing vibration.

Of course, Gregory and the other VS-300 pilots had no standard of comparison except aeroplanes. There were no helicopter training courses or licences, and it was impossible to learn except by strapping in and doing it. But the VS-300 at last suggested that the helicopter was about to become a worthwhile and practical vehicle, with adequate performance, adequate payload and satisfactory, if far from brilliant, flying qualities.

So, in January 1941 Sikorsky and his chief engineer Mike Gluhareff began the design of a development of the VS-300A intended as a product for sale. They called it the VS-316A, and it was somewhat larger than the experimental machine, with a 165-hp Warner Super Scarab radial engine driving a 36-ft rotor. The fuselage was longer and of better shape, and the two crew members sat side-by-side in the enclosed nose cabin, with dual controls. The VS-316A flew for the first time a month after America entered the war, on 14 January 1942. It flew quite well, and on 18 May the same machine left Stratford en route to the US Army Air Force. It was now called the XR-4, and it flew by itself the 761 miles to Wright Field in easy stages, in all kinds of weather, with very little trouble. This impressed everyone.

A service-test batch of YR-4 helicopters was ordered, and these were sent to gain experience in Alaska, Burma and other arduous places, and to the US Navy and Coast Guard and to the Royal Navy. An order for 100 production machines followed, designated R-4B by the Army Air Force, HNS-1 by the Navy and Hoverfly I by the British RAF and Fleet Air Arm. This was not the first production helicopter – that honour goes to the German Fl 282 – but it was the first helicopter whose development continued unbroken into the modern era.

To build the R-4, Sikorsky Aircraft was set up in January 1943 as a separate division of UAC, henceforward to concentrate entirely on rotorcraft. The new division left Stratford and took over a leased factory at nearby Bridgeport which was swiftly tooled up for helicopter production. It was probably the first time in the world that a new aircraft factory had been planned without any airfield. Instead it had what Sikorsky called 'the world's smallest airport', a flat area about as big as a typical parking lot from which all the helicopters built at the plant flew. By early 1944 the R-4B was coming off the line at the planned rate, flights had been made from the restricted deck of a tanker, pilot training schools had been set up in America and Britain and the prototypes of two more advanced machines, the R-5 and R-6, were engaged in flight development. As one of Sikorsky's top men put it, 'Before Igor Sikorsky flew the VS-300 there was no helicopter industry; after he flew it there was'. So, though he did not play any part in inventing the helicopter, Igor Sikorsky did more than any other man to make it work.

Sikorsky R-6A (RAF Hoverfly II, USN HOS-1)

First flown in October 1943, the R-6 began as a development of the R-4, but was already showing typical modern helicopter features – the streamlined tadpole fuselage and a Plexiglas bubble cockpit

Engine: 245 hp Franklin O-485-9 *Max speed:* 96 mph *Weight fully loaded:* 2600 lb *Number of seats:* 2

HELICOPTERS AT WAR

Flettner Fl 282 Kolibri
Representing a real advance in helicopter technology when it first flew in 1940, the Fl 282 was the only helicopter to be actually used operationally during the Second World War
Engine: 140 hp Siemens-Halske 14A *Max speed:* 89 mph *Range:* 106 miles

It must, however, be acknowledged that the German helicopter teams had created a helicopter industry even earlier than Sikorsky, and by December 1941 were in series production with helicopters that could outperform the R-4B by a wide margin. Indeed, one of the German machines was in a size and weight class that was not reached in the United States until the 1950s. Yet it is the smaller of the German production helicopters that deserves the greater praise, because this machine, the Fl 282, can claim to have been the first fully developed helicopter, the first in production and the first in operational service. It will be recalled that Anton Flettner gave up the single-rotor Fl 185 in favour of two intermeshing rotors with slightly inclined axes close together. His first 'egg-beater', the Fl 265, flew in May 1939, but despite a German Navy production order placed in 1938 Flettner decided he could do better. By July 1940 he had developed the 265 into the two-seat 282, able to fly either solo or, without need for retrimming, with an observer seated behind the rotors.

To speed development the German Navy ordered 30 prototypes and 15 production aircraft, designated Fl 282 *Kolibri* (hummingbird). After three were built in 1941 with streamlined enclosed cockpits the main run of *Kolibris* had an open pilot seat in front and open observer cockpit at the rear. This was the only helicopter used operationally during the Second World War. At least 20 had been delivered by 1943, and these were used from various ships including cruisers and merchant vessels for scouting and anti-submarine reconnaissance in the North, Baltic, Aegean and Mediterranean Seas. Luftwaffe transport units also used the Fl 282 for liaison and general utility, and helicopters of this type are believed to have made some hair-raising rescue and supply missions in the closing stages of the war. By 1944 the BMW company was engaged in fulfilling an order for 1000 of these highly developed machines, but were frustrated by Allied bombing. Flettner was never able to build the Fl 339, designed to carry about 20 passengers, and all that is left of his outstanding work is a pair of *Kolibris*, one at Cranfield, England, and the other in the US Air Force Museum.

Transport Helicopter

Flettner's rival, the Focke Achgelis company, stole a march on him when in 1938 they gained a Lufthansa order for the world's first transport helicopter. Designated Fa 266 *Hornisse* (hornet), this was a scaled-up Fa 61 with 39·4-ft left and right rotors driven by a 1000-hp Bramo Fafnir 323Q-3 radial engine in the mid-fuselage. At the rear was a T-tail, as in the Fa 61, but the forward fuselage was an unobstructed load-carrying section, with two pilots side-by-side in the completely glazed nose.

When the prototype was finished in late 1939 it was far in advance of any other helicopter, but owing to the outbreak of war it was taken over by the Luftwaffe as a multi-role military machine called Fa 223 *Drache* (kite). Free flight trials began in August 1940, but the programme was constantly set back by Allied bombing. Development was successful, and a few of these impressive machines entered Luftwaffe service as transports, reconnaissance machines (often with comprehensive radio and a nose MG 15 for defence) and for front-line supply and casualty evacuation often carrying slung loads. Despite great efforts, including tooling up a new factory at Berlin to make 400 a month, possibly no more than a dozen Fa 223 were completed and flown, though many were destroyed by bombing. In 1945 one was flown by its German crew to the Airborne Forces Experimental Establishment at Beaulieu, near Southampton. Others were flown in Czechoslovakia, while Focke himself went to France and helped SNCASE start building helicopters.

Focke Achgelis also made several rotagliders – engineless towed autogyros – the

Left: D-OCEW, the second prototype Fa 223, undergoing acceptance trials in July 1942. Only a few of these advanced machines ever reached the Luftwaffe. Right: Flettner Fl 282 Kolibri. Twin intermeshing, contra-rotating rotors cancelled out the engine torque and gave the Fl 282 remarkably good handling

Focke-Achgelis Fa 223 Drache
Twin contra-rotating rotors on outriggers and a powerful radial engine buried in the fuselage promised a large utility helicopter for the Luftwaffe. Allied bombing however crippled the production programme
Engine: 1000 hp Bramo Fafnir 323Q-3 *Weight fully loaded:* 9502 lb *Cruising speed:* 75 mph *Range:* 199 miles *Number of seats:* 6

best known being the Fa 330 *Bachstelze* (water wagtail) of which about 200 were delivered. The German Navy had considered using small folding Arado floatplanes from its larger U-Boats, but decided the Fa 330 was much more cost effective. It was probably the cheapest military aircraft in history, for it had no engine and was a one-man autogyro kept aloft by being towed by the parent U-Boat (usually a Type IX). It could hold an altitude of about 400 ft, and the pilot (a member of the U-Boat crew) could see about 25 miles with powerful binoculars and report by telephone. In emergency he could jettison the rotor and recover by parachute. These simple machines were used in various theatres of war from the North Atlantic to the Indian Ocean, but were put out of business by the growing Allied air power which demanded crash dives too fast for the poor autogyro pilot to be recovered.

Focke Achgelis made many experimental rotorcraft during the war and conceived numerous projects far more advanced than anything thought of among the Allies. The Fa 284, abandoned in 1943 or 1944 because it was obviously not going to help the desperate German war effort in time, was to have been an outstanding example of a new class of helicopter, the 'flying crane'. This type of helicopter carries its load externally, either slung on a cable or packed into a container which is then attached under the helicopter.

Big and Powerful

No such machine had ever previously been attempted, but the German designers planned it big enough and powerful enough to be really useful. The slim fuselage carried two outrigger wings with 58·5-ft rotors on their tips. About halfway along each wing was the main landing gear and two 1600-hp BMW 801 radial engines (no helicopter of such power was contemplated elsewhere until long after the war). The pilot and winch operator sat in the glazed nose, and one payload pod took the form of a huge bin, with hinged glazed nose and opaque rear doors. After the project was dropped, the company worked on a 'twin Fa 223' with two sets of rotors in tandem joined by a long fuselage.

An even more significant project, which was reluctantly dropped because of the pressures of war was for the world's first convertiplane. Designated Fa 269, this was again a new species of flying machine. In VTOL and hovering flight it was to be a helicopter, with two wing engines (probably liquid-cooled DB 603s) geared to small but highly loaded rotors tilted to thrust upwards from below the wings. Once well clear of the ground the pilot would gradually tilt the rotor shafts to the rear so that eventually they lay horizontally, driving pusher propellers. In forward flight the Fa 269 was thus an aeroplane, lifted by its small wing, driven by two propellers and controlled by a conventional set of aeroplane control surfaces. Cruising speed was estimated at 373 mph. Again, it was to be many years before other nations attempted such a bold proposal.

Germany – or, rather, Austria – achieved a further success during the war. The Doblhoff WNF 342 was the world's first successful tip-drive helicopter, and rested on a remarkable amount of completely original research. Tipdrive imparts no

Doblhoff WNF 342
Engine: 140 Siemens-Halske Sh 14A *Weight fully loaded:* 1411 lb *Number of seats:* 2

torque tending to rotate the fuselage, and the first full-scale tip-driven rotor was tested by the Frenchmen, Papin and Rouilly, during the First World War. They had inadequate resources, but Baron von Doblhoff and his team were able to develop the principle at the Wiener Neustadt plant near Vienna, where the Bf 109 was a staple product. After running a static rig to prove their method of tip drive, they built a succession of prototype helicopters which were nearing the operational stage at the end of the war. A piston engine, typically a 140-hp BMW (Siemens) radial, drove an air compressor which discharged air from jets at the tips of the three hollow blades, fuel being burned at the tips to increase rotor power. In cruising flight the rotor drive was stopped and engine power switched to a pusher propeller, converting the WNF 342 into an autogyro. This was a much better scheme than carrying small engine/propeller units on the rotor, and accomplished the objective of providing torqueless drive.

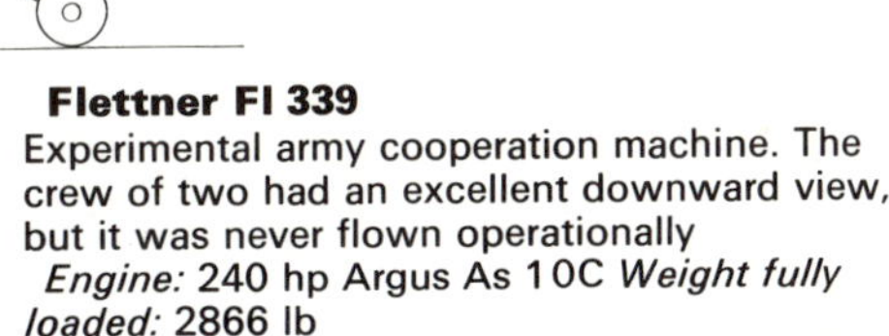

Flettner Fl 339
Experimental army cooperation machine. The crew of two had an excellent downward view, but it was never flown operationally
Engine: 240 hp Argus As 10C *Weight fully loaded:* 2866 lb

Fa 330 Bachstelze rotor-kite climbing from a U-Boat

Focke-Achgelis Fa 330 Bachstelze
Designed to give a surfaced U-Boat a flying 'crow's-nest', the Fa 330 was a lightweight, collapsible rotor kite
Weight: 180 lb *Min speed:* 16 mph

Rotary wing Gliders: A Precision Means of Airborne Assault

Focke-Achgelis Fa 325
The fuselage of a DFS 230 glider and the rotor from an Fa 223 produced this rotary-wing 'glider.' It was designed to be hauled behind a Ju 52/3m at speeds up to 120 mph and land within 20 yards. It was never used operationally

Rotaplane
Developed by the Airborne Forces Experimental Establishment, the Hafner Rotaplane was designed to carry a paratrooper armed with a Bren gun
Weight fully loaded: 295 lb *Max speed:* 93 mph

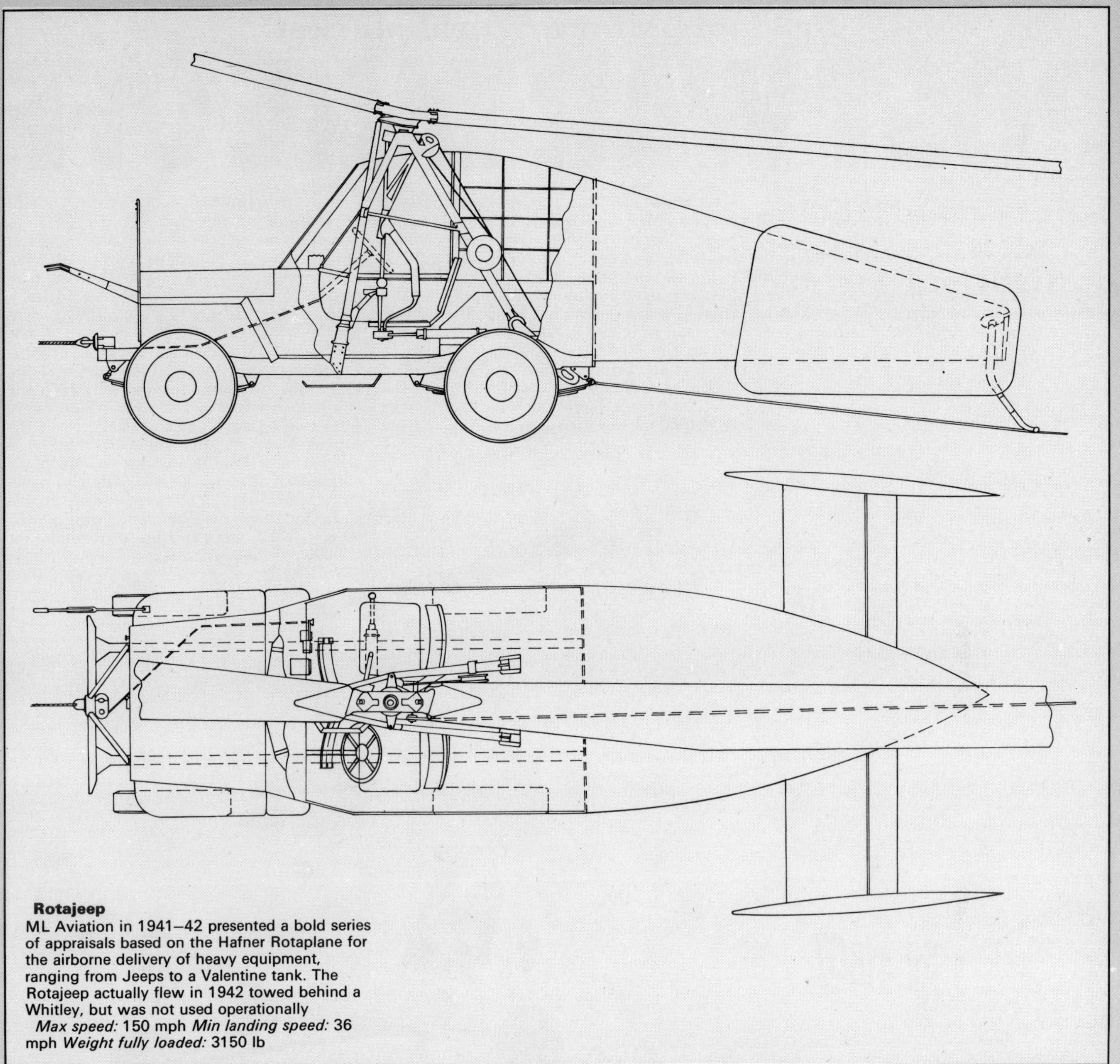

Rotajeep
ML Aviation in 1941–42 presented a bold series of appraisals based on the Hafner Rotaplane for the airborne delivery of heavy equipment, ranging from Jeeps to a Valentine tank. The Rotajeep actually flew in 1942 towed behind a Whitley, but was not used operationally
Max speed: 150 mph *Min landing speed:* 36 mph *Weight fully loaded:* 3150 lb

The one thing the Allies did try was the rotaglider for tactical assault. Focke Achgelis also proposed this idea, the theory being that in making an airborne assault on a fortified place one needs a vehicle able to land as steeply as possible and come to rest in the minimum distance. In the Low Countries in May 1940 the Germans used the DFS 230 glider, but this needed about 200 ft for a full-load landing even assuming the glider was demolished in the process. So in 1942 a DFS 230 had its wings replaced by a three-blade autogyro rotor, converting it into the Fa 225. This proved successful, landing in a total distance of about 60 ft after an almost vertical descent. On the other hand it could not be towed as fast as the glider, and in any case Germany had no more need of such aircraft in the almost wholly defensive final three years of the war.

Britain, on the other hand, did make interesting and little-publicised progress in the field of rotagliders between 1942 and 1945, mainly at the Airborne Forces Experimental Establishment. Here plans were hatched for the addition of free-wheeling rotors to all kinds of payloads including palletised cargo, troop pods, jeeps, heavy trucks and, as a final objective, a Valentine tank. Trials with the jeep began in 1944. With its rotor removed the jeep could be parked anywhere without exciting attention, unless someone happened to notice it had a turn/slip indicator and airspeed indicator. Various rotors were used, including one with a single blade and counterweight that looked rather like a sycamore seed, but most of the AFEE rotagliders had two-blade rotors. Trials behind a Whitley were partially successful, though there were severe problems with stability and no jeep flying was accomplished except on tow. The 155-ft rotor for the Valentine tank was built but not flown.

Precision Delivery

At the other end of the scale the Rotachute was highly developed for the precision delivery of individual troops or supply packages, with the advantage of an extended glide and more accurate landing than is possible with a parachute. Slingsby, Cierva and other companies participated in this work, which halted soon after the end of the war.

Of all the German rotary-wing machines built during the war the smallest were the little prototypes of another Austrian, Bruno Nagler. During the 1930s he had built attractive helicopters and autogyros in Britain, and had worked with Hafner, but as the pre-war crisis worsened he returned to Germany and set up a company with Franz Rolz. Several Nagler-Rolz helicopters flew, all small single-seaters and therefore not of great interest to the Luftwaffe. This was a pity, because they worked better than any other small helicopters of their day. The NR 54 of 1941 weighed a mere 80 lb unladen, lighter than any other powered rotorcraft until after the war, yet could reach about 50 mph. Today Nagler builds baby helicopters in the United States.

Helicopters for a World Market

POST WAR TAKE OFF

One of the few pre-1945 non-German helicopter programmes to accomplish real advances led to the most successful and long-lived rotary-wing aircraft of all time. In June 1941 Bell Aircraft Corporation, at Buffalo, NY, began the development of a small utility helicopter. The work was privately funded and no government contract was sought. The most important feature of the Bell helicopter was its novel rotor. The two blades were connected to collective and cyclic pitch controls but the hub was not articulated. There were no flapping, drag or any other hinges. Instead there was a stabilizer bar, typically five feet long and weighted at each end, mounted at 90° to the blades and rigidly attached to the hub just below them. This bar tended to dictate the plane of the rotor, and the complete rotor could tilt about the drive shaft and mast. Otherwise the Bell scheme was a straightforward one, with a small anti-torque tail rotor.

Bell do not appear to have any record of when their first helicopter flew, contemporary accounts stating merely that the first of five Model 30 prototypes flew in 'mid-1943'. These had finely streamlined bodies with two seats side-by-side in front of the vertically mounted 160-hp Franklin engine. There were two wheels at the nose and one under the long rear fuselage. By 1945 the engine power had increased to 178 hp, there were two sets of wheels at each end of the centre fuselage, and the tail rotor was carried on a long triangular-section boom which was often unskinned. The two occupants were either in open cockpits or inside a large Plexiglas 'bubble' forming the whole front end, setting a fashion for

Bell Model 30
Bell's first helicopter, built in early 1943, introduced the right-angled stabilising bar characteristic of all early Bell helicopters. Since then Bell has built more helicopters than any other company (21,000)
Engine: 160 hp Franklin *Number of seats:* 2

Bell 47G
The first Model 47 was flown in 1945. 5000 examples later it was still being built in 1972, and even in 1976 it was still being made by Agusta in Italy
Engine: 200 hp Franklin 6V4-200-C32 *Weight fully loaded:* 2350 lb *Max speed:* 100 mph *Range:* 215 miles

Smithsonian

Bell 47G-2. This model was delivered to the US Army from 1955 to 1961 as the OH-13H Sioux, most often used for armed reconnaissance, liaison, wire-laying, light supply and, as seen here, for casualty evacuation equipped with twin stretcher panniers

helicopters which has been ever popular.

On 8 March 1946 the Bell 47 received the first-ever CAA certificate for commercial operation of a helicopter, and since that time more than 6000 of this same basic design have been constructed in more than 60 versions by Bell (now Bell Helicopter Co) and licensees in Britain, Italy and Japan. Continual 'product improvement' kept this helicopter saleable for more than 30 years, the engineering being refined through a process of more than 6000 often seemingly trivial changes, and the useful load being increased from 200 lb to 1200 lb. Most Bell 47 versions have been military, used for training, liaison and utility roles; a few have borne arms and one Italian version even carries a torpedo. Civil variants range from the early 47B-3 agricultural version of 1947 to today's plush 47J Ranger carrying four people plus baggage in great comfort. Final versions introduced many major refinements including hydraulically powered controls to give featherlight pilot controls under the most adverse conditions.

Another important American helicopter family was begun in 1941, when Frank N Piasecki and some associates formed PV Engineering Forum, which was incorporated two years later. They swiftly designed an extremely neat single-rotor single-seat helicopter, the PV-2, powered by a 90-hp Franklin mounted as in the Bell with its crankshaft vertical. First free flight came earlier than that of the Bell, on 11 April 1943. In September 1943 the PV-2 made the second public helicopter flight in the United States (Sikorsky was first), and Piasecki also gained the No 1 Helicopter Pilot certificate issued by the CAA.

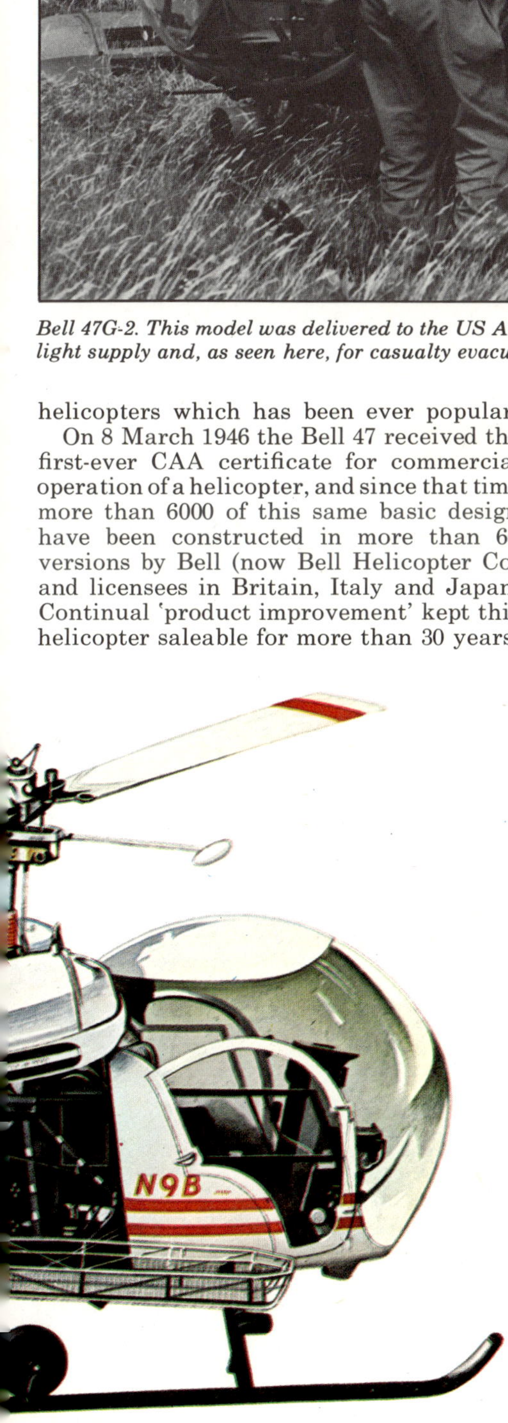

Bell 47D, with faired-in engine and tail boom, supplied to the US Navy in 1949 as the twin-float HTL-2

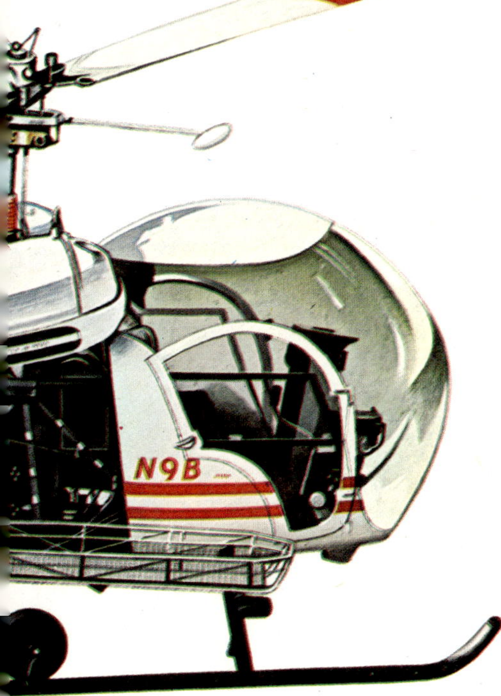

Smithsonian

E C P. Armées

France's war in Algeria from 1956–62 was the first large-scale test of the combat helicopter supporting ground forces. Here a Vertol (Piasecki) Model 43 (US Army H-21C) of the Aviation Légère de l'Armée de Terre flies over the arid Bled *of Algeria*

The expertise of the infant company was recognised by a secret contract from the US Navy for the PV-3, a helicopter much more ambitious than any previously attempted in the United States. For this big utility transport and rescue machine Piasecki chose to mount a 600-hp Wasp engine in the middle of a long, apparently sagging fuselage – people called it 'the flying banana' – supported by a rotor at each end. He did this so that a modest and easily developed rotor should be used in multiple to lift the required load of a crew of two and ten passengers, with the added benefit that the load could be shifted fore and aft over a wide cg range. This was the first helicopter ever built with the now common tandem-rotor configuration.

The first PV-3 flew in March 1945 and 22 were subsequently built and saw service with the Navy, Coast Guard, Marine Corps and civil operators. They were designated HRP-1 Rescuer, and were unique at that time in providing a large unobstructed cabin for passengers, cargo up to 2000 lb or six stretchers (litters). Their landing gear comprised twin rear wheels and a single nosewheel, used plain or surrounded by a large inflatable buoyancy bag in overwater operations. Alternatively, the wheels could be replaced by permanently inflated floats.

The success of the PV-3 resulted in a succession of further orders. In 1945 work began on a much smaller tandem-rotor machine for utility use aboard surface ships, and this became the HUP-1 and HUP-2 Retriever series with a 525- or 550-hp Continental radial engine, stumpy fuselage, rear rotor carried on top of a huge fin and tailwheel-type landing gear. More than 430 of this family were delivered for many Navy, Air Force, Army and foreign duties, land-based H-25 versions being called Army Mule (an unofficial designation).

One of the last highly developed piston-engined helicopters, the Vertol (Piasecki) HUP-2 Retriever is shown aboard an Essex *class carrier serving as liaison transport and plane guard*

Smithsonian

Vertol H-21
Ten of these tactical and logistic transports were delivered to the French Aéronavale
Engine: 1425 hp Wright R-1820-103 Cyclone *Weight fully loaded:* 14,704 lb *Max speed:* 125 mph *Range:* 403 miles

Westland Dragonfly HR I
Licence-built development of the Sikorsky S-51, specially modified for air-sea rescue with the Fleet Air Arm
Engine: 540 hp Alvis Leonides 50 *Weight fully loaded:* 5374 lb *Max speed:* 105 mph *Range:* 300 miles *Number of seats:* 4

A much bigger and more powerful family began with the HRP-2, a development of the original flying banana but with a straight body and long sloping fin. From this machine, flown in April 1952, stemmed the very important H-21 family, later called the Work Horse and Shawnee, as well as the civil Model 44. These were powered by 1425-hp Cyclone engines and could carry 14 passengers or 12 stretchers. From 1955 various H-21 versions became the main Western helicopters in heavy casualty-evacuation, Arctic rescue, radar station support and similar 'outback' roles involving heavy lifting. (Production was in full swing when Piasecki became Vertol Aircraft in 1956; in 1960 Vertol became a division of Boeing.) Altogether more than 600 of this series were built, and a few continued in service into the last quarter of the century.

Having begun helicopter development with the much-rebuilt VS-300, Sikorsky followed the production R-4 with the bigger R-5, first flown on 18 August 1943. Powered by a 450-hp Wasp Junior radial, this was ordered as the R-5A for the US Army and as the HO2S-1 for the US Navy, both being two-seat tandem observation machines with twin front wheels and a stilted rear wheel at the root of the long tail boom. The 48-ft rotor was a notable advance over the R-4, and gross weight was 5000 lb, just twice as great. Instead of steel tube and fabric, the R-5 was made chiefly of light-alloy monocoque. Eventually about 300 were delivered, plus 139 built in England as the Westland Dragonfly with modified airframe and Alvis Leonides engine. Nearly all the production machines had tricycle landing gear, and small batches were sold for commercial purposes, British European Airways using this type on 1 June 1950 for the world's first scheduled passenger helicopter service (on an odd route: Liverpool-Cardiff).

Sikorsky's next production machine was the R-6, flown on 15 October 1943, a streamlined successor to the R-4 with a same-size rotor driven by a 225-hp Lycoming. On 2 March 1944 the prototype set world helicopter records by flying 387 miles non-stop from Washington to Dayton and climbing to 5000 ft over the Alleghenies. Most of the production R-6 machines were built by Nash-Kelvinator, the Navy version being the HOS-1 and the British name being Hoverfly II.

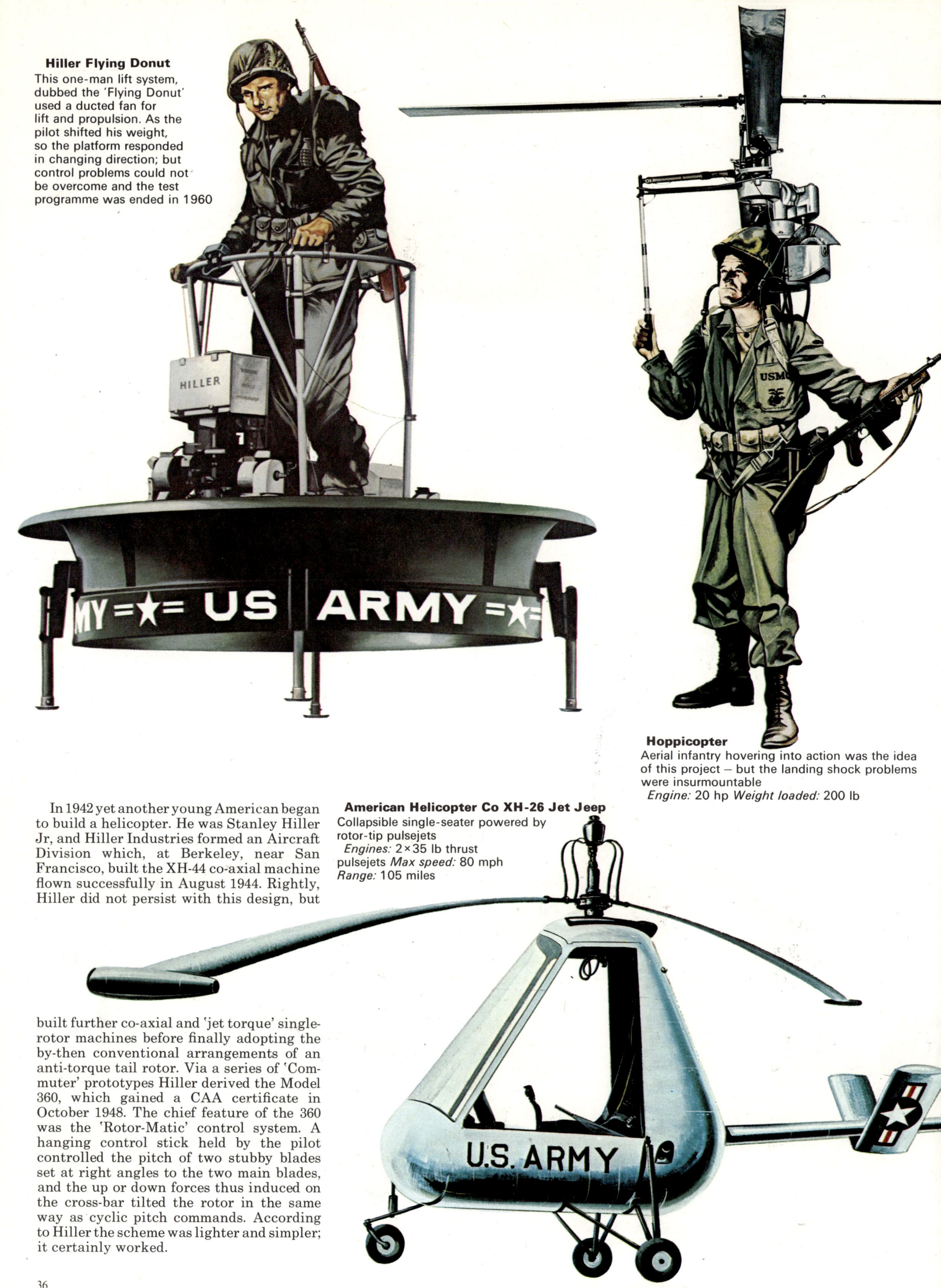

Hiller Flying Donut
This one-man lift system, dubbed the 'Flying Donut' used a ducted fan for lift and propulsion. As the pilot shifted his weight, so the platform responded in changing direction; but control problems could not be overcome and the test programme was ended in 1960

Hoppicopter
Aerial infantry hovering into action was the idea of this project – but the landing shock problems were insurmountable
Engine: 20 hp *Weight loaded:* 200 lb

American Helicopter Co XH-26 Jet Jeep
Collapsible single-seater powered by rotor-tip pulsejets
Engines: 2×35 lb thrust pulsejets *Max speed:* 80 mph *Range:* 105 miles

In 1942 yet another young American began to build a helicopter. He was Stanley Hiller Jr, and Hiller Industries formed an Aircraft Division which, at Berkeley, near San Francisco, built the XH-44 co-axial machine flown successfully in August 1944. Rightly, Hiller did not persist with this design, but built further co-axial and 'jet torque' single-rotor machines before finally adopting the by-then conventional arrangements of an anti-torque tail rotor. Via a series of 'Commuter' prototypes Hiller derived the Model 360, which gained a CAA certificate in October 1948. The chief feature of the 360 was the 'Rotor-Matic' control system. A hanging control stick held by the pilot controlled the pitch of two stubby blades set at right angles to the two main blades, and the up or down forces thus induced on the cross-bar tilted the rotor in the same way as cyclic pitch commands. According to Hiller the scheme was lighter and simpler; it certainly worked.

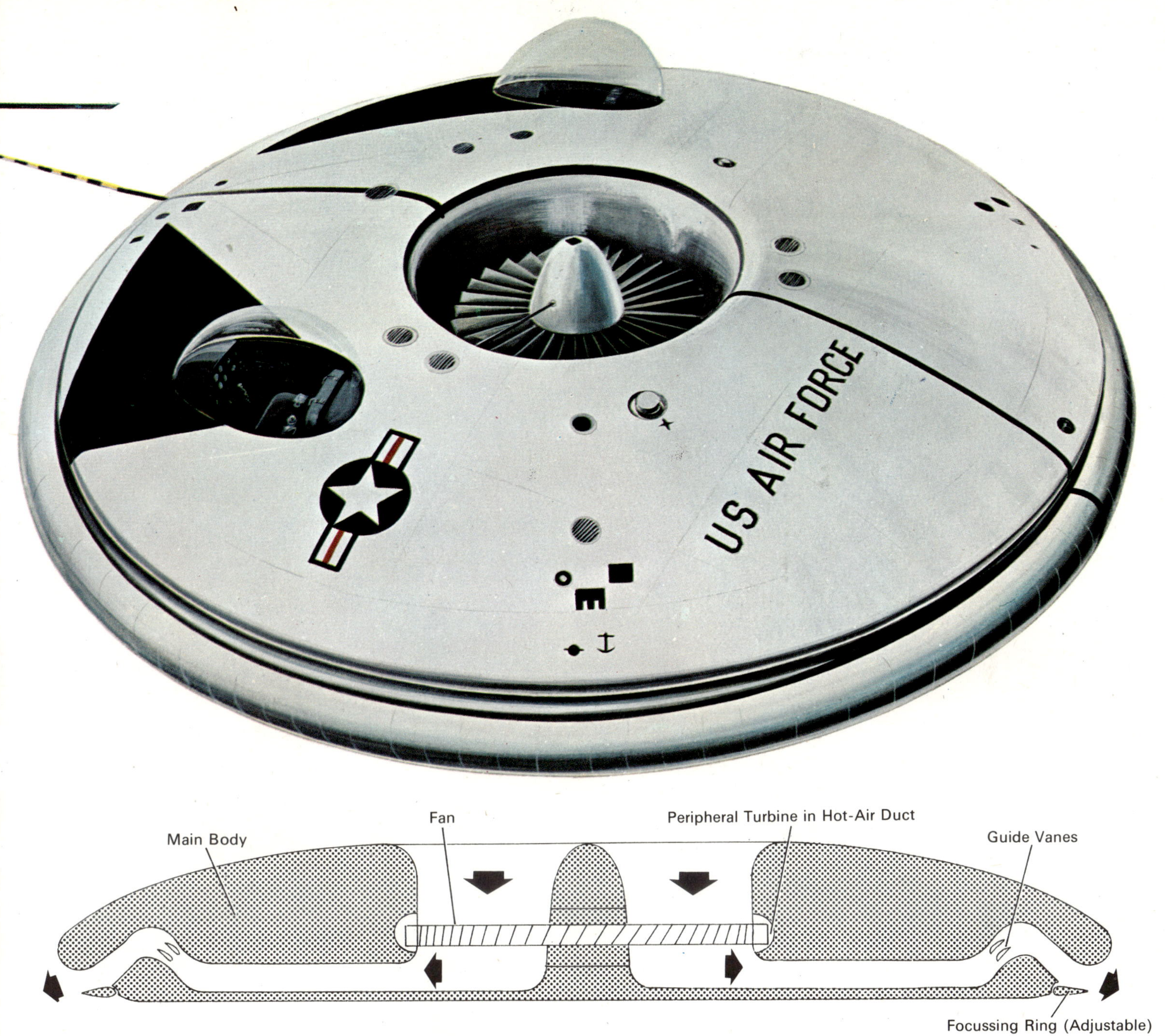

Avro Avrocar
Built by Avro Canada for the USAF. Intended to fly at high speed and at altitude, it never did more than hover within ground effect
Engine: 3×1000 hp Continental J69-T-9 turbojets *Max forward speed (planned):* 300 mph *Range:* 1000 miles

Redesignated Model 12, this machine went into production in 1949, and by 1965 more than 2000 had been built, in many versions. Most were trainers for the US Army, there often being more than 200 Hiller H-23B, H-23C or H-23D trainers at Fort Wolters alone. This cheap and robust Hiller was also a favourite for agricultural spraying and dusting, pipeline and power-line patrol and many other tasks not calling for heavy-lift capability. Seating varied from two to four. Hiller also shared in the great boom in baby helicopters immediately after the war, building the HJ-1 Hornet in 1950 with stubby body and twin Hiller ramjets on the tips of the rotor blades.

This craze for small rotorcraft was expected to give almost every citizen his own personal helicopter. Designs by the dozen proliferated in the United States, most either being simple machines with baby piston engines or even simpler ones with various kinds of jet unit on the tips of the blades. One of the earliest was the Hoppi-Copter, flown in 1945. This weighed a mere 90 lb, and was strapped to the pilot's back. The second, Hoppi-Copter 101, had a seat, the co-axial rotors growing from 12 ft to 15 and then to 17 ft.

There followed at least nine similar ultra-light US helicopters, as well as the following with tip drive: American Helicopters XA-5 Top Sargent, flown in January 1949 with 8·75-in pulsejets on the two blades; American Helicopters XA-6 Buck Private, flown in February 1951 with improved pulse jets funded by the USAF; American Helicopters XH-26, flown on 30 June 1952, meeting a USAF need for a single-seat folding machine capable of being air-dropped, with weight of 700 lb and speed of 80 mph on two 6·75-in pulsejets; Bensen Mid-Jet, flown in 1954 by yet another former Russian, Igor Bensen (of whom much will be heard later), powered by two ramjets and weighing a mere 120 lb empty; Capital Hoppi-copter, flown in 1954 with Naval Research Laboratory pulsejets; Jervis Bay J, tested in 1954, with valved pulsejets; Kellett KH-15, flown in 1954, with Reaction Motors XLR32 rockets on the tips; McDonnell XH-20 Little Henry, flown on 5 May 1947 with two Marquardt ramjets; McDonnell Model 82 XV-1, a large converti-plane with fixed wing, pusher propeller and twin tail booms, with auxiliary compressor supplying air to pressure jets (fuel/air combustion) at the tips of the three blades, flown under Army contract in 1954; Nagler 130 Convert-a-Craft, an autogyro flown in 1954 with three small rockets to speed up the tip of each of the two blades prior to vertical takeoff: Marquardt M-14, flown in 1946, the world's first pulsejet helicopter with an 8-in unit on each tip; Rotor-Jets RJ-1, flown in 1947, with single counter-balanced blade with a tip ramjet; Rotorcraft RH-1 Pinwheel, flown in 1954, with XLR32 rockets and intended to have the skid removed and be strapped on; and Schmidt Paracopter, flown in 1953, with a Schmidt pulsejet on each tip.

Cierva W-9
Experimental design of 1944. Torque compensation was by ducted exhaust efflux instead of a tail rotor
Engine: 1205 hp DH Gipsy VI *Weight fully loaded:* 2647 lb *Number of seats:* 2

A Bristol 171, later called Sycamore, inaugurates the short-lived BEA London (Heathrow)–Southampton helicopter shuttle service on 15 June 1954

Bristol Sycamore HR 14
One of a batch of 36 (of a total of 87 of this mark) delivered to the RAF in 1954. The bulged side panels accommodated two transverse stretchers
Engine: 1520 hp Alvis Leonides 524/1 *Weight fully loaded:* 5400 lb *Cruising speed:* 92 mph *Range:* 268 miles *Number of seats:* 4–5

To a great degree this wealth of radical little rotorcraft, with no 'engine' other than a thruster on the blade tips, happened simply because it was technically possible, and because in the United States the environment was fertile. In other countries there was no such outburst, though steady progress continued. In the Soviet Union Bratukhin had taken over the *vertolet* (vertical flight) section at the TsAGI in 1940 and under his direction work went ahead – slowly, because of the war – on helicopters derived from the Fa 61. Called the Omega series, these were not outstanding machines, though from No 2, flown in August 1941, they had two engines – the first rotorcraft with two engines. The twin rotors were of under 23-ft diameter and consequently were heavily loaded. Even in the powerful G-4, flown in October 1947 with a pair of 500-hp Ivchenko AI-26 radials, the rotors were of only 25·25-ft diameter despite the gross weight of over 6600 lb. The Bratukhin team never produced a really good machine, though later models of 1948–50 had fixed wings and were compound helicopters (helicopters provided with wings and tails and able to fly from one place to another in the same way as an aeroplane).

In Britain the Cierva company recommenced operations in 1943, two of the directors, J G Weir and C G Pullin, having long experience of earlier designs. Two later recruits were Jacob Shapiro and former aeroplane designer Harold Bolas. They built a helicopter called the W 9 which was unusual in that instead of an anti-torque tail rotor it had a long tail boom terminating in a side-facing jet nozzle through which cooling air from the 200-hp Gipsy Queen engine was discharged. The greater the engine power, the faster went the cooling

British Airways

Cierva W-11 Air Horse
Powered by a single Merlin engine buried in the fuselage, the W-11 was the largest helicopter in the world when it first flew in December 1948
Engine: 1620 hp Rolls-Royce Merlin 24 *Weight fully loaded:* 17,500 lb *Cruising speed:* 110 mph *Range:* 330 miles *Number of seats:* 26

fan and the greater the side-thrust at the tail. This was followed by a totally different and rather ill-conceived monster, the W 11 Air Horse, the only helicopter ever built with three rotors driven by one engine. The Rolls-Royce Merlin of 1620 hp was in the big fuselage, just behind the flight deck. Shafts drove the 47-ft rotors arranged at the bow and to left and right at the rear. The Air Horse was intended to carry 24 passengers, freight up to 3755 lb (with full tanks) or to do crop spraying. Unhappily a vital part broke through fatigue and the giant machine crashed, killing pilots H A Marsh and Sqn Ldr Cable.

Cierva also began a light helicopter, the W 14 Skeeter. Though seemingly simple, this little machine demonstrates how difficult it is for a not particularly outstanding team to make a helicopter safe and reliable enough for delivery to customers. In the case of the Skeeter the job took over ten years. Design began in 1946, and the prototype flew at Southampton Airport on 8 October 1948, after extensive rig tests and ground running. The Cierva team might have expected production to begin within two years, but in fact no Skeeters were delivered until September 1958. By this time the company had long since been acquired by Saunders-Roe, and the design of the Skeeter had been subjected to countless modifications. Only 74 were delivered, the last in 1960 by which time the name of the firm had changed yet again – this time to Westland, the company that eventually absorbed virtually all British helicopter activities.

Biggest of the British post-war helicopter teams was that built up from nothing by Bristol Aeroplane Company (later Bristol Aircraft Ltd). The technical director was Hafner, who had never ceased to dream of commercial helicopters and even proposed great moth-like VTOL machines which would have rotated through 90° to hang on vertical walls. But the work began in a much simpler way with a straightforward single-engine, single-rotor machine designated Bristol 171 and later named Sycamore. Design began in 1944 and deliveries were made from 1951 to 1959, total output being 177. Virtually all were military, though BEA used two. Though conventional, this Leonides-powered five-seater was fast and smooth, a notable feature being the high rotational speed of its three-blade rotor.

After getting the 171 into production it seemed natural to double up and produce the Type 173. This was designed to a Ministry of Supply specification, was fully funded by the government and took shape in 1947–51, finally completing its static testing and taking to the air on 3 January 1952. At that time it was possibly the most advanced helicopter in the world, and the nearest thing yet to a VTOL airliner. It looked rather like a railway carriage, with a long parallel-sided fuselage, four wheels, a huge fin and two sets of Sycamore engine/rotor systems in tandem, linked together to give some single-engine capability. Unfortunately the 173 could not fly on one engine, and the Bristol Janus turboshaft engine was never fully developed. The result was an appalling waste of time and money, with five years being spent fiddling with various problems and countless more advanced projects, and no eventual product was produced until the turboshaft-powered Westland Belvedere entered service in 1961.

Saunders-Roe Skeeter AOP 10
The Skeeter was a two-seater light observation helicopter designed initially by Cierva, and built by Saro (later Westland). It served with the RAF and the German forces
Engine: 200 hp DH Gipsy Major *Weight fully loaded:* 2200 lb *Cruising speed:* 101 mph *Range:* 260 miles *Number of seats:* 2

Dead-End Developments

TAIL-SITTING FIGHTERS

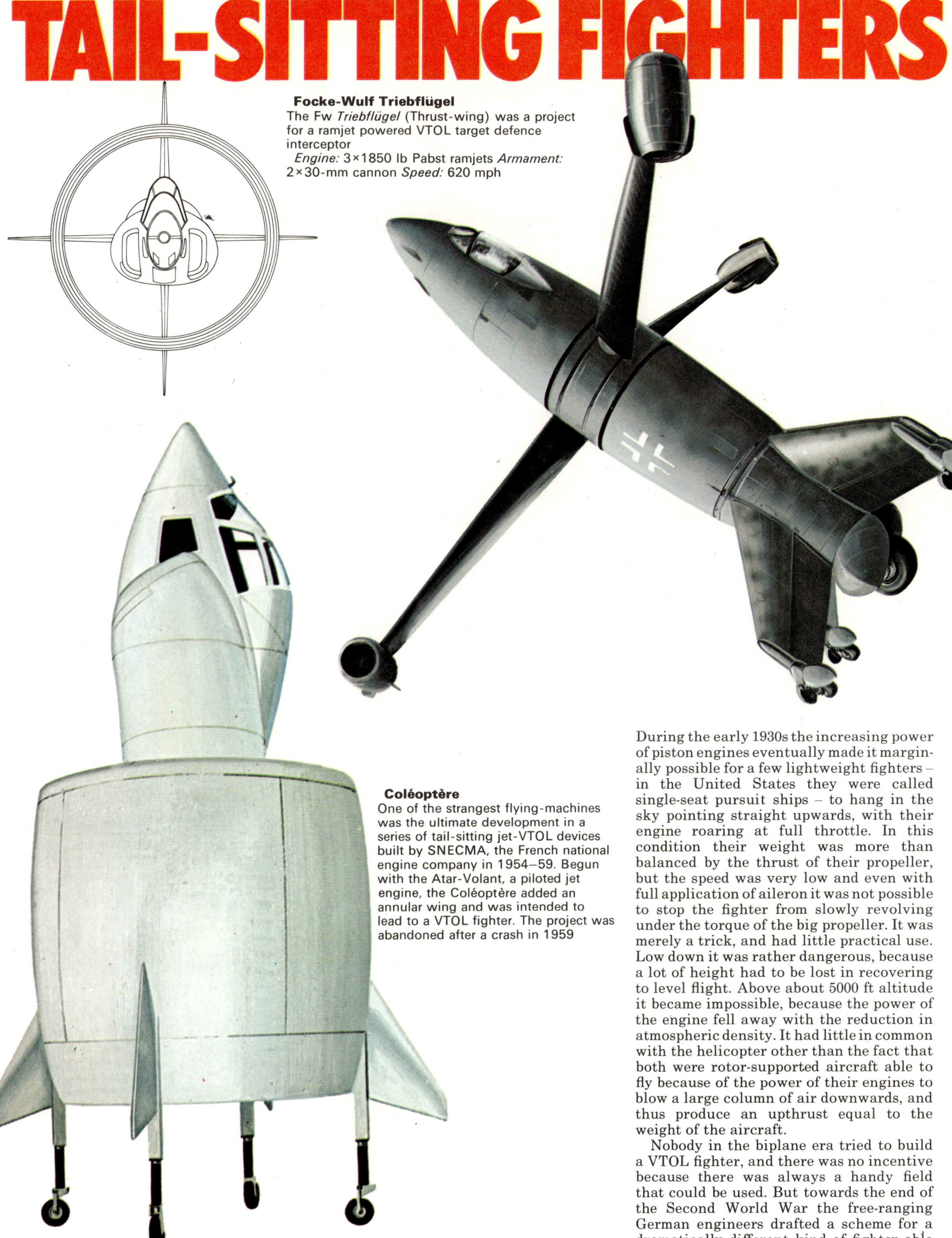

Focke-Wulf Triebflügel
The Fw *Triebflügel* (Thrust-wing) was a project for a ramjet powered VTOL target defence interceptor
Engine: 3×1850 lb Pabst ramjets *Armament:* 2×30-mm cannon *Speed:* 620 mph

Coléoptère
One of the strangest flying-machines was the ultimate development in a series of tail-sitting jet-VTOL devices built by SNECMA, the French national engine company in 1954–59. Begun with the Atar-Volant, a piloted jet engine, the Coléoptère added an annular wing and was intended to lead to a VTOL fighter. The project was abandoned after a crash in 1959

During the early 1930s the increasing power of piston engines eventually made it marginally possible for a few lightweight fighters – in the United States they were called single-seat pursuit ships – to hang in the sky pointing straight upwards, with their engine roaring at full throttle. In this condition their weight was more than balanced by the thrust of their propeller, but the speed was very low and even with full application of aileron it was not possible to stop the fighter from slowly revolving under the torque of the big propeller. It was merely a trick, and had little practical use. Low down it was rather dangerous, because a lot of height had to be lost in recovering to level flight. Above about 5000 ft altitude it became impossible, because the power of the engine fell away with the reduction in atmospheric density. It had little in common with the helicopter other than the fact that both were rotor-supported aircraft able to fly because of the power of their engines to blow a large column of air downwards, and thus produce an upthrust equal to the weight of the aircraft.

Nobody in the biplane era tried to build a VTOL fighter, and there was no incentive because there was always a handy field that could be used. But towards the end of the Second World War the free-ranging German engineers drafted a scheme for a dramatically different kind of fighter able to stand on any patch of ground – even a cleared patch in a city bombed to rubble – and roar vertically up into the sky. After shooting down enemy bombers it could again revert to the propeller-supported mode and gingerly lower itself back on to the ground, again in the vertical attitude. It has not been mentioned before because it was not built during the war; but the idea was of such extreme technical interest that it inspired the Americans to build VTOL fighters in the decade after 1945.

The company involved in the wartime project was Focke-Wulf. The main purpose of the *Triebflügel* (thrust-wing) project was target defence, and it was expected that such aircraft could operate anywhere (needing no airfield) and climb very rapidly to intercept hostile formations. The fuselage was of circular section, and almost perfectly streamlined. In the nose was the pilot's pressurized cockpit, and two 30-mm cannon. At the rear were four large fins and an array of five landing wheels on which the craft could stand pointing vertically upwards. Around the centre of the fuselage was a freely rotating collar, running on rings of wheels carried on ball/roller-bearing shafts arranged round the fuselage. This collar carried three radial wings, each slightly twisted like the blades of a monster propeller. On the tip of each wing was a Pabst ramjet with a thrust of about 1850 lb.

The intention was that the wings should be pivoted in their sockets until their mean angle of incidence was zero. The collar was then driven round by an electric starter motor, or by rockets attached to the ramjets, until the three wings were rotating at high speed, like the rotor of a helicopter. The fuel was then admitted to the ramjet burners, ignited, and the rockets jettisoned or the starter de-clutched. The ramjets would then drive the wings even faster, making a ring of flame around the aircraft. The pilot would take off by applying positive pitch to the wings; the fighter would rise vertically and climb into the sky.

The pilot then had the difficult task of effecting a new manoeuvre called a transition; from vertical flight with the nose pointing skyward to horizontal flight with the fuselage in the normal attitude. At full power and maximum wing (propeller) pitch the speed was expected to be 620 mph. Obviously there were severe problems to be overcome, but the basic idea was sound and of great interest. To land, the pilot adjusted the pitch of the tail controls to bring the aircraft into a level hovering attitude roughly above its landing area. He then had to look down over his shoulder and juggle with the throttle until the aircraft had touched down gently on its tail landing gears.

In the immediate postwar years the US armed forces carefully studied the concept of a VTOL fighter. It seemed that, before long, the increasing thrust of jet engines would enable a fighter to rise straight off the ground and fly away (as the Harrier can indeed now do). But before that became possible it seemed likely that a VTOL aircraft could be made using a powerful turboprop. Driving large propellers, engines can generate static thrust much greater than the thrust of an equivalent turbojet. The main drawback, apart from the weight, complexity and likelihood of failure of the propeller, was that the maximum speed was

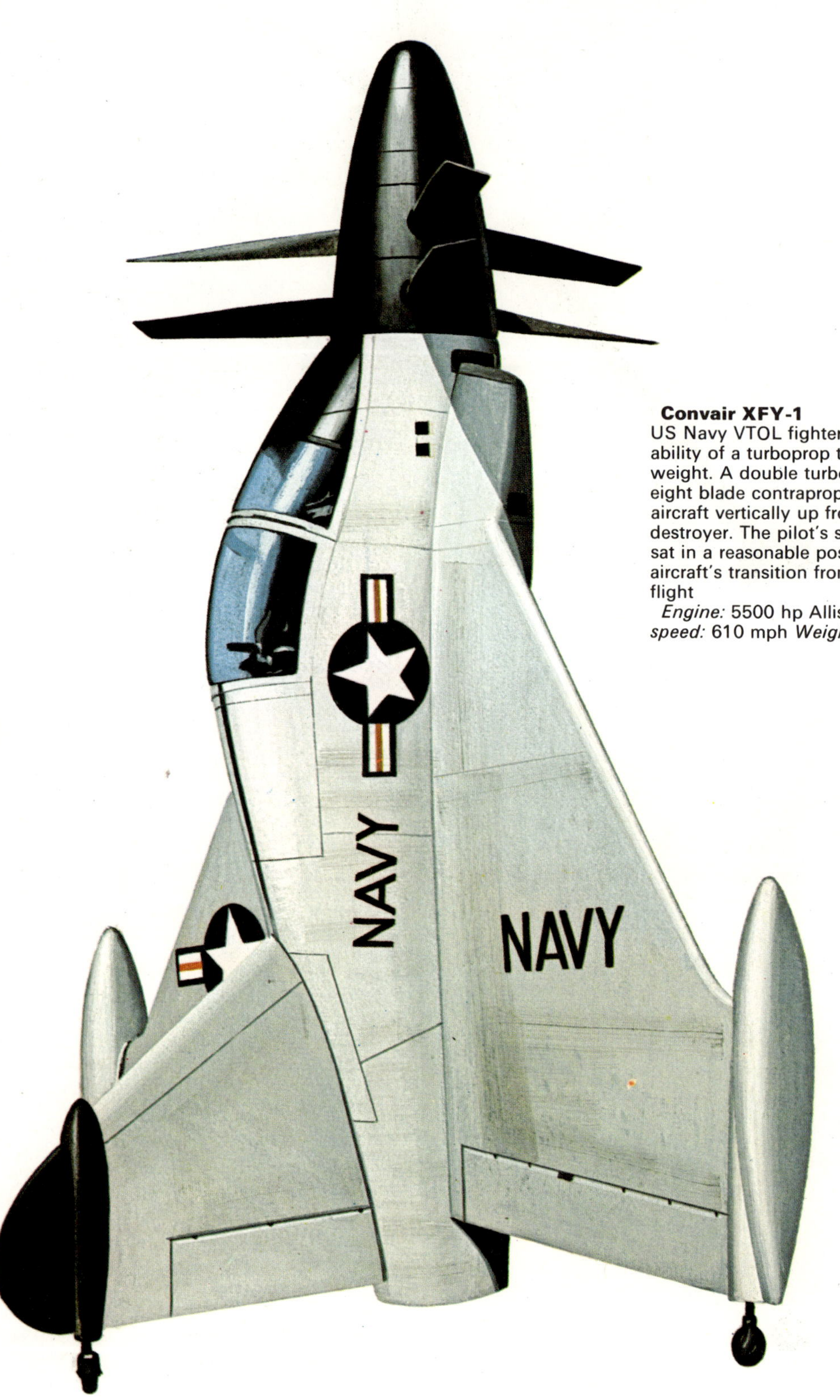

Convair XFY-1
US Navy VTOL fighter made possible by the ability of a turboprop to lift several times its own weight. A double turboprop driving a large eight blade contraprop was intended to pull the aircraft vertically up from the deck of a frigate or destroyer. The pilot's seat was pivoted so that he sat in a reasonable position throughout the aircraft's transition from vertical to horizontal flight
Engine: 5500 hp Allison XT40A-A-6 *Max speed:* 610 mph *Weight fully loaded:* 16,250 lb

unlikely to be as high as that of a jet fighter.

Despite this, the US Navy decided in 1950, after two years of study, to invite submissions from industry for VTOL 'fighters' powered by turboprops. There was no background of prior experience, no notion of what problems would be met and, not least, no suitable turboprop. But in March 1951 submissions were chosen from two manufacturers and designated the Convair XFY-1 (nicknamed the Pogo) and Lockheed XFV-1 (called Salmon after the chief test pilot Herman 'Fish' Salmon). Both submissions specified the Allison XT40, a coupled turboprop with two power sections jointly putting out about 5500 shaft horsepower. By paring the projects to the bone, and cutting out most fuel and armament, it was expected that this would be enough for safe vertical flight.

The XFV-1 and XFY-1 were like no other aircraft before or since. Standing on their tails they towered over people on the ground, and it was quite a frightening climb up a multi-storey maintenance platform to reach the cockpit and climb into the pivoting ejection seat. Both aircraft were investigated carefully in model tests in special wind tunnels. Then the Lockheed, fitted with a temporary 'horizontal' landing gear, flew as an aeroplane from a runway, while the Convair, tethered to a safety harness, lifted off vertically inside a hangar.

Eventually the Convair succeeded in making free flights during 1954, and in completing the difficult transitions to forwards wing-supported flight and back to a vertical landing. Gross weight of both machines was around eight tons (an operational fighter would have been heavier) and maximum speed about 600 mph. One of the reasons why the concept was abandoned was the sheer piloting difficulty of landing. Taking off was straightforward: the pilot merely opened the throttle and steered straight up until beginning the forwards transition to wing-borne flight. But landing was difficult and dangerous. The pilot had a poor over-the-shoulder view, had to judge height very accurately and, most difficult of all, had no direct check on descent. An unskilled pilot would have yo-yoed up and down or crashed. Later, however, there were jet tail-sitters.

Lockheed XFV-1
Rival to the XFY, the Lockheed XFV-1 Salmon first flew as a conventional aeroplane with a large temporary landing gear. Like its competitor intended as a ship-based fighter, development problems were too great and the eventual aircraft too compromised to be useful
Engine: 5500 hp Allison XT40A-A-6 *Max speed:* 580 mph *Weight fully loaded:* 16,221 lb

U.S. EXPANSION

In the late 1940s helicopters were built by many American companies, most of them having no previous aircraft experience. Gyrodyne Company of America adopted the co-axial configuration, and tried to combine this with the fixed wing and pusher propeller to yield a compound helicopter or convertiplane. McDonnell, formed in 1939, received a Navy contract in 1944 for the world's second twin-engined helicopter, the XHJD-1 Whirlaway. Weighing six tons, this flew in 1946 and had the exact configuration of a scaled-down German Fa 284, with wings, engines at mid-span, tip rotors, tricycle landing gear and glazed nose.

Another team that copied the Germans was that of Charles H Kaman, one of the few to stay in the helicopter business right up to the present. Basing the design on the Flettner scheme, with intermeshing rotors on close tilted axes, Kaman flew the K-125A on 15 January 1947. His main contribution was to dispense with all articulation save the lag hinge. Instead he rigidly attached blades of solid spruce, fitted at three-quarters span with servo flaps hinged to the trailing edge and moved by the pilot's controls. These flaps twisted the blades, which also had appreciable flapping resilience. Surprisingly good results were obtained, and by 1949 the pre-production K-225 utility vehicle, with 225-hp Lycoming, had been certificated and was being used from Maine to Florida in the control of insect pests and in other spraying and dusting agricultural duties.

Later the K-225 was fitted with a Boeing XT50 turbine and on 10 December 1951 became the first of the new and dominant generation of rotorcraft driven by turboshaft power. A modified K-225 was built in small numbers for the Navy as the HTK-1 trainer and utility machine, and on 26 March 1954 an HTK-1 flew on the power of two inter-geared Boeing YT50 turboshaft engines. Kaman believe this to have been the first helicopter ever to have true 'engine-out' capability, ie, it could go on flying indefinitely after failure of one engine. From this time on, the light and compact gas-turbine engine was to exert the largest single beneficial influence on the whole family of rotary-wing aircraft, at last giving them more than marginal

Hughes XH-17
Experimental heavy-lift helicopter first flown in October 1952. Turbojets provided compressed air for blade-tip pressure jets. The XH-17 had enormous potential, but its range was too short to be practical
Engines: 2×GE J35 turbojets *Weight fully loaded:* 52,000 lb *Cruising speed:* 60 mph *Range:* 40 miles *Number of seats:* 2

Kaman H-43B Huskie
Specially designed as an airborne crash and fire-rescue vehicle, the Huskie was ready with a range of rescue equipment at all major USAF bases
Engine: 860 hp Lycoming T53-L-1B *Weight fully loaded:* 8800 lb *Cruising speed:* 109 mph *Range:* 270 miles *Number of seats:* 12

Kaman H-43A crash-rescue helicopter with ball of extinguishant on its hook

payload and ample flight performance.

During 1950 Kaman won a Navy design competition for a utility helicopter for the Marine Corps. The K-600 developed the eggbeater layout to a larger size, with 47-ft rotors and gross weight exceeding 7000 lb. The production HOK-1 was first delivered in 1958, with a 600-hp Pratt & Whitney Wasp, large cabin for two crew and five passengers, and improved ability to fly safely even in bad weather. In the same year deliveries began of the H-43A version to the US Air Force for crash/fire rescue use. Some of these carried a large red ball slung underneath filled with chemical extinguishant. Ultimately several hundred of these fine machines were delivered for many purposes to many customers, the majority having the new Lycoming T53 free-turbine engine derated to 825 hp and providing much better performance, more interior space and a lower noise level. All were eventually designated in the H-43 series, with the family name Huskie. The turbine-powered Huskies could seat up to 11 passengers.

By far the most impressive of all rotorcraft in the early 1950s was a strange monster designated XH-17. This was planned and taken through the design process by Kellett, but hardware trials were transferred to Hughes Aircraft at Culver City. Already the aircraft firm of billionaire Howard Hughes had a reputation for being quite undeterred by the most formidable development problems, and certainly the XH-17 made sense on paper. In any case, it was part-funded by the US Air Force. It was a flying crane, the specialized category pioneered by the German Fa 284 and intended to lift cargo weighing up to 24,700 lb, more than ten times as much as any other rotorcraft of its day. To do so it had a radically new form of lift power.

Limited Range

There was not very much to the XH-17 apart from the gigantic two-blade rotor, with a diameter of 136 ft. This was carried on a stubby but lofty structure, on a tall multi-wheel landing gear. On each side was a General Electric TG-180 turbojet, later redesignated J35, modified so that instead of giving just jet thrust it supplied an enormous flow of compressed air, tapped off through a large duct between the compressor and combustion chambers. The air trunks led up to the mighty rotor hub and then delivered the air along the hollow blades to General Electric GE33F pressure-jet burners arranged along the outer part of each blade. Here fuel was injected and burned for VTOL, though it was hoped fuel burning at the tips could be reduced or even eliminated in cruising flight. The giant machine spent 1949–51 in ground tests and then made a successful free flight on 23 October 1952. Eventually plans for the projected production version, the H-28, were cancelled. The limiting range of around 40 miles was a great handicap, because the XH-17 was too big to be airlifted at that time and thus had to fly to wherever it was needed or travel by ship. But it was bigger and had more rotor power than any helicopter since built outside the Soviet Union.

British Development Falters

FRANCE LEADS EUROPE

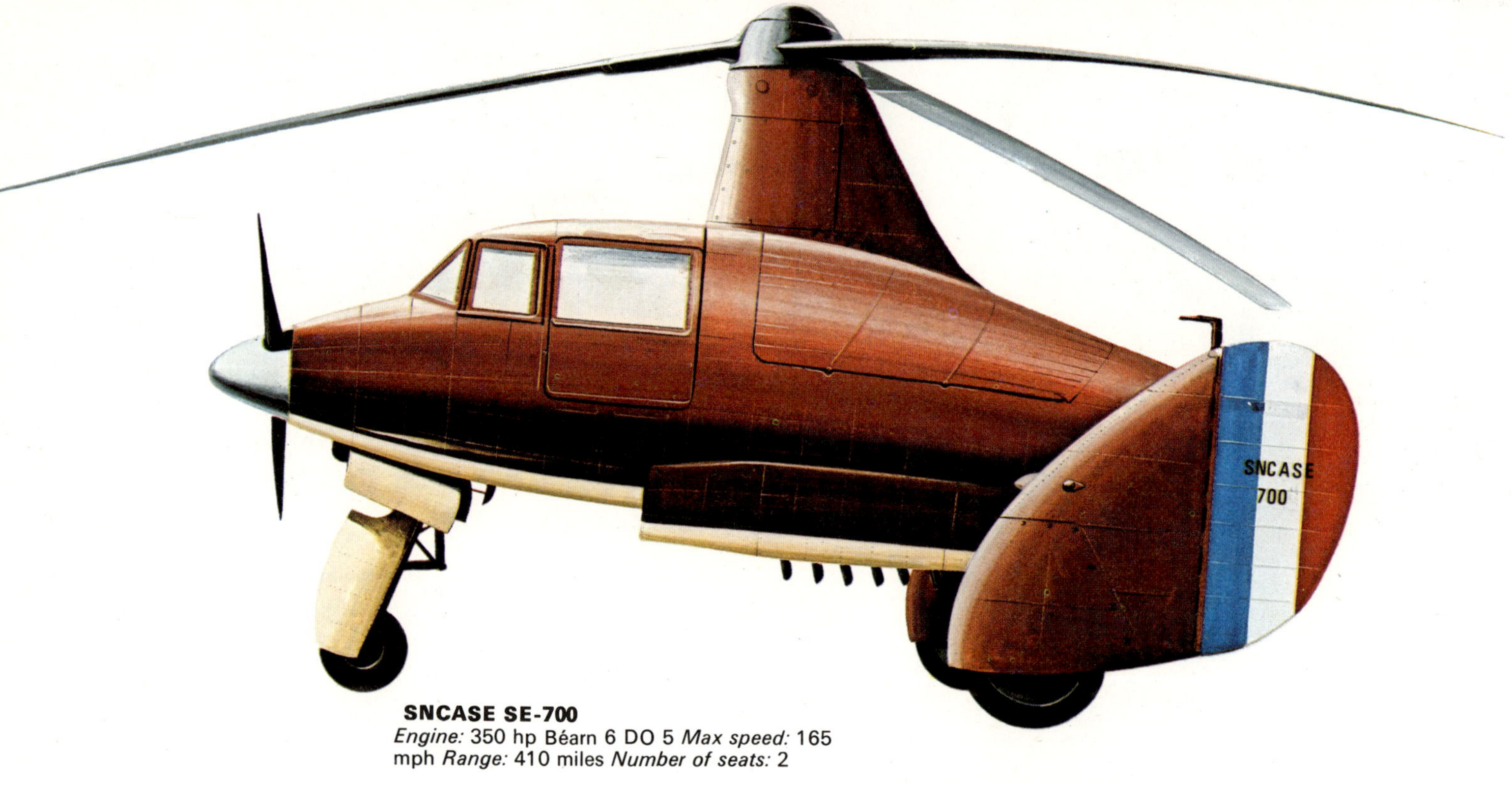

SNCASE SE-700
Engine: 350 hp Béarn 6 DO 5 *Max speed:* 165 mph *Range:* 410 miles *Number of seats:* 2

Outside the United States the biggest rotorcraft effort in the postwar years took place in France, where teams worked heroically in a very difficult environment to get back in the aviation business after years of enemy occupation. All the aircraft produced in France for the Germans had been aeroplanes, and there was no background of rotary-wing experience except at Breguet. Yet, oddly, Breguet's postwar helicopter development came to nothing, while rival teams gradually evolved the best-selling helicopters of the whole of Europe. Breguet built the Gyroplane IIE in 1949 with coaxial rotors driven by a 240-hp Potez radial, then rebuilt it as the III with 450-hp Wasp engine, but never achieved production.

The nationalized group SNCASO (Sud-Ouest) had no experience in this field when, in 1947, it embarked on the design of the novel SO 1100 Ariel I. Looking rather like an orange, being of that colour and almost spherical, the Ariel I flew in 1949 with an unusual tip-drive scheme. A 220-hp Mathis G8 piston-engine drove a Turboméca compressor delivering air to combustion pressure-jet burners at the tips of the three blades. As there was no torque there was no tail rotor, but the engine also drove a propeller in a ring shroud at the back of the stumpy body. Within weeks this was followed by the SO 1100 Ariel II, with a long tail boom carrying a tailplane and twin fins. Turboméca then produced a self-contained gas-turbine compressor engine, the Arrius, which gave more power for much less weight, and with this the SO 1120 Ariel III was flown on 18 April 1951. The number of seats was increased from two to three, and the tail boom carried just a single fin and jet nozzle.

Quiet and Nimble

SNCASO also experimented with other drive systems. The SO 1310 *Farfadet* (sprite), flown on 9 June 1953, was a beautiful little convertiplane (compound helicopter), with a streamlined lightplane-type fuselage with 3/4-seat cabin, nose turboprop (Turboméca Marcadau), small wings, tricycle landing gear and conventional tail. Behind the cabin was the Arrius compressor serving the Ariel-type rotor. This trim little machine achieved its design speed of 150 mph, but was not taken any further.

The SO 1220 Djinn, however, was built in quantity for the French ALAT (*Aviation Légère de l'Armée de Terre)* and civil customers. A neat utility machine, it comprised an open frame carrying a Turboméca Palouste compressor delivering plain air to cold tip jets (ie, without additional combustion). Quiet and extremely nimble, the Djinn was one of the few European helicopters to have no counterpart elsewhere. SNCASO also made a research helicopter to fly the Lepère system of co-axial ducts along the blades for cold compressor air and hot engine exhaust, all mixed and discharged at the tip.

Another national group, Nord, built the Nord 1750 in 1954 with shaft drive from a Turboméca Artouste turbine rated at about 400 hp. Nord soon abandoned helicopters, and so eventually did SNCASO. The SNCASE (Sud-Est) group, on the other hand, began in the least impressive way yet finally became the leaders. Their works at La Courneuve, in northern Paris, began by flying a Focke Achgelis 223 and, after making some improvements, called it the SE 3000. The SE 3101 was a much smaller single-seat open-girder machine with a 110-hp Mathis engine and a curious tail-rotor scheme with twin oblique rotors. The SE 3110 used this scheme in a two-seat civil machine with streamlined body and new-technology blades having steel-tube spars and moulded-plastics shells. This was in turn developed into the SE 3120, powered like the 3110 by a 200-hp Salmson radial. Intended for agricultural spraying and dusting – tasks for which the helicopter is well suited, partly because the rotor downwash blows the chemical on to the normally inaccessible undersides of the leaves or crops – the 3120 was named Alouette (lark). It set several world and national records in July 1953.

Then the SE team did the obvious thing and exchanged the radial piston engine for a Turboméca Artouste turboshaft. The turbine gave 400 hp instead of 200, and was considerably lighter, and though it burned fuel faster the result transformed a fair helicopter into a world-beater. Designated SE 3130 Alouette II, the first production helicopter in the world with a turbine engine was built in France mainly because Joseph Szydlowski had by dogged determination managed to develop a suitable power plant. Since that time Szydlowski's Société Turboméca has been able to hold its own, even against the competition from the United States, as a leading supplier of small turbine engines for helicopters.

Apart from its totally different sounds – a screaming whistle instead of a throbbing roar – the Alouette II was very straightforward. It had an open girder frame, totally exposed engine just behind the rotor hub

Dorand DH-011
A flying test-bed for low-pressure tip-jet drive
Engine: Turboméca Aspin 1 *Weight fully loaded:* 2260 lb *Range:* 124 miles

and skid landing gear. On the front a plastic bubble housed the pilot and up to four passengers. Various versions have carried two stretchers, slung loads up to 1100 lb, guns, missiles and even homing torpedoes. The first SE 3130 (now designated SE 313B) flew on 12 March 1955, and in June 1955 set a new world helicopter record by climbing to 26,932 ft. Eventually 923 of the original version were sold to customers in 33 countries. Assembly and marketing licences were sold to the USA and Sweden, and in 1963 an Alouette II becme the first commercially used turbine helicopter in North America.

In January 1961 the first SA 318C Alouette II Astazou flew, powered by the new Turboméca engine of that name. Normally rated at 530 hp, the very neat Astazou is derated to 360 hp, giving constant power under almost any conceivable combination of high temperature and high altitude where other engines would give much less than their full output. Production of the Alouette II finally came to an end in 1975 after just over 1300 had been sold to customers in 46 countries. The SA 315B Lama remains in production, with 195 sold by late 1975, and more are being built as the HAL Cheetah in India. This combines the airframe of the Alouette II with the engine/rotor system of the Alouette III, and has lifted a slung load of 2205 lb to over 8200 ft and actually made takeoffs and landings in the Himalayas at heights over 24,600 ft.

The Alouette III first flew in 1959, and compared with the II has a much bigger cabin and more powerful engine. The main rotor is increased in size from 33·4 ft to 36·1 ft, and the engine is the Artouste (870 hp, derated to 570 hp) in the SA 316B version, and the Astazou XIV (870 hp, derated to 600 hp) in the SA 319B. This seven-seat helicopter proved an even greater success, and by 1975 was still in production with 1340 sold to customers in 69 countries. India, Rumania and Switzerland are making further Alouette III versions under licence.

In Britain such success with helicopters was conspicuously absent. The Auster company toyed with a small tip-ramjet helicopter for use as an Army observation machine but never flew it. Fairey made a very neat little helicopter, called the Ultra-Light, for the same British Army requirement, powered by a Blackburn Palouste compressor made under licence from Turboméca. Though smaller, more nimble and a better performer than the French Djinn, the Army decided it did not want such a thing after all, and the programme was dropped after six years of work.

Fairey Rotodyne

Fairey also built a very fast helicopter, the Leonides-powered Gyrodyne, which instead of having a tail rotor had an anti-torque rotor thrusting forwards on a stub wing on the right side. Flown in 1947, the Gyrodyne set a world helicopter speed record at 124·3 mph in June 1948. In January 1954 the second of these machines flew in completely rebuilt tip-drive form, using Doblhoff technology. The Leonides drove the supercharger from a Griffon piston engine to deliver air to a new rotor with only two blades with combustion pressure jets at the tips.

By this time the Hayes, Middlesex, company was well advanced with the design of a very large compound helicopter with two 2800-hp Napier Eland turboprops mounted on the fixed wing, driving propellers as well as delivering air to the pressure-jet main rotor. Sound engineering development ensured the scheme's viability, and eventually promised to yield the most efficient high-speed VTOL vehicle attainable with contemporary technology. The first Fairey Rotodyne flew on 6 November 1957, lifting off with pressure jets making a noise like a hardworking steam locomotive. In April 1958 it first converted into cruising flight, with the engine power all going into the propellers and the 90-ft rotor autorotating. The same aircraft set a closed-circuit speed record in January 1959 at 191 mph.

In 1960, after much further rebuilding and refinement the Rotodyne was taken over with the Fairey company by Westland, who continued this promising but very challenging machine and abandoned their own twin-Eland Westminster, a fine straight-forward shaft-drive helicopter first flown in 1958. Under the pressure of continually increasing demands from such apparent customers as BEA and the British Army the Rotodyne grew to a 75-seat size, with a different airframe and two Rolls-Royce Tyne engines each rated at 5250 hp. Civil and military operators around the world showed intense interest, and three even an intent to order, but eventually the British government did as it has invariably done since 1945 and simply got cold feet. It decided to abandon the whole thing, and work had to cease in 1962. For a supposed 'saving' of £10 million BEA was denied the use of an advanced city-centre airliner and the British forces were denied a heavy-lift helicopter. To show the quality of British official planning, the latter shortcoming was rectified in 1968 by ordering the American Chinook helicopter, and reversed by cancelling this order only weeks later, at a substantial penalty in dollars!

Yet another totally mismanaged British helicopter project was begun by Percival Aircraft in 1949, using two Napier Oryx turbine engines to deliver a mixture of cool air and hot gas through ducts to a large two-blade rotor. The scheme was tried in the P 74, which over a period of years (1954–58) steadfastly refused to fly. Eventually the proposed production P 105 was dropped, and with it the government-funded Oryx. One need hardly comment on the parallel Westland projects for huge helicopters with either shaft-turbine drive or, in the monster W 90, a Sapphire turbojet on the tip of each rotor blade. It would have weighed 206,000 lb and carried 450 troops.

Sud-Aviation SO-1221 Djinn
The Djinn was the first production helicopter to use simple compressed-air tip-jets without further combustion, and was outstanding in its simplicity
Engine: Turboméca Palouste IV gas turbine
Weight fully loaded: 1764 lb *Max speed:* 81 mph
Range: 112 miles *Number of seats:* 2

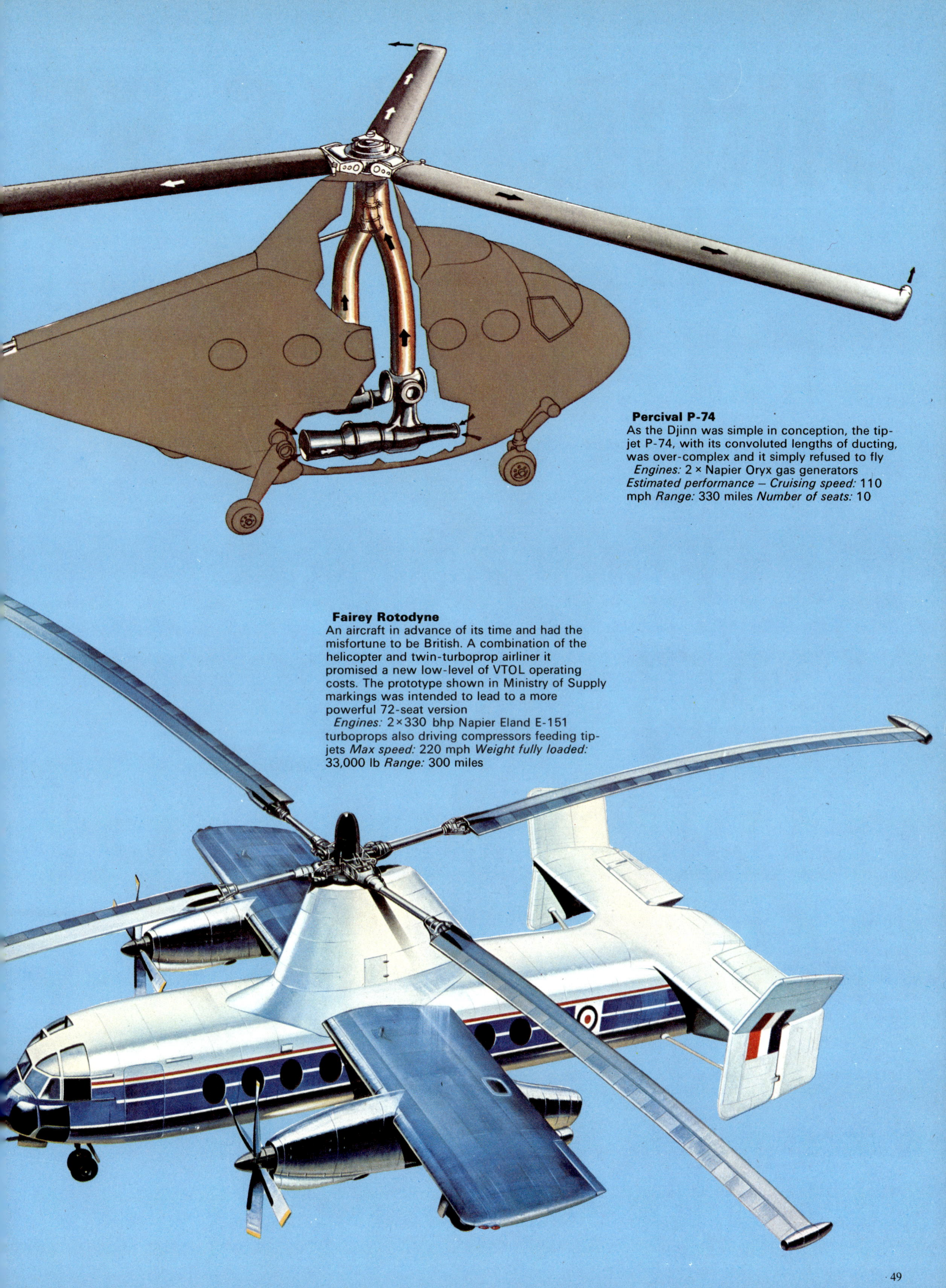

Percival P-74
As the Djinn was simple in conception, the tip-jet P-74, with its convoluted lengths of ducting, was over-complex and it simply refused to fly
Engines: 2 × Napier Oryx gas generators *Estimated performance – Cruising speed:* 110 mph *Range:* 330 miles *Number of seats:* 10

Fairey Rotodyne
An aircraft in advance of its time and had the misfortune to be British. A combination of the helicopter and twin-turboprop airliner it promised a new low-level of VTOL operating costs. The prototype shown in Ministry of Supply markings was intended to lead to a more powerful 72-seat version
Engines: 2×330 bhp Napier Eland E-151 turboprops also driving compressors feeding tip-jets *Max speed:* 220 mph *Weight fully loaded:* 33,000 lb *Range:* 300 miles

SIKORSKY S-55

September 1951 and US Marines practise the new military art of helicopter airborne assault at Camp Pendleton, Calif. The Sikorsky S-55 (Marine Corps designation HRS-1) was beginning its long career as a military and civil workhorse

Most British helicopters were Sikorsky designs, made by Westland. After the R-5 and R-6 the next big step was taken with the first flight of the Sikorsky S-55 in November 1949. In retrospect this was an odd design, but it marked a great advance in helicopter capability. With it Sikorsky tried to find the best answer to what was then a very difficult problem: how to arrange the parts of a helicopter for the best overall result.

As in all aircraft, the lift of a helicopter (which in a type with a single main rotor is close to the axis of that rotor) has to act along a line fairly close to the centre of gravity. It is also important for the place where the useful load and the fuel are carried to be centred about this same vertical line, otherwise the nose-up or nose-down trim would be altered according to the amount of load or fuel on board. In the early Sikorsky helicopters the load comprised only about two people, and ballast could be carried to compensate for an empty seat, so the seats could be in the nose. But with the S-55 it was intended to lift loads of up to 2800 lb. To carry such a load demanded a roomy cabin, and this had to be under the rotor.

Sikorsky looked at the various places an engine could be put, and even examined the pros and cons of two engines on the sides of the fuselage. Piston engines tended to be heavy and bulky, especially the air-cooled radial types which were the only ones available in the required 600-hp class. A further important point was that this helicopter was intended to be a robust and easily maintained workhorse for arduous use away from airfields, and it was essential that the engine (or engines) should be easily accessible, ideally without ladders and trestles being needed.

Eventually a unique arrangement was selected. The fuselage was made in the form of a large box, mounted on four landing wheels or large inflated float pontoons, with the tail rotor on the end of a slender boom quite high off the ground. The engine, a 600-hp Pratt & Whitney Wasp radial, was placed in the nose, access to it being via two clamshell doors which formed the entire nose of the helicopter. The engine was installed at a diagonal angle, with the drive shaft leading back and up to the main-rotor gearbox under the hub. Most of the box consisted of unobstructed cabin, with 340 cubic ft of space and a large sliding door on each side.

New Tradition

The cabin was directly under the rotor, and if evenly loaded did not disturb the cg position. Fuel was contained in a 159-gallon tank forming the cabin floor. The two pilots sat side-by-side above the cabin and engine, with the drive shaft casing passing diagonally between them, and got to their places by climbing up the outside. It was with the S-55 that the tradition was firmly established of seating the pilot on the right, with the co-pilot on the left if dual controls were fitted. This is the reverse of the conventional arrangement in aeroplanes.

Seated in an S-55 the pilot is more than ten feet off the ground before he starts the engine. As in all except a few ultra-light machines, the engine has to be fitted with a powered starter, the usual type being electric. This cranks the engine, but does not have to turn the whole ponderous rotor system because at rest the latter is de-clutched. The engine can be run at about 1000 rpm to have its dual ignition systems checked (by switching off first one and then the other) without the drive being engaged. Only when the pilot wishes to take off do the rotors begin to turn: opening up the throttle engages a centrifugal clutch which transmits the drive through to the main gearbox. From this, output shafts turning much more

Flight

Igor Sikorsky in the mid 1950s. The Russian born aviation pioneer's VS-300 was the prototype for modern machines and the helicopter industry

Sikorsky H-19 (Armée de l'Air markings)
The S-55 was licence-built in France by SNCASE
Engine: 600 hp Pratt & Whitney R-1340-57
Weight fully loaded: 7200 lb *Range:* 405 miles
Number of seats: 12

slowly drive the main and tail rotors, at least one of these shafts (usually that to the tail rotor) being fitted with a hydraulic brake to clamp the rotors when the helicopter is on the ground.

It is because there is a centrifugal clutch that the helicopter can autorotate freely after failure, or deliberate shutting-down, of the engine. In autorotation the engine is turning slowly or not at all, and the clutch is completely disengaged. The main and tail rotors can then spin freely, still geared together through the main gearbox, under the action of the airflow.

Sikorsky flew the first S-55 in November 1949. It was a timely flight, because in June 1950 war broke out in Korea, and this was to be the first conflict in which the helicopter played a major part. Nearly all the first S-55 versions were military. The first production type was the US Air Force H-19A, with a 550-hp Wasp engine and seats for two pilots, up to ten passengers or six stretchers. The Army and Marines bought basically similar models respectively designated H-19C and HRS-1 and -2, while the Navy bought the HO4S anti-submarine version (though it was not capable of carrying both search and strike gear). The US Coast Guard bought the HO4S-2G rescue version with a power-operated hoist which was also specified by nearly all other military customers. Since then a high proportion of utility helicopters have been fitted with a hoist, used chiefly for winching survivors from the sea or from wrecked ships or other dangerous places.

Slung Loads

Early hoists were electric, and could lift about 600 lb on a 250-ft cable; today many hoists are hydraulic, and some have higher performance in both weight limit and cable length. Many modern helicopters can also carry slung loads, but these are invariably merely secured to a strong hook on the belly approximately beneath the centre of gravity and axis of the main rotor. A few helicopters used aboard naval vessels are also provided with one of several kinds of hold-down system working like a load sling in reverse. The helicopter is winched down to the pitching deck of its parent ship by a cable and self-centring anchor device, and finally held by the same system so that it does not move even in a heavy sea.

Two Sikorsky HRS-1s (Marine Corps S-55) undergoing tests with experimental rotor hubs

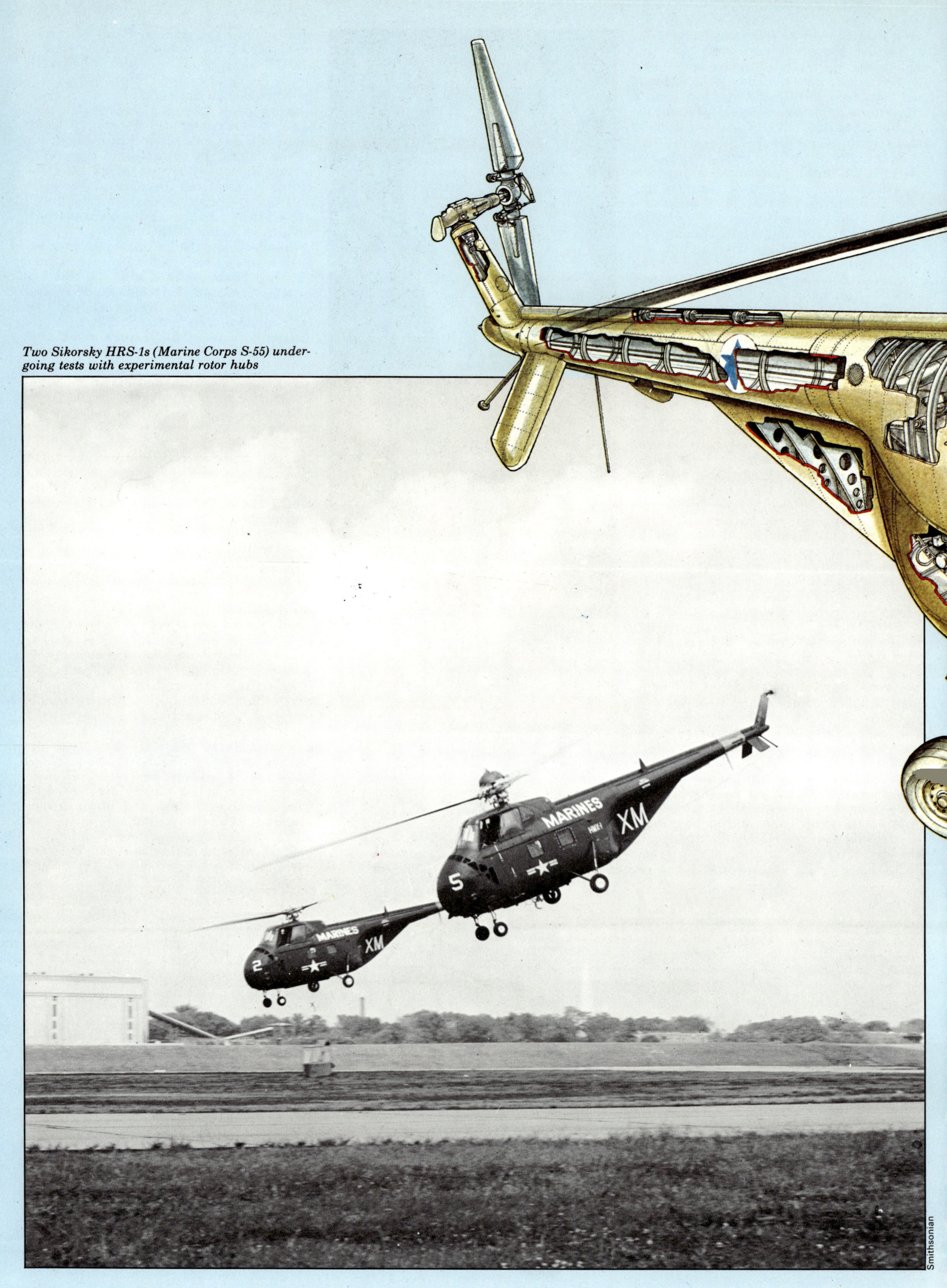

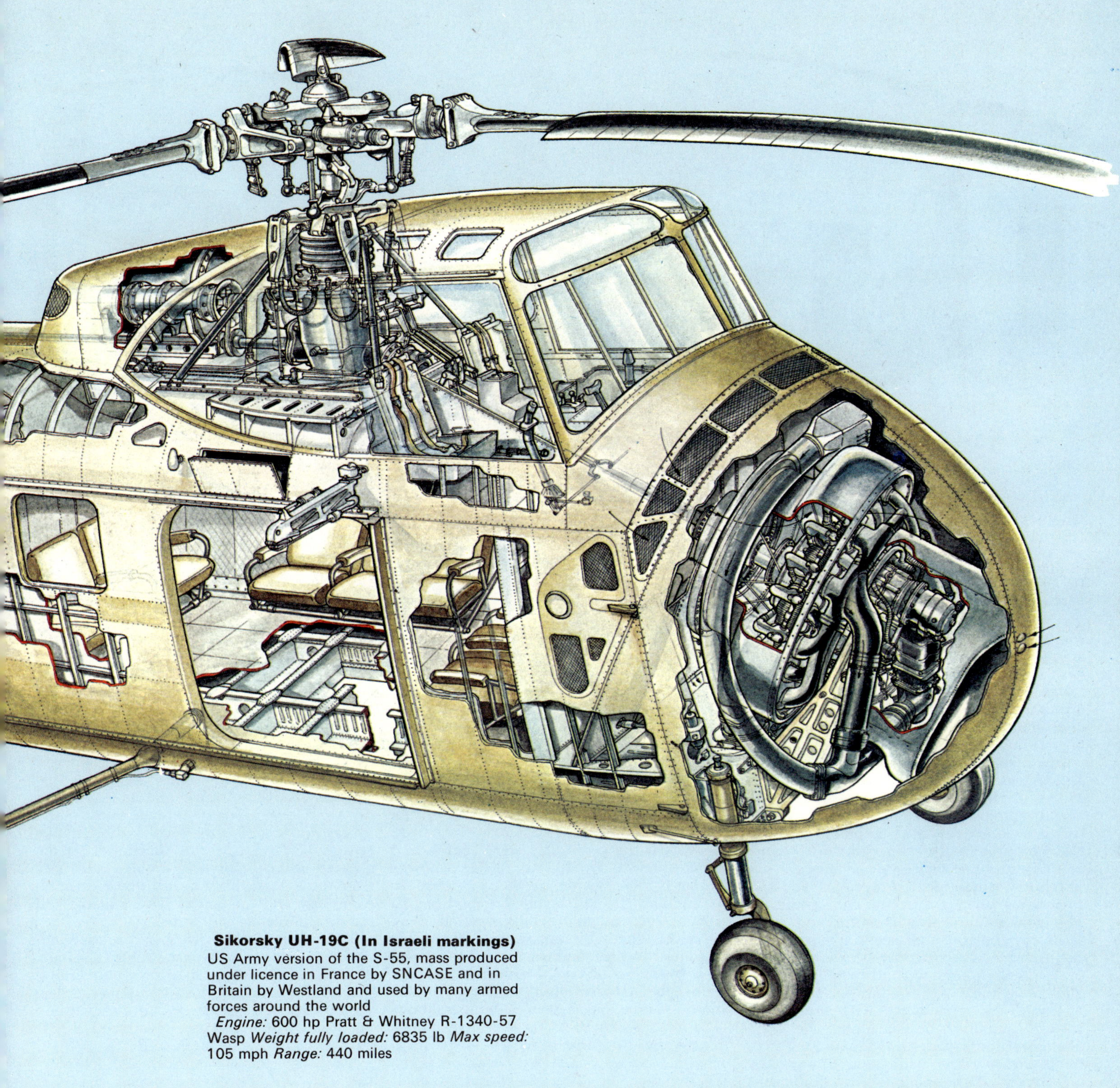

Sikorsky UH-19C (In Israeli markings)
US Army version of the S-55, mass produced under licence in France by SNCASE and in Britain by Westland and used by many armed forces around the world
Engine: 600 hp Pratt & Whitney R-1340-57 Wasp *Weight fully loaded:* 6835 lb *Max speed:* 105 mph *Range:* 440 miles

By the early 1950s the S-55 had become the world's premier type of utility transport helicopter. A few were civil machines, some of which were used by the Belgian airline Sabena to inaugurate the world's first VTOL international air routes between city centres. This operated throughout the 1950s between Brussels and other European cities as far away as Paris and Amsterdam. In Britain BEA used the S-55 and the British-built Westland WS-55 Whirlwind to inaugurate their own scheduled passenger and mail services in several areas, including a route between London Helicopter Terminal (then conveniently located on the South Bank in central London) and Heathrow airport. Several other commercial operators used the S-55 civil version, which had large rectangular windows on each side of a comfortable eight-seat cabin. Most, however, were military.

Experience in Korea

By 1952 the more powerful H-19B was flying with the 700-hp Wright R-1300 Cyclone seven-cylinder engine, the last new type of aircraft piston engine in the high-power radial class ever to be developed in the West. This enabled the gross weight to be increased from 6800 lb to 7200 lb, with 7500 lb in some versions. Stretchers were hung on the outside to bring back injured troops quickly from front-line positions in Korea, and over a period of a few busy months Allied helicopters, led by the S-55 versions, blossomed forth as tactical vehicles of immense value.

At first they were used merely for observation and light transport duties, but their ability to operate from almost any patch of reasonably firm and level ground

Bell HSL-1
The first helicopter designed from the start for anti-submarine warfare
Engine: 2400 hp Pratt & Whitney R-2800-50 Double Wasp *Weight fully loaded:* 26,500 lb *Max speed:* 138 mph *Range:* 350 miles

was gradually appreciated by army commanders on the spot, who discovered that here was a completely new front-line capability. The helicopter was swift and direct, needed no roads, and though vulnerable could survive much better than had been thought, even in an active battle area.

During 1951 the technique of airlifting troops was perfected by the US Army and Marines, who began to refine methods of aerial envelopment, logistic resupply and 'vertrep' (vertical replenishment) which had not previously been possible. Troops could be supplied with food and ammunition in places where no truck could go, and sometimes where not even a mule could go. The S-55 could carry mortars and light artillery, and in tough areas troops began the practice of sitting in the open doorway of the helicopters with cocked machine-guns ready to keep the enemy's heads down. A few H-19s were fitted with multi-tube rocket launchers bolted along the sides above the doors, though it took a long time to learn how to use them safely and effectively. Although realisation did not come in a flash, a new weapon of war was slowly being forged, which in the course of time would come to be as important to the land battle as the gun or the tank.

In the rescue role even light helicopters, such as the H-13 and HTL versions of the Bell 47, literally made the difference between life and death across the entire Korean front. An especially useful task was bringing back downed aircrew, even those shot down deep in enemy territory. With a fast winch aircrew could be retrieved in seconds, and many dramatic rescues were effected in the midst of enemy troops, in jagged mountains, in offshore waters and in rice paddies and forests. Skill, nerve and luck played a part in trying to ensure that the helicopter crew did not simply add themselves to the list of personnel to be rescued. Many helicopters were shot down before the best techniques were perfected, but the American pilots eventually brought the snatch of a downed aircrew to a fine art.

Altogether Sikorsky delivered 1281 of the military S-55 versions, which in 1962 were all redesignated in the H-19 series according to a new Department of Defense numbering scheme which unified the three US service designation systems. Thus, the USAF UH-19B was a utility machine, the Marine CH-19E a logistic cargo carrier and the Navy SH-19 an anti-submarine version; those with the prefix HH were search and rescue versions. During the 1950s the power of the R-1300 engine in the S-55 rose to 800 hp, and the tail boom was modified to prevent catastrophic accidents caused by the main blades hitting it. The boom was tilted downwards, and the tail rotor carried on a swept fin of useful area instead of a plain tube. Gross weight rose to 7900 lb, and maximum speed from 90 mph to about 112 mph. In Japan versions were made under licence by Mitsubishi, while in Britain other models were made by Westland as the Whirlwind. The British company soon exchanged the original Pratt & Whitney or Wright engine for the locally produced Alvis Leonides Major, a 750-hp two-row radial which gave an improved performance. These Series 2 Whirlwinds were supplied to the Royal Navy, RAF and several other air forces, but in 1958 the important decision was taken to build a turbine-engined Whirlwind called Series 3.

Turbine Power

The chosen engine was the General Electric T58, made under licence in Britain as the Bristol Siddeley (later Rolls-Royce) Gnome. The Gnome differed from the US engine in many respects, one being that it incorporated a Hawker Siddeley Dynamics electronic control system which virtually allowed the helicopter pilot to let the engine look after itself. The adoption of turbine power transformed the Whirlwind, the Gnome giving 1050 hp while weighing less than 400 lb with all its accessories, much less than half the weight of the piston engines. It also enabled high-octane petrol to be replaced by kerosene or a range of other less-volatile fuels including, in certain cases, the same diesel oil as that burned by a naval vessel's main engines. Distinguished by its longer and more pointed nose and large circular exhaust outlet – and by the quite different noise – the Gnome-powered Whirlwind was built both from scratch and by converting older machines from the 400 plus already built by Westland. Many are still in use as RAF coastal and mountain rescue machines.

The Gnome Whirlwinds had higher performance and could carry more payload, but the chief reason for turbine conversion was to improve reliability and safety. Ten years later an American turbine conversion appeared, the Aviation Specialties S-55T, with a 700-hp AiResearch TSE 331.

The only other American helicopter of the same period that could exceed the S-55's performance was a curious machine that marked a complete, and not wholly successful, break in Bell's single-rotor philosophy. In 1950 the US Navy wanted a helicopter that could do an ASW hunter-killer job, a task which called for great lifting power. Bell won the resulting contest with the Model 61, which went into limited production in 1955 as the HSL-1. It had quite a small fuselage, very narrow and less than 40 ft long overall, but a gross weight of 26,500 lb. The engine was a 2400-hp Pratt & Whitney Double Wasp which drove a 51·5-ft rotor at the extremities of the nose and tail. Inside or underneath were more than 4000 lb of sonar and weapons. This little-known machine also pioneered all-weather helicopter operation with an autopilot and use of large helicopters from restricted areas aboard surface ships.

Parallel Development

SOVIET HELICOPTERS

The scene in the Soviet Union had been discouraging, but in 1947 Mikhail Mil, who had not achieved notoriety at TsAGI, but did well in an air force autogyro squadron, was at last given charge of a design bureau. His bureau's very first design, the GM-1, flown in September 1948, was built by the thousand and gave rise to direct developments that are still in production – a remarkable achievement.

The GM-1 was a neat stressed-skin single-rotor machine bearing considerable similarity to the Sycamore in shape, size, power and weight. By 1951 it was in mass production as the Mi-1 for military and civil customers in 17 countries. Most versions were utility transports, ambulances and agricultural machines, powered by the 575-hp Ivchenko AI-26 radial behind the cabin. In 1955 the whole programme was transferred to Poland, and since that time the WSK-Swidnik plant has delivered many hundreds of SM-1 helicopters powered by the LiT-3 engine, these being the Polish designations for the original Russian designs. From 1959 to final delivery in 1963–64 the majority were SM-2 versions with a larger cabin seating five.

In 1951 Mil's bureau began design of a much bigger helicopter obviously inspired by the S-55. It had exactly the same layout, with nose-mounted diagonal engine, cabin under the rotor, flight deck above the nose and four wheels, but it was on a larger scale of size and power. Designated Mi-4, it was by far the most useful helicopter of its era, with a 1700-hp engine, gross weight of 17,600 lb and excellent all-round performance. Clamshell rear doors can admit small vehicles and palletised freight, while a typical passenger load is 18 civilians or 14 equipped troops. ASW versions carry radar, sonar, torpedoes and in some cases other sensors such as a magnetic-anomaly 'bird' on a long cable. Civil versions have spatted wheels and square windows, and many hundreds still form an important means of communication in remote areas of the USSR, especially in Siberia. Altogether at least 5000 of these capable machines have been built, all in the Soviet Union, and large numbers have been exported.

It should be emphasised that copying someone else's helicopter design does not solve the real problems. When Mil laid out the Mi-4 he adopted the same configuration as the S-55 (he might, of course, have arrived at the same arrangement independently, but the S-55 had been announced three years earlier and was obviously a sound idea), but this was the least of his problems. The items that take the development time and money are the dynamic parts: engine, drive shafts, fans, clutches, gearboxes, bearings, hubs, blades and rotor control systems. Mil could not copy these, and in any case was making a much bigger helicopter.

Capable Russian

The engine was a version of an established aeroplane engine already built in vast numbers for wartime fighters and bombers and post-war transports. Nevertheless, the different demands of helicopter operation necessitated a major development effort by A D Shvetsov's engine bureau, with reliable high power at low flight speeds assisted by a powerful cooling fan, and with a completely different arrangement of accessories and a high-speed direct-drive output shaft. Though conventional, the gearbox and rotor were major undertakings, and Mil's design staff adopted an unusual blade form with the outer 40% tapered to a quite pointed tip. There are four blades, and trimming surfaces are provided on the outer trailing edge. Despite the use of four very efficient blades the diameter of the main rotor settled at 68·92 ft, allowing the rotational speed to be quite low, even with a gross weight much more than twice that of the S-55.

As with so many Soviet developments, this helicopter looked so conventional when it appeared in late 1952 that it was greatly underestimated (the rotor was estimated at 52 ft and then at 56·5 ft). Only when the power of its engine was made known was it appreciated to be so much more capable than Western machines of similar general size and layout. Consequently, the Mi-4 remains in service in all the Warsaw Pact forces and in at least 14 other countries. The Mi-4S is a specially equipped agricultural version, and other special versions have served in Arctic and Antarctic exploration.

Development of the Mi-4 was started after a sudden summons to the Kremlin of the nation's chief helicopter designers in 1952. One of those who attended was the former aeroplane designer Aleksandr Yakovlev, who – without having much choice in the matter – found himself saddled with a machine twice as big as the Mi-4. Like Mil, he had to promise the prototype would fly in a year, and he just made it. The first Yak-24 flew on 3 July 1953, despite the fact that another was completely destroyed by resonance during ground running.

Resonance has been the curse of many otherwise good rotorcraft. It arises from the fact that, unlike an aeroplane, a helicopter has very large rotating masses which can make the whole structure shake in sympathy until it begins to break up. The cure may be to change the rotor speed, change the design of the landing gear or do several other things, but finding the cure can cost millions, and waste months or even years. Yakovlev's problem was acute, because the Yak-24 was very big, had an Mi-4 engine and rotor system at each end and was needed by the Russian armed forces in a great hurry.

It is only natural that design and development of the Yak-24 should have been urged ahead with such frantic haste, because this was a time when the Cold War was at its iciest and the Korean War could well have

PZL-Swidnik SM-1 (NATO = Hare)
Polish-built Mil Mi-1
Engine: 575 hp LiT-3 *Weight fully loaded:* 6429 lb *Cruising speed:* 115 mph *Range:* 342 miles *Number of seats:* 4

Mil Mi-4 of the AV-MF (Soviet Navy Air Force) takes a crewman off a Soviet Whisky-class submarine

Novosti

Yakovlev Yak-24U (NATO = Horse)
The Soviet Union's first large transport helicopter was beset by teething troubles in 1953-56 and finally entered service in 1958. The civil Yak-24A version carries 30 passengers
Engines: 2×1700 hp Shvetsov ASh-82V
Weight fully loaded: 34,899 lb *Cruising speed:* 109 mph *Range:* 298 miles

Mil Mi-4 (NATO = Hound)
Built for both Soviet and satellite air forces and Aeroflot, in larger quantities than any other Soviet helicopter of its day. The Aeroflot version shown is the 11–18-passenger Mi-4P
Engine: 1770 hp Shvetsov ASh-82V *Weight: fully loaded:* 17,196 lb *Max speed:* 130 mph *Range:* 155 miles

escalated. Though the techniques of using large helicopters in warfare were in their infancy, the Soviet leaders had no doubt such a machine was an immediate requirement – in the first instance for the armed forces, but also to help open up the vast undeveloped areas of the Soviet Union where there was no method of surface transport. Bearing in mind the panic situation at the Yakovlev bureau, and the fact that designing a helicopter was something the bureau had never before attempted, – apart from two baby research machines – the problems were solved relatively quickly. In contrast, the British team at Bristol, which embarked on a smaller and much less powerful helicopter with the same layout, did not succeed in delivering a single machine to a customer until ten years after the first flight.

The vital difference was that in the Soviet Union the engineers were being driven night and day by an impatient customer, whereas the British Ministry of Supply appeared to overlook the fact that the purpose of aircraft development is to produce aircraft that can be used. The curse of the tandem-rotor Bristol machines was resonance, just as in the case of Yakovlev, but the Russian had only one year, not ten. At the original Kremlin meeting he had asked for 24 hours in which to give his answer to the government request that he should build a big helicopter. On his return the next day he reported that his design staff, led by Nikolai Skrzhinskii (the pioneer helicopter/autogyro designer at TsAGI), agreed that the task could be done, and he explained that they had estimated final design drawings could be made ready in just one year. The Kremlin response was that the matter had already been decided: Mil would quickly complete his 12-passenger machine, which became the Mi-4, and Yakovlev would build one twice as big to carry 24 – and he would have it flying in a year, not just drawn on paper.

Unlike most designers, Yakovlev managed to write a book about his experiences, and he commented on the fact that the helicopter posed quite new problems. Instead of having to go faster and higher and further it made life difficult by having to hover motionless. 'The combination of our experience with profound scientific analyses prevented grave errors, but, when the helicopter was built and underwent static engine tests, it turned out that it was impossible to plan everything theoretically. Many new problems cropped up, engine cooling being one of them. We had to make the heavily loaded helicopter hover in the air, and therefore its engine cooling had to be forced. But vibration (resonance) was the main difficulty that caused us no end of trouble. Four helicopters were built simultaneously: one for laboratory static-strength tests, one for dynamic tests at the airfield when endurance of the engines and rotors of the tethered machine was proved, one for plant flight tests and the fourth for state flight tests. Satisfactory results with one machine did not exclude the possibility of failure with one of the others. For example, the static test machine could, and sometimes did, pass its complete test programme, while its brother failed to make the dynamic tests and had to be improved for years afterwards.'

Resonance Problem

Like other tandem-rotor machines, the Yak-24 had a long body supported by two similar rotors linked into a common dynamic system, so that each engine could drive both rotors. With most twin-engined helicopters, which in 1952 were very rare indeed, the objective is to be able to continue flying even at gross weight after failure of either engine. This became almost simple in the modern gas turbine era, but in 1952 with heavy piston engines it was a great challenge, and Yakovlev enlisted the help of several state laboratories. Even though they were based on the blades of the Mi-4, the Yak-24 rotor blades were fatigue-tested at TsAGI, being bent and twisted 12 million times. The vital gearbox was exhaustively tested at the plant where the Shvetsov engines were made. The complete engines, fuel systems and cooling arrangements were all simulated at the Aircraft Engine Research Institute and run day and night.

All this was done to schedule, but as soon as the endurance-test helicopter began to operate out on the airfield the vibration reared its head. In Yakovlev's words 'The machine vibrated at various rpm and there was nothing we could do about it. As soon as we got the vibration under control in one place it would invariably crop up somewhere else. . . . We had to pass the 300-hour endurance test on the ground, before proceeding to test the captive helicopter hovering above the ground on mooring lines. Our confidence was gradually mounting as the test proceeded, but then one day an excited voice came over the telephone from the airfield: "There's been trouble. The helicopter disintegrated on the ground and is burning up. Nothing can be saved. The cause is unknown." – "What about the people?" – "They are all safe."

Vibration Overcome

After 178 hours of running, the first Yak-24 was a heap of charred rubble. Eventually it was discovered that the resonance and vibration had made the mountings of the rear engine fail by fatigue. The rear rotor had pulled the rear gearbox and engine clean out and, as it travelled along the fuselage, the rear rotor chopped the big helicopter to pieces. Gushing petrol from several pipes poured on to the hot engines and caught alight.

This kind of thing was all too common in the early days of rotary-wing craft, which can be said to have finished at about 1955. Throughout that time the helicopter was, fundamentally, still not a fully tamed beast. Its combination of aerodynamic and structural problems were too difficult for complete solution until, after 1955, engineers could at last master them with a combination of deeper understanding and much greater computer power. Even small helicopters posed terrible problems, so those that finally achieved production were not necessarily better than the others, just luckier. Small teams of only a handful of designers sometimes achieved complete success, as did Stanley Hiller with the Model 360, while big and experienced aeroplane companies struggled for years amidst a funeral pyre of wrecked rotors, lost blades sailing over the rooftops and in-flight disasters.

Much more so than with an aeroplane, trouble with a helicopter tended to be catastrophic. In-flight failures were more difficult to ride down to a safe landing, and even accidents occurring during ground running all too often had fatal results. Insurance premiums were therefore extremely high, making all helicopter operations an unnaturally costly business until, well after 1960, confidence slowly grew.

Of course, in the Soviet Union in 1952 nobody was much bothered about insurance premiums, and for harassed Yakovlev there was no such word as 'can't'. He did not even have the option of standing back for a moment and seeing whether there might not be a case for major redesign. True, he had escaped official disgrace by getting his Yak-24 flight prototype into the air in a year, before the catastrophe with the ground-running machine; but test pilots Brovtsev and Milyutichev kept mentioning 'a tiny bit of vibration' in certain conditions. Gradually it became clear that they were trying not to disappoint the design team; the truth was that the whole frame of the monster was shaking dangerously.

In Yakovlev's words: 'For five solid months we tried to get rid of that vibration. Five months of intensive research, calculations, dozens of experimental flights – all in vain. . . . We began to lose every vestige of hope that we could ever eliminate the hated vibration, because it would suddenly appear in the most unexpected places. The time came when, upon meeting each morning, instead of a greeting we would ask "Well, does it still vibrate?" and be told "It sure does!" There were scientists who bent their learning to present the most convincing proof that, generally speaking, we were trying to cure an incurable disease. . . . Many pointed out "The Americans failed to get rid of vibration in the YH-16, Hafner is still wrestling with the same problem in his Bristol 173. You think you are smarter than anyone else. Don't waste time. . . ." But we were not wasting time. . . . What if we changed the dynamics of the main rotor blades? I suggested we should chop half a metre from each blade tip. . . . The engines were started, blades whirled. . . . Brovtsev and Milyutichev stayed in the air for 20 minutes. . . . We could see from the ground their smiling faces, and knew we had scored a bull's eye.'

Even then there were troubles and occasional catastrophes in store, but eventually four service-cleared Yak-24s were publicly flown in 1955. By this time the 'flying wagon' was in full production at last, and several hundreds were built. The machine still needed tinkering with, the flight control system being changed and the vee tail replaced with twin fins, but its capabilities were tremendous.

As a troop carrier it could lift 40 men with personal equipment and weapons. At the rear was a large hatch, extending across the two metres width of the fuselage and forming a strong ramp up which could be driven two GAZ-69 command cars or light artillery and crews. Total cargo load was almost four tons (over 8500 lb), and especially bulky loads could be slung below. In 1956 a Yak-24 gained world records by lifting two tons of cargo to 16,670 ft, and four tons to 9520 ft.

Twice as Powerful

It was also a remarkably fast machine, with a speed of up to 158 mph. Examples made non-stop flights between Leningrad, where the production line was at first set up (later it moved to the Urals), and Moscow, and with improved radio navaids missions were often undertaken at night. Compared with the outwardly similar Vertol H-21 the Yak-24 was only fractionally larger but much more than twice as powerful, and it could carry at least twice as much. Ultimately Yakovlev fitted two 2700-hp gas-turbine engines in a redesigned model in 1960, but by this time the rival Mil bureau had gained the ascendancy with a gigantic single-rotor machine, the Mi-6.

Much of the burden of the original design of the Yak-24 was borne by Skrzhinskii, Kamov's partner in 1929. Kamov himself surged ahead after the Second World War with a succession of helicopters which began with the tiny 27-hp Ka-8 of 1947. This one-man machine was followed in 1949 by the 55-hp Ka-10 which was developed into a simple pontoon-equipped reconnaissance helicopter for the Soviet Navy.

In 1952 the much larger Ka-15 flew on the 255 hp of an Ivchenko AI-14V radial. Seating two side-by-side, the Ka-15 was used in quantity by the armed forces (especially the navy) and Aeroflot for many utility and training purposes. The same basic layout, with co-axial three-blade rotors, was taken further in the Ka-18 of 1957, which on the same engine carried four people in a longer cabin. Most Ka-18 versions had the 275-hp AI-14VF, and with a roomy cabin could carry stretchers, freight or agricultural chemicals and fly hard in adverse conditions.

Piston-Engined Heavyweights

BIGGER AND BETTER

In the West no attempt was made to follow the defunct XH-17 with a giant weightlifter, though for six years Piasecki strove to build the US Air Force an acceptable XH-16 with tandem rotors driven by 2750-hp Allison T38-6 turboshaft engines on each side of the vast fin. The project never succeeded, partly owing to Allison's failure at that time to produce a reliable turbine engine.

Sikorsky, on the other hand, did succeed in building a useful large helicopter, though it was handicapped by the burden of two large piston engines. The S-56, first flown on 18 December 1953, was developed as the HR2S-1 for the Marine Corps, with clamshell nose doors for rapid loading of 26 troops or vehicles and weapons. The 72-ft five-blade folding rotor was a major advance which was to serve as the basis for many important Sikorsky machines in the 1960s. It was driven by a pair of 1900- or 2100-hp Double Wasp radials mounted on the ends of stub wings in large nacelles which also housed the retracted twin-wheel main gears. Most of the 150-odd production machines were CH-37 Mojave versions for the Army, though two were fitted with giant APS-20 surveillance radars for use as radar pickets with the fleet.

At the same time, Sikorsky achieved a product sold in far greater numbers as the next stage in mainstream development after the S-55. Designated S-58, and flown on

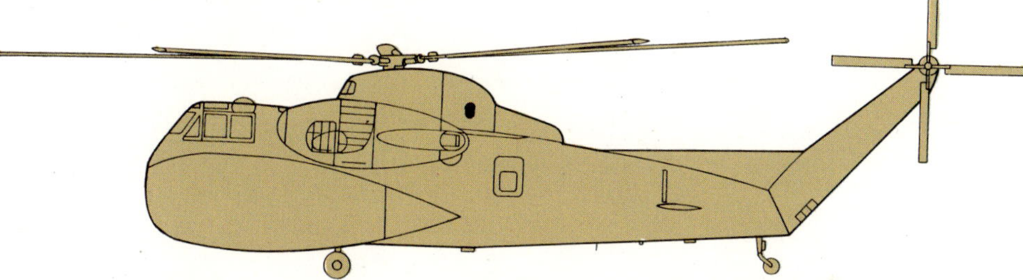

Sikorsky HR2S-1W
Radar-picket (AEW, airborne early warning) modification of S-56 with APS-20E search radar in bulbous nose radome
Engine: 2×1900 hp Pratt & Whitney R-2800-50 Double Wasp *Weight fully loaded:* 31,000 lb
Max speed: 122 mph *Range:* 220 miles

The Sikorsky H-37A Mojave US Army heavy transport helicopter represented a peak in piston-engined helicopter design, transporting 36 fully armed troops or an 11,000 lb lift. The US Army bought 94 in 1956–60, later switching to the greatly superior CH-54 Tarhe (Skycrane) with turbine engines.

Smithsonian

November 1967 and a UH-34B (US Marine S-58) disgorges ARVN soldiers during fighting around Phu Bai, S Vietnam

8 March 1954, this was a much more conventional machine but still significantly bigger than the S-55. Its dynamic system was quite straightforward, and followed S-55 philosophy in having the engine at a diagonal angle in the nose. But the form of the fuselage was subtly different. Instead of being made up of a pod and boom, the airframe of the S-58 was a proper fuselage, of finely streamlined form and with the bottom quite close to the ground all the way to the tail. At the back was a tall slanting fin, and the anti-torque tail rotor was mounted atop this. Like the 56-ft main rotor the tail rotor had four blades, compared with only two in the S-55, and the detail design of the blades was improved for longer life. Compared with the S-55, the -58's rotor hub was considerably more advanced in concept and bigger and stronger, and its larger gearbox resulted in a much bigger fairing on top of the fuselage behind the cockpit. Another difference was the use of three landing wheels arranged just as in tailwheel-type aeroplanes.

Sikorsky designed the S-58 at the request of the US Navy, which in 1952 had asked for a more powerful machine than the S-55 to handle ASW missions. Designated XHSS-1, and inevitably called 'Hiss 1', this was eventually developed into the production HSS-1 (since 1962 restyled SH-34G and named Seabat) used from late 1955 in the ASW role and for various utility tasks. The 1525-hp Wright R-1820-84 Cyclone engine is twice as powerful as typical S-55 engines, and though the S-58 family weigh up to 13,000 lb or more they offer much better performance than an S-55. By 1955 the H-34 Choctaw was in production for the US Army as a 16-seat troop and cargo carrier and the HUS-1 (now UH-34D) utility machine for the US Marine Corps, able to carry a far greater range of loads in amphibious assault than earlier equipment.

In the late 1950s the HSS-1N (now called SH-34J) introduced autostabilization equipment, day/night instruments, improved

Sikorsky S-58 (Aéronavale markings)
To meet the needs of the Algerian war, Sud-Aviation assembled 135 and later (1960–61) built 166 more S-58s under licence
Engine: 1525 hp Wright Cyclone R-1820-84
Max speed: 134 mph *Weight fully loaded:* 12,700 lb *Range:* 225 miles *Number of seats:* 16

Smithsonian

Sikorsky HSS-1N (later styled SH-34) Seabat in automatic flight dunks its sonobuoy

navaids and other equipment, one of the completely new capabilities being a hover coupler. When switched in, this automatically steers the helicopter to a preselected position and lets the machine down to hover motionless at a height of 50 ft. This was a great advantage to ASW crews, because it let them get on with their search and sensing tasks – for example, with dunking sonobuoys and passive sonar devices into the ocean to listen for submerged submarines – while the helicopter automatically rode out the gusts at exactly the right height.

The ASW mission was one that the helicopter was found to accomplish extremely well. During the 1950s the submarine made remarkable technical progress. With the German Type XXI of 1944 it had doubled its underwater speed, and with the coming of nuclear propulsion the submerged submarine was becoming a very formidable opponent, often capable of outrunning any open-sea surface ships. Aeroplanes were faster still, of course, but they found it difficult to search for submerged submarines. Their radar was useless, the science of magnetic-anomaly detection (MAD) was in its infancy (but promised eventually to be able to find submarines by noticing the extremely small disturbance they cause to the Earth's magnetic field) and the only way they could use sonar detection devices was the costly method of dropping numerous sonobuoys into the ocean.

The helicopter, on the other hand, could get to close grips with its underwater enemy and could follow it and, at intervals, dunk a tethered sonobuoy into the sea and listen. The buoy or sonar receiver was not thrown away, and so could be large and very sensitive. Once helicopters were powerful enough they could carry both ASW search gear and weapons. And no submarine could hope to outrun, nor turn quicker.

The Sikorsky HSS-1N was the first really formidable ASW helicopter in history, and it was bought in useful numbers. Sikorsky kept receiving additional and repeat orders from all the US forces and from many other air forces, and when production of this simple, robust and popular machine finally ended after 1960 the total built had reached 1821, a record for any Sikorsky helicopter. But this was by no means the total of S-58 versions. One batch comprised civil airline versions for Sabena of Belgium, with square windows along a cabin seating 18, while the French ALAT was another customer.

During their bitter campaign in Indo-China the French had learned the potential value of the helicopter as a multi-role tactical machine in a land battle, though they were hamstrung by shortages and lack of helicopters. Later, during the war in Algeria, the French were to find that the helicopter can often be the most valuable vehicle of all, carrying troops and fire units, logistic supplies, enemy prisoners, radar, casualties and almost anything else to places inaccessible by other means. Guns could be mounted on helicopters in many ways, either fixed to fire ahead, or obliquely down, or manually aimed from the doorway; and France had also developed the first wire-guided anti-tank missiles, for which the helicopter appeared a natural carrier.

For Algeria France needed all the helicopters it could get, and the S-58 was first choice. It bought 90 direct from Sikorsky, and Sud-Aviation (now Aérospatiale) also built 166 under licence for the ALAT and Aéronavale. Many of these French S-58 versions are still in use in the final quarter of the century. In addition, a larger number of developments of the S-58 were built in Britain as the Westland Wessex.

One of the least-known production types of Sikorsky helicopter was the S-52, first flown on 12 February 1947. This was designed immediately after the Second World War to compete with the small Bell 47 and Hiller helicopters in what appeared likely to be the large market for private and light utility operations. An extremely neat machine that still looks modern today, it had a three-blade rotor of 33 ft diameter, considerably smaller than any previous Sikorsky machine. These blades were of radically new all-metal construction, previous blades having been of composite construction with a metal spar (often a steel tube), solid wood leading edge and built-up rear part with fabric covering.

During the 1950s several US helicopter companies, plus the specialist Parsons company, were to devote great efforts to finding the best way to make a helicopter rotor blade that would give long trouble-free life; even today new methods are continually being introduced. The all-metal S-52 had two rear main wheels and either one or two wheels at the front, and in civil form seated up to four. It was fast for its day, exceeding 105 mph on a 178-hp Franklin.

Most S-52 versions were military, the largest batch being 79 two-seat trainer/utility machines for the Marine Corps designated HO5S-1. A few HO5S-1G versions served with the Coast Guard, and small batches were supplied to the Army. One of the Army machines was rebuilt into the experimental S-59, with Army designation XH-39, with a French Turboméca Artouste 250-hp turboshaft engine in a fairing above the fuselage under the rotor (the engine was imported by Continental Motors, who designated it XT51-T-3). This was the first helicopter in history to have the modern style of turbine engine installation.

This was the state of the art of helicopter design on the eve of the revolution made possible by the turboshaft engine.

How a Helicopter Flies

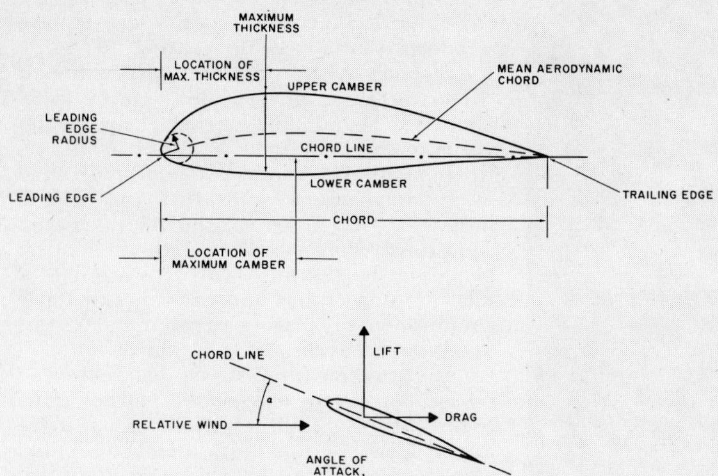

1 Rotor Blade

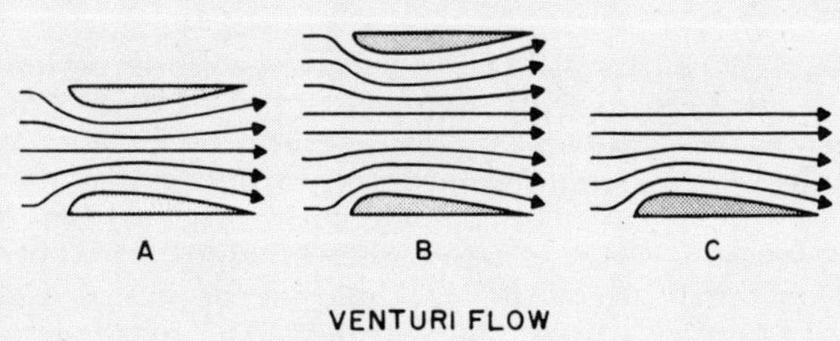

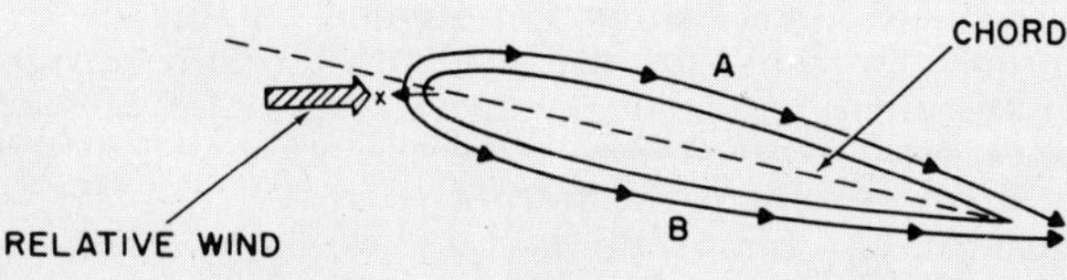

AIRFLOW AROUND AIRFOIL

2 Airflow

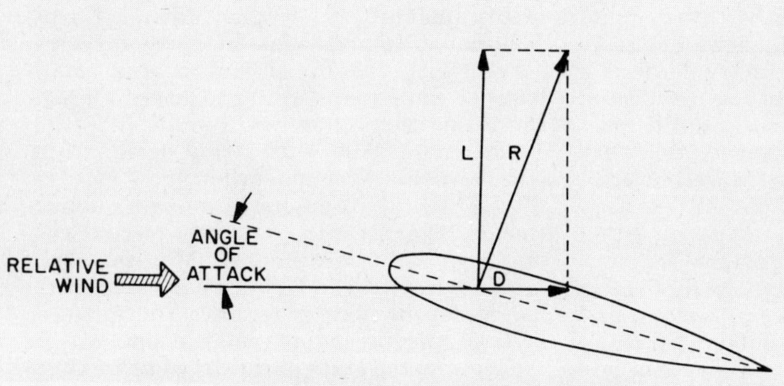

3 Forces Acting on Rotor Blades

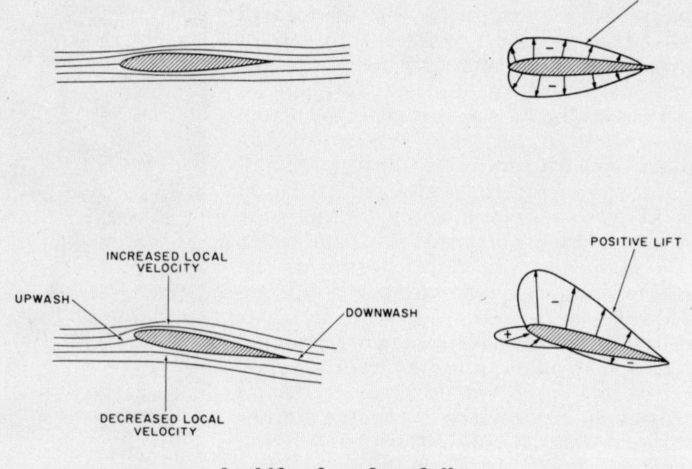

4 Lift of an Aerofoil

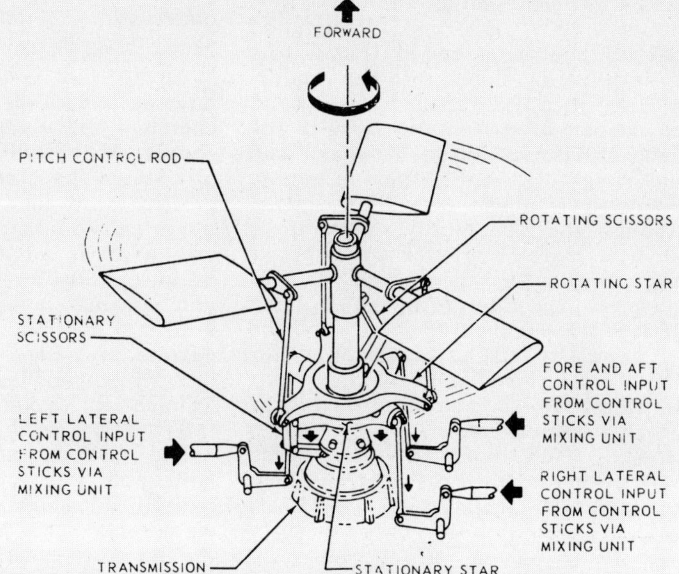

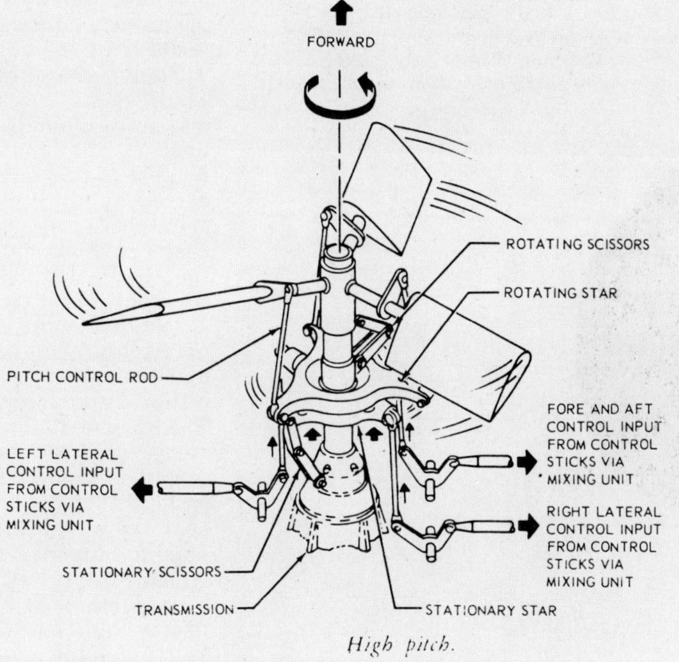

High pitch.

5 Collective Pitch

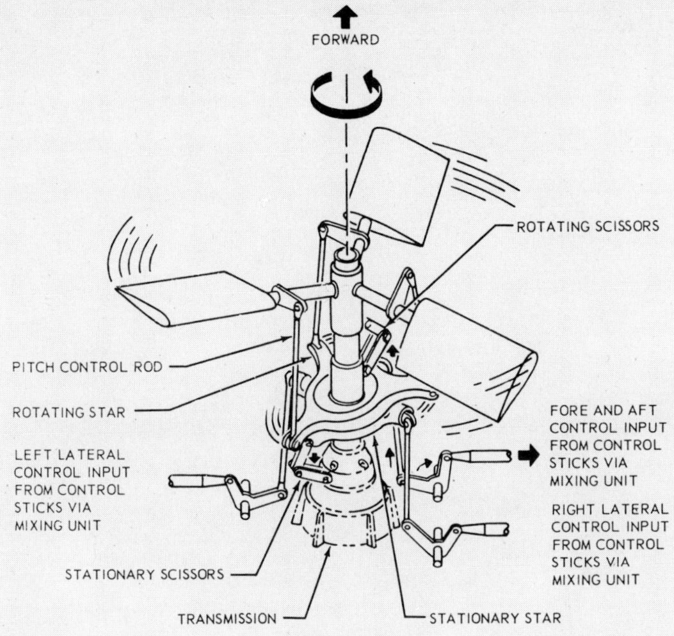

6 Cyclic Pitch

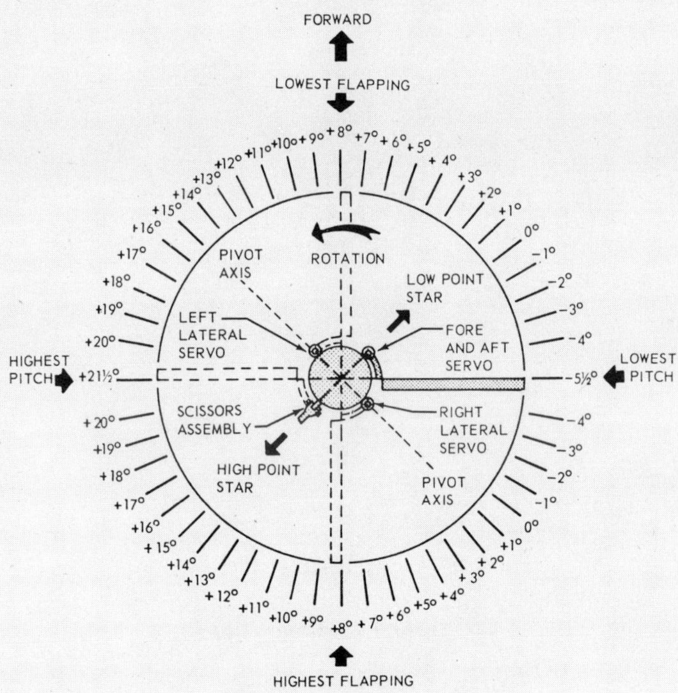

7 Blade Angles

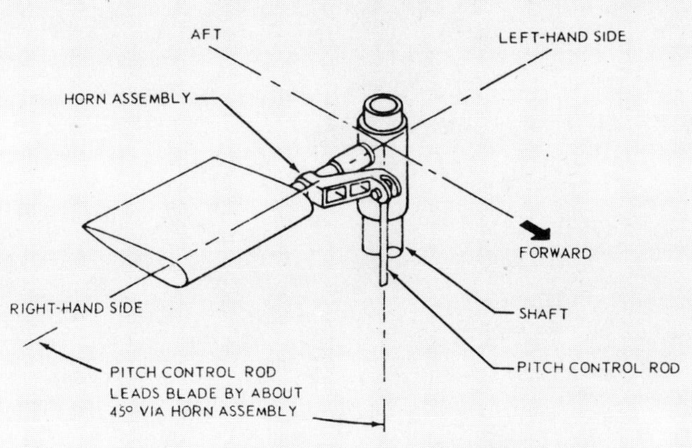

Blade pitch control linkage.

Sikorsky Aircraft

8 Rotor Hub: 1

1: A rotor blade is an aerofoil (US = airfoil) or wing, and has the same profile (cross-section shape). The upper drawing shows the meanings of basic aerofoil words. Camber means curvature, while the mean aerodynamic chord is the theoretical line through the centre of the profile equidistant from the upper and lower surfaces. The smaller drawing shows how the blade is usually set at a positive (nose-up) angle of attack so that it generates lift.
2: Airflow contains energy due to its presence and velocity. If no energy is added or taken away (for example, by heating or cooling) the total energy must remain constant. It follows that if the velocity increases, the pressure must fall. This means that if air flows through a constriction, such as the specially profiled tube called a venturi, the pressure at the narrowest point is not increased (as one might think at first glance) but reduced. A single piece of a venturi resembles a wing (C), showing how the faster air above a wing has reduced pressure; thus, the wing lifts. Even when both surfaces of an aerofoil have similar camber (lower drawing) the airflow generates lift at a positive angle of attack. The relative wind striking the leading edge at X is theoretically brought to rest. The rest of the air goes over the top (A) or underneath (B), and the greater distance over the top means more speed and lower pressure.
3: Forces acting on rotor blades due to a surrounding airflow are really distributed all over its surfaces, as in the previous illustration. For convenience aerodynamicists add together all the forces, taking account of the fact that some are positive and others negative, and the direction in which each force acts (always at 90° to the surface of the aerofoil), and can represent the total as a single force called the resultant (R). This can then be further resolved into two components, the lift (L) perpendicular to the relative wind, and the drag (D) parallel to the relative wind. Designers try to make L greater and D less, for greater efficiency.
4: Lift of an aerofoil depends upon its angle of attack. At a zero setting (upper left) the airflow, represented by parallel lines called streamlines (each showing the path of a tiny particle of the air), is slightly constricted as it passes above and below the rotor blade or wing, but it is not deflected bodily either up or down. Thus a plot of pressure round the aerofoil (upper right) shows negative pressure (suction) on both surfaces, which cancel out. But at a positive angle of attack (lower left) the airflow is bodily deflected downwards. Plotting pressures all round gives the positive lift shown.
5: Collective pitch, one of the two primary flight controls of a helicopter, and it has the effect of increasing or decreasing the lift of the rotor by pivoting all the blades in unison. It thus does not make the helicopter move in any direction except vertically. The collective control is a lever on the left of the pilot, hinged at the rear and pulled up or down. Pushing it down causes a control demand to be sent to the mixing unit which pushes on all three of the input linkages acting on the stationary star. This bodily pulls the stationary star downwards, pulling the rotating star with it and thus pivoting all the blades to lower pitch (left). Pulling up on the collective has the opposite effect: the stars are pushed up, pivoting all the blades to increased pitch (right). Normally, increased collective also calls for increased engine power, obtained by rotating the throttle twist-grip on the end of the collective lever.
6: Cyclic pitch is the other primary flight control. It causes the pitch of each blade in the rotor to oscillate continually between high and low values, and it does so by tilting the stationary and rotating stars. The pilot's cyclic-pitch control is a control column ('stick'), which can be moved in any direction. Its motion is passed through a mixing unit and the output used to move any of three levers connected to the stationary star, the fourth point of which is pivoted to the transmission case by the stationary scissors. The drawing shows the result of pulling the cyclic stick back, to make the helicopter slow down or move backwards. The pull on the fore/aft input tilts the stars, reducing the pitch of each blade as it passes round the left and rear of the disc and increasing it again round the right and front. This tilts the whole rotor disc to the rear, so that the force on the rotor pulls not only upwards but also backwards.
7: Blade angles are constantly changing, except when the helicopter is hovering and has zero airspeed. This diagram shows the rotor disc, seen from above, of a helicopter in forward flight. The cyclic stick is held forward, pushing up the star assembly at the left rear (the opposite of the previous figure). The effect this has on the pitch as each blade makes one revolution can be seen from the successive pitch angles. These range from 21½° on the left to minus 5½ ° on the right. The resulting powerful variation in blade lift makes the blades rise as they pass round the left half of the disc and fall as they pass round the right half. The disc is thus tilted, up at the rear and down at the front, to pull the helicopter along.
8: A rotor hub may carry from one to eight blades, which may be rigidly attached or articulated (hinged), but all hubs have to provide means of controlling the helicopter's flight. This is done by

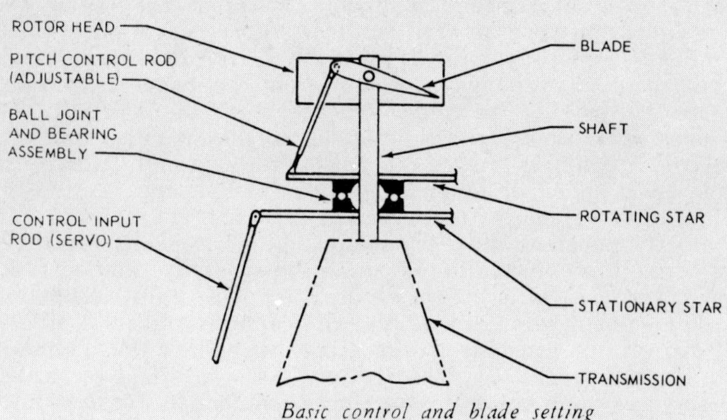

Basic control and blade setting

8 Rotor Hub: 2

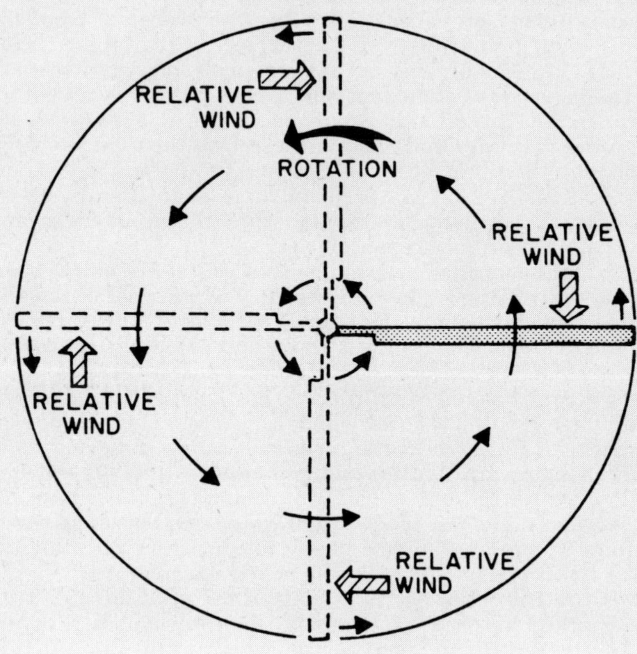

9 Blade Airspeed

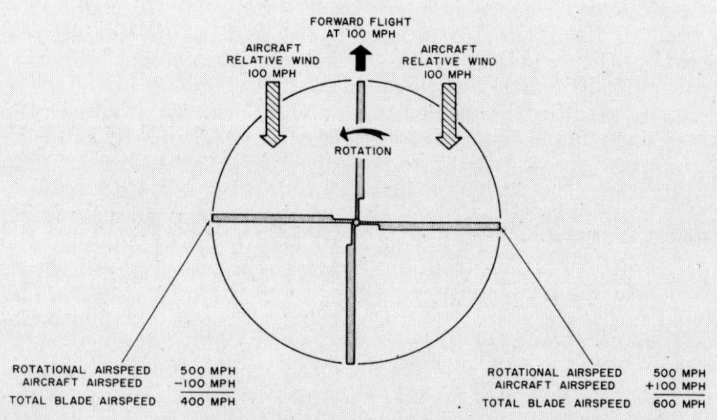

10 Blade Airspeed: Forward Flight

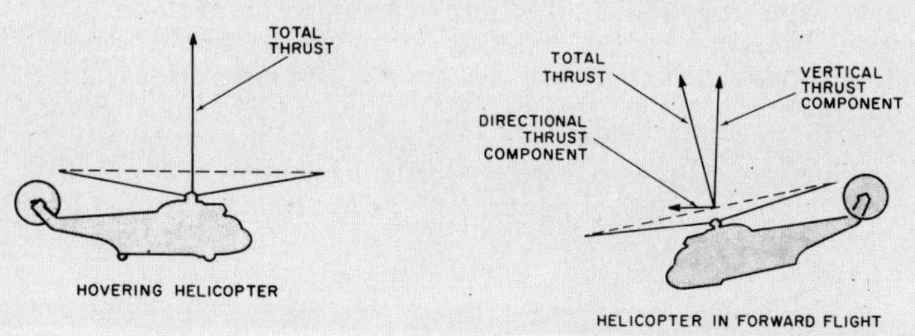

11 Flight Control

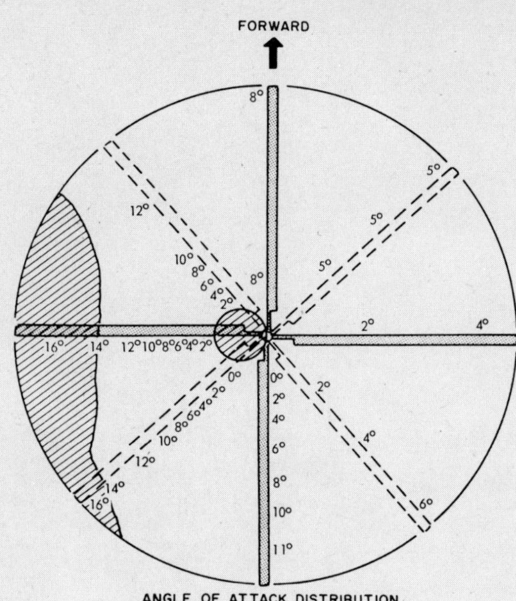

12 Blade Stall

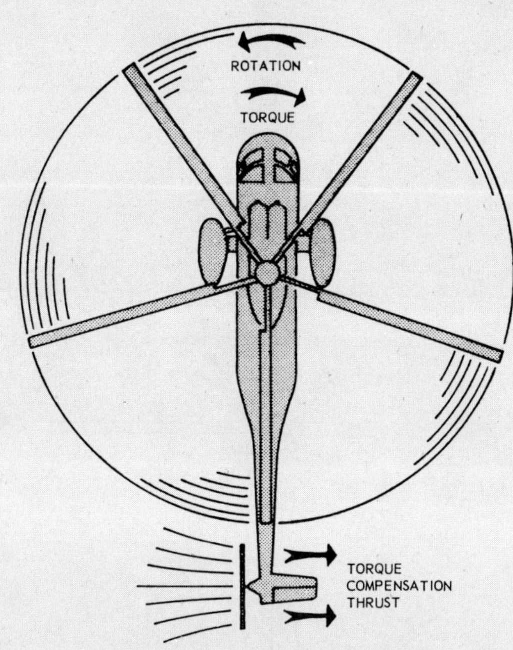

13 Torque Compensation

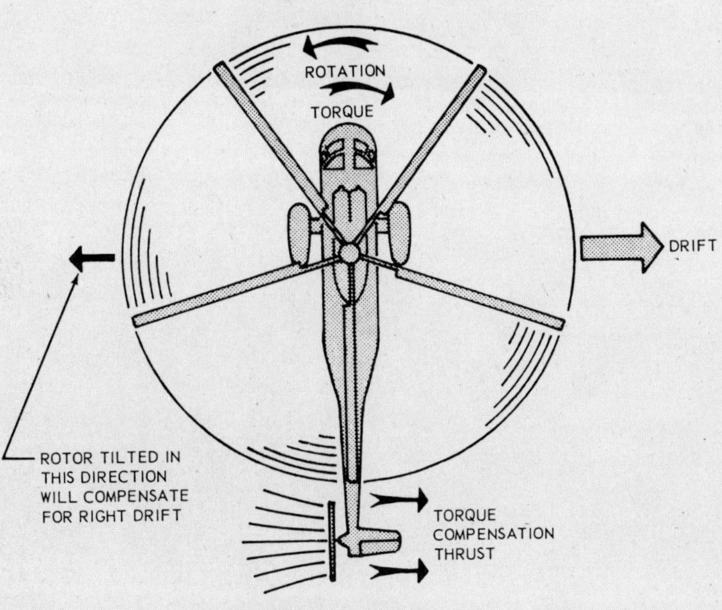

14 Lateral Drift Compensation

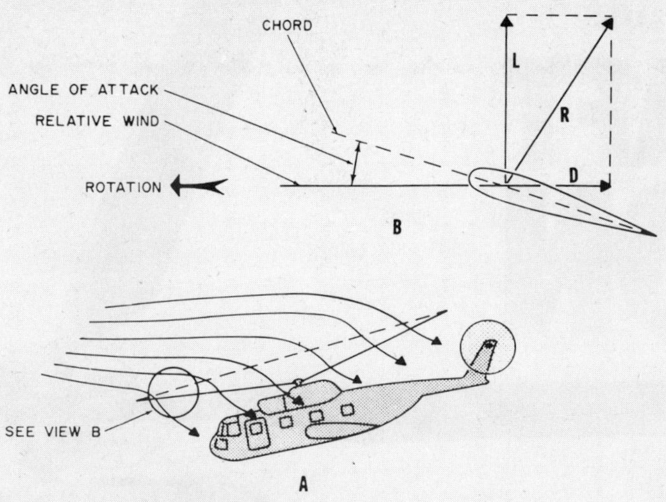

Normal Flight

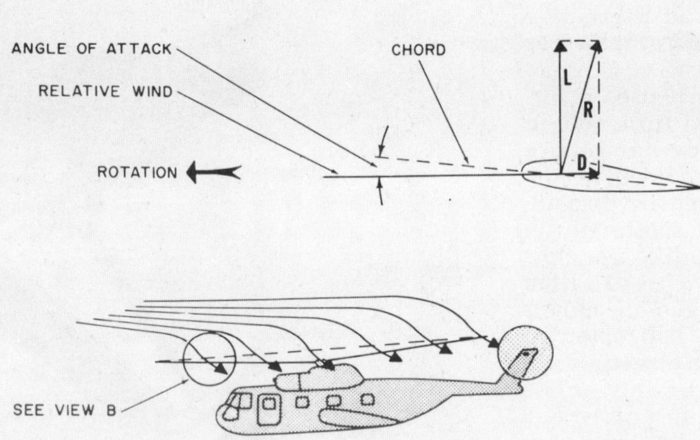

Loss of Power

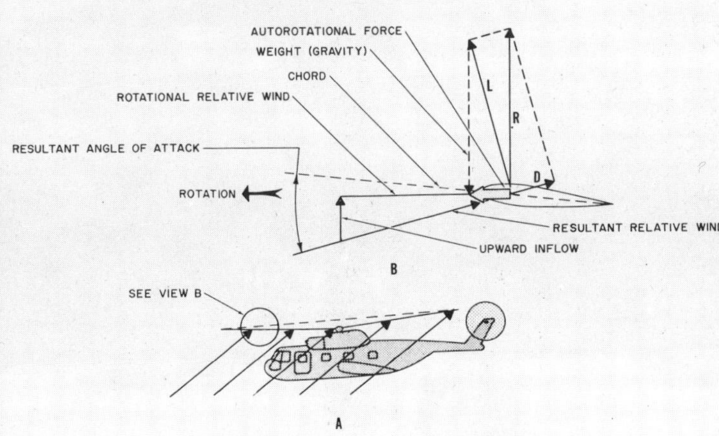

Autorotation

Sikorsky Aircraft

altering the pitch (angular setting) of the blades, which are held in pivoted mountings, so that they can be rotated from a negative pitch through zero to a positive pitch by a horn fixed at the root (the inboard end of the blade). This horn is driven by a vertical (push/pull rod pivoted to the 'upper rotating star' seen more clearly in the next figure. The upper and lower stars are connected by a large ball bearing and are tilted in different directions by the pilot's control demands. The upper star rotates with the rotor.

9: Blade airspeed remains constant in hovering flight at any particular position along the blade, but varies greatly with radius. At the root (the inboard end) the airspeed may be only 30 or 40 mph, whereas at the tip it may be 500 mph. For this reason most blades have some twist incorporated, with greater pitch at the root than at the tip (like a propeller). When hovering in still air the blade operates under the same conditions of angle and airspeed all round the disc, and the disc is horizontal. Hovering in a wind is similar to flying in the opposite direction through still air, calling for some cyclic control to be applied to tilt the rotor disc and give a horizontal thrust on the helicopter to cancel out the wind.

10: In forward flight blade airspeed varies constantly, between a maximum on one side of the disc and a minimum on the other. As each blade passes through the fore/aft direction its airspeed at any station is the same as in hovering flight in still air. The 'advancing blade,' however, has an airspeed equal to this value plus the speed of the helicopter. The 'retreating blade' has an airspeed equal to this value minus the speed of the helicopter. Obviously there must be some point (X) on the retreating blade at which the two speeds cancel out, giving a net airspeed of zero. Inboard of this point the airspeed is negative, the air flowing to the leading edge.

11: Flight control of most helicopters is effected by changing the magnitude (strength) of direction of the total thrust generated by the main rotor. In a hovering helicopter (left) this thrust acts vertically, and its magnitude is exactly equal to the weight. The cyclic stick is central, and the rotor disc is horizontal. If the pilot increases or decreases collective, the hovering helicopter will go up or down. In forward flight the picture is quite different (right). The cyclic stick is forward, causing constant change in helicopter blade angles, resulting in the rotor disc being tilted forwards. The total thrust vector is thus rotated forwards, giving a vertical component (still equal to the weight) plus a directional thrust component to pull the helicopter along.

12: Blade stall is difficult to avoid in forward flight, and the faster the helicopter the bigger the stalled region may be. In this view looking down on the rotor disc the helicopter is flying at full speed in the direction marked at the top. The angle of attack of the retreating blade increases to a maximum at the left 90° position. The outer part of the blade is then at such a coarse angle to the air that it stalls (in the example, the blade stalls at an angle of 14°). There is also a small stalled area at the inboard end of the retreating blade. The angle here is small, but the blade stalls because its airspeed is negative, as explained in figure 11.

13: Torque compensation is essential to stop the helicopter spinning round in the opposite direction to the main rotor. Some helicopters have co-axial or intermeshing rotors, or tandem or side-by-side rotors turning in opposite directions in such a way that the torque needed to drive one rotor cancels out the torque needed to drive the other. Most helicopters, however, have a single main rotor, and a separate tail rotor, geared up from the main-rotor gearbox, giving a lateral (sideways) thrust.

14: Lateral drift from the tail rotor must be taken into account. The side-thrust tends to push the helicopter sideways, causing an unwanted lateral drift. To compensate for it the designer does not make the axis of the main rotor quite vertical. Instead, it is tilted slightly to one side, so that the total-thrust axis contains a small lateral component (side-thrust) which under most flight conditions approximately balances the thrust of the tail rotor.

15: In normal flight (A) a helicopter has its nose tilted downwards, and the main-rotor disc is tilted even more sharply to pull the machine along. The air encountered by the rotor passes downwards through the disc, and is deflected powerfully down by the blades. Typical force vectors on any blade station (B) show a large angle of attack and large lift and drag forces.

16: Loss of power immediately changes the airflow through the rotor, and the force vectors. The pilot reduces the collective pitch to keep the rotor speed from falling too rapidly, which reduces the rotor downwash, the tilt of the disc and the blade angle of attack. All force vectors are greatly reduced in magnitude, but act in approximately the same directions as before. This is a transition stage prior to autorotation.

17: In autorotation the helicopter descends in a controllable way, without power input from the engine(s).

Smaller Engines, Bigger Payloads

THE TURBOSHAFT REVOLUTION

Prior to 1955 all helicopters suffered from some ills, and some from many. Among the problems were vibration and resonance, both in flight and on the ground – severe mechanical and aerodynamic design problems, made more difficult by the fact that the basic theory had still not been fully worked out. Solving these problems was largely a matter of hit-and-miss. The underlying poor ratio of thrust or power to weight meant that helicopters carried small payloads and flew slowly.

Taken together these shortcomings were serious enough to hold back the use of man's only practical VTOL (Vertical Take Off and Landing) vehicle developed up to that time. The fact that large numbers of helicopters were nevertheless put into service is explained by the ability of military services to pay very large sums in order to achieve limited extra capabilities. The extra capabilities the helicopter offered were real enough: it could hover around suspected targets on land or at sea, land on any small reasonably flat clearing, hurry casualties from the heart of the battle straight to the field hospital, carry urgent supplies to front-line troops or the smallest ship, and snatch a downed aviator from the heart of enemy territory. But none of these things could easily be done on a large scale, except at costs that soon became a real deterrent.

The commercial operators, who were concerned to make business profits, generally gave helicopters a cool look and decided to wait until the breed improved. Though a few airlines and state organizations bought a few helicopters, this was mainly an educational exercise rather than a commercial one. It was possible to carry a handful of people or a few sacks of mail in a very convenient door-to-door way, but only at a cost that had to be covered by some other source of revenue.

Everyone knew, even from the earliest days, that rotorcraft were likely to prove similar to almost all man's earlier creations and improve with time. So it proved: week by week, imperceptibly or in massive leaps, the helicopter became more reliable, more efficient and a better performer. Most of the running was made in the United States. Sikorsky led in the engineering of the big helicopter (though pushed hard by Vertol), while Bell and Hiller managed to assemble simple hardware priced low enough to appeal to a vast range of military and civil customers – for example, to patrol pipelines or power lines, or carry a newsreel or TV camera – so that, for the first time, the helicopter became a viable commercial product able to sustain a continuing production line.

All these early helicopters were powered by otherwise conventional aviation piston engines. Such engines were extremely refined and quite attractive products, with half a century of development behind them. But after the Second World War an alternative came increasingly into the picture: the gas turbine.

Most of the first gas turbines used in aircraft were of the kind called turbojets, in which all the power surplus, over and above that needed to run the engine itself, is supplied in the form of a high-velocity propulsive jet. Such engines make sense only in rather fast aircraft, quite unlike the slow helicopter; but there is much more to it than this. Many engineers sought to mount turbojets on the blades of a helicopter, so that the rotor could be driven directly without the need for heavy and failure-prone gearboxes and shafting, or an anti-torque tail rotor. Pioneers had been making such 'tip-drive' rotors since the Austrian Doblhoff had started using the first 'gas-drive' with tip-jets fed by a piston-engined compressor in 1942. After the Second World War the attractions of tip-drive schemes, allied with the sudden emergence of a shoal of simple jet-type engines such as the cold rocket (using decomposing chemicals to give a gas jet much cooler than a normal

Westland Belvedere
The Belvedere should have provided a capable ASW helicopter for the Royal Navy and a large utility machine for the RAF. The turbine installation however was inconvenient and the aircraft had only a brief service career
Engines: 2×1650 shp Rolls-Royce (Napier) Gazelle Mk 101 turboshafts *Max speed:* 140 mph *Weight fully loaded:* 18,000 lb *Range:* 420 miles *Number of seats:* 20

Westland Wessex HAS Mk I
Engine: 1450 shp Rolls-Royce (Napier) Mk 161 *Max speed:* 132 mph *Weight fully loaded:* 12,600 lb *Range:* 391 miles *Number of seats:* 14–18

rocket flame), the flap-valve pulsejet, the resonant valveless pulsejet, the ramjet, and the gas-drive tip-jet fed by air or gas pumped along the hollow blade from a compressor in the helicopter fuselage, all these brought forth a mass of technically interesting and often attractive small tip-drive helicopters. Many were flown in the United States and a few in Western Europe. Compared with piston-engined machines they were usually simpler, lighter and cheaper, and often smoother and faster to fly. But they suffered from inadequate development, from unpleasant noise and, above all, from high fuel consumption. Almost the only thing common to all of them was that none went into wide use.

Obviously, all tip-drive units have the unique property of 'flying' at high speed even in a slow helicopter, or one hovering motionless. This largely overcomes the problem of slow flight speed which makes it difficult to use these simple jet units in slow fixed-wing aircraft. But many visionaries could see, even before 1950, that none of these would be the most important engine for future helicopters. Far and away the most important power unit today is the turboshaft engine, which is essentially a turbojet with extra turbine power to extract more energy from the jet and deliver it via a rotating shaft. Another way of regarding the turboshaft is to view it as a turboprop without the reduction gear and propeller. Experience has confirmed that the shaft drive is the best answer even for the largest helicopters.

It makes for a more efficient blade, for minimal transmission losses, lower fuel consumption, and generally results in a smaller and lighter machine to fly a given mission. On the other hand, this traditional form of drive retains the need for a tail rotor or other anti-torque system, as well as the gears and shafts that can be heavy, costly and vulnerable.

Bearing in mind that in nearly all modern helicopters the possibility of doing away with the gears and shafting has been ignored, what are the advantages of the turboshaft, compared with the efficient and fully developed piston engine? By far the biggest advantage, for most customers, is ratio of power to weight. This factor is set out in numerical terms in an accompanying table, when the superiority of the turboshaft can be judged. In early gas turbines of

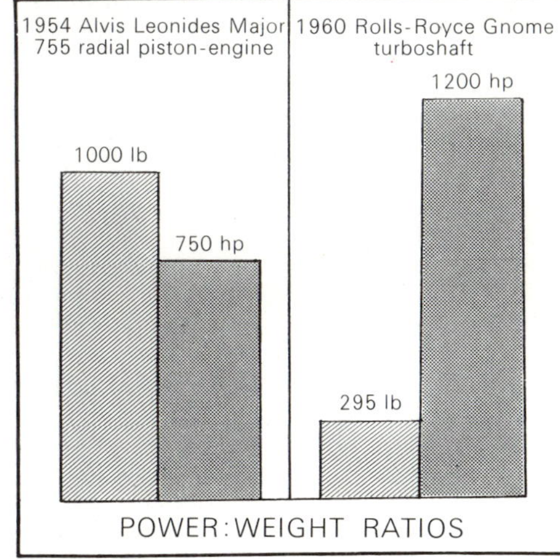

twenty and more years ago the fuel consumption was high, so that this good power/weight ratio was to some degree offset by the need to carry a heavier mass of fuel to fly a given mission. Today the specific consumption (the rate at which fuel is burned for a given output of power) has been brought down by countless small improvements. Compressors have been made more efficient, turbines developed to withstand higher operating temperatures, mechanical efficiency improved, and the clearance between rotating parts reduced to fine tolerances to cut down gas leakage. As a result the fuel consumption of modern turboshaft engines is getting near the much heavier piston engine's.

A second advantage is that, whereas the piston engine needs expensive high-octane gasoline (typically 100/130 grade), the turboshaft runs on a wide range of turbine fuels which are cheaper and in general use throughout navies, armies and air forces, besides being found on nearly all major civil airfields. These fuels range from gasolines through kerosenes (paraffin) to diesel oil and even ships' bunker fuel. A third advantage is that helicopters have to be able to hover at sustained high power, which is very difficult for an air-cooled piston engine (which was originally intended to operate in a constant high-speed slipstream) but poses no problem to a gas turbine which needs no cooling. A fourth advantage is one of bulk: in the high-power categories, the contrast in size between piston engines and the modern turboshaft is truly dramatic.

Bulky and Massive

High-power piston engines are bulky and massive. The only way they can reasonably be installed in a helicopter is inside the fuselage (where they occupy the whole cross section, so nobody can get past) or in pairs on the end of stub wings, which means high drag and long shafting with several angle-gearboxes at the corners. In contrast the turboshaft is light and slim enough to be snuggled up close beneath the hub of the main rotor. The transmission could hardly be simpler, and in modern helicopters it is normal for the high-speed input pinion on the engine drive-shaft to act directly on the main ring gear under the rotor. Drag is minimal, because the engine can be streamlined into the profile of the fuselage. Not least, the engine installation does not in any way intrude into the useful interior space, which for reasons of centre of gravity position has to lie under the main rotor (or in a tandem-rotor machine be midway between the two hubs). An incidental advantage is that the turboshaft installation can be enclosed by large hinged doors to provide perfect all-round access, either from the ground or by climbing steps in the side of the fuselage. The access doors can serve as platforms for servicing crews and their tools. This was much more difficult to arrange with any previous installation of piston engines.

Though most of these advantages were predicted in the immediate post-war years, remarkably little attention was paid to doing anything to realize them in practice. In Britain, then the world leader in aircraft gas turbines, the government ignored the turboshaft for almost ten years after the Second World War. Westland, the aircraft firm trying to gain helicopter experience by building the American Sikorsky designs under licence, proposed the W.81 of its own design with two turboshaft power sections (the engine was the Armstrong Siddeley Double Mamba, already developed as a coupled turboprop for the Gannet anti-submarine aircraft) but could not whip up any official enthusiasm. All the public money – and it was not much – was spent on gas drives and on various projects for ramjets and pulsejets by such firms as Auster, Fairey, King Aircraft, Napier and Saunders-Roe. By 1954 considerably greater funds were being voted for a Percival helicopter, the P.74, powered by two Napier Oryx engines. For some reason best known to the government these were arranged to drive the rotor by discharging gas from the blade tips, yet they were mounted right at the bottom of the tall fuselage on each side. A less-sensible way of using gas turbines in a helicopter could hardly have been invented, and it was little wonder the P.74 never managed to lift itself off the ground.

Bold Projects

In the United States two enormously bold and impressive projects likewise failed to deliver the goods, but simply because they were ahead of the available technology. The potentially valuable heavy-lift Hughes XH-17 was killed by its very short range. It was almost impossible to get it a long distance to where it might be needed. The other big American project was a pure helicopter, the PV-15 Transporter by Piasecki. Like all that company's production machines it had tandem rotors; but the PV-15 was far larger, being a 40-seater, bought by the US Air Force as the XH-16. It cried out for turboshaft engines, and was intended to fly with two Allison T38 turbines, one on each side of the large fin, driving the rear rotor and a shaft to the front rotor. Unfortunately, Allison, though a division of the mighty General Motors, did not then possess the engineering talent to make the T38 work.

It was left to a tiny French company, spurred by the vision of one man, to make the turboshaft helicopter an accomplished fact. Joseph Szydlowski founded the Société Turboméca in 1938. At the end of the war – as soon as his factory, pillaged by the Germans, had been re-equipped – he began developing small gas turbines for many purposes, which he had worked on throughout the war. His first units were the 140-hp Orédon and 220-hp Artouste, both of which were type-tested under official conditions in 1949. By 1952 he had developed two forms of Artouste, the Mk I which had grown to 280 hp, and the II of 400 hp. Both were extremely simple, consisting of a single rotating assembly comprising centrifugal compressor, two-stage turbine and a slinger which sprayed fuel droplets into the annular combustion chamber. Though still primitive and relatively undeveloped, the 1952 Artouste II weighed only 253 lb, much less than half the weight of the best 400-hp piston engine. Its best specific fuel consumption was just under 1 lb per horsepower per hour.

Only one other company at that time was as far ahead with small gas turbines to power aircraft. Mighty Boeing had initiated a small development programme for engines in the 200-hp class, receiving USAF support and the official engine designation XT50. Boeing could not equal Turboméca's compressor performance, but it was a turboshaft XT50, rated at 175 hp, that powered the first gas-turbine helicopter in the world. The helicopter was a Kaman 'eggbeater' K-225 of the US Navy, and it flew on 10 December

Avco Lycoming T53-L-13
One of the first engines in the world designed and developed specifically for helicopter propulsion, the T52 free-turbine turboshaft was planned in the early 1950s at about 700 shp and is today in service at powers close to 2000 hp
Length: 47·6 in *Diameter:* 23 in *Weight:* 549 lb
Power: (max at sea level) 1400 hp plus residual jet thrust

1951. Later Kaman fitted two YT50 engines, each rated at 210 hp, into the improved Kaman HTK-1, flying this in March 1954. But some years later Boeing abandoned the T50 engine, and for most of the 1950s and 60s the field was left to Turboméca. In 1952 a licence for the French engines was purchased by the American firm then called Continental Motors, and the Artouste became also the Continental T51. In 1954 XT51 engines powered two American helicopters, the Bell XH-13F and Sikorsky XH-39, the latter gaining a world helicopter altitude record at nearly 35,000 ft, well above anything then possible with a piston engine.

French Success

However, the really important helicopter was French, like its engine. Sud-Aviation (today called Aérospatiale) had built several contrasting tip-drive turbine helicopters, but it found worldwide success when it simply fitted an Artouste to its Alouette (Lark), with shaft drive. First flown on 12 March 1955 this simple machine, the Alouette II, sold all over the world and was even licensed as the Republic Lark in the United States. When production was complete in 1975 over 1400 had been sold, not including examples made in the USA, Sweden and India.

By 1954 Szydlowski had made a further

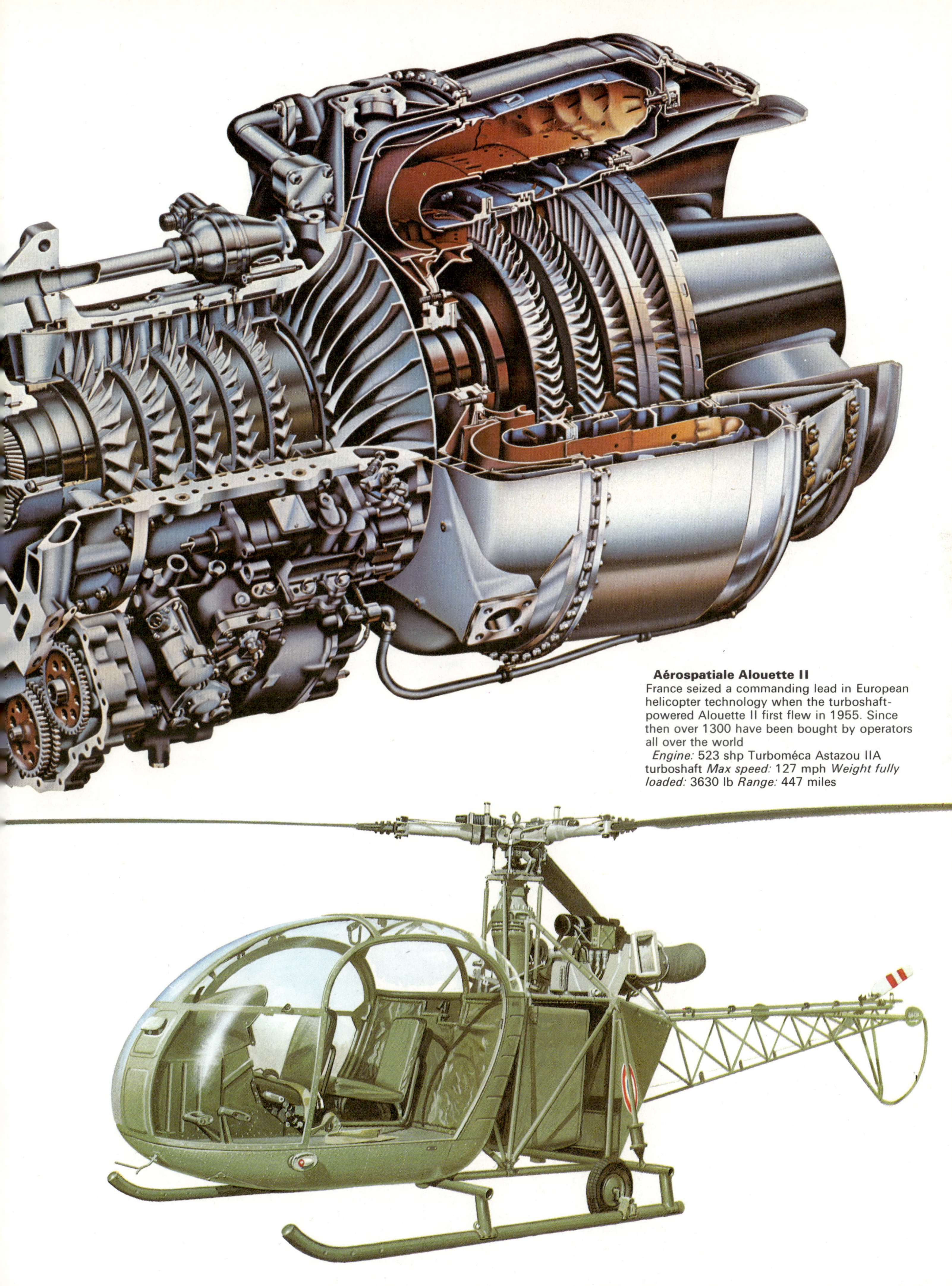

Aérospatiale Alouette II
France seized a commanding lead in European helicopter technology when the turboshaft-powered Alouette II first flew in 1955. Since then over 1300 have been bought by operators all over the world
Engine: 523 shp Turboméca Astazou IIA turboshaft *Max speed:* 127 mph *Weight fully loaded:* 3630 lb *Range:* 447 miles

great advance which revealed yet another fundamental advantage of the turboshaft engine. Since early wartime days various engine companies, notably Bristol, had made 'free-turbine' engines in which there were two quite separate turbines. One drove the compressor while the other drove the propeller or output shaft. As the two rotating assemblies were free to turn at their own speed, being linked only by the gas flow past their blades, the result was an engine eminently suited to use in a helicopter. On starting, the starter had to crank only the engine compressor and its associated turbine. The free turbine and helicopter rotor could remain at rest, with no need for the large clutches fitted to all earlier rotorcraft. As the engine power increased, so did the rising gas flow begin to accelerate the free, or 'power', turbine and the helicopter rotor. In flight the helicopter rotor could turn at its best speed, with the transmission, gearbox and free turbine mechanically unconnected to the power section, or gas-generator, portion of the engine. This gave perfect flexibility, improved efficiency and in most cases a simpler control system and better response to changed power demands and flight speeds. The first free-turbine helicopter engine was the Turboméca Turmo (a name coined from *turbine motoriste* or 'power turbine'). The Turmo is still in full production, in greatly improved forms, more than 20 years later. It inspired many later free-turbine engines for helicopters, notably the American Lycoming T53 and General Electric T58 and the British Napier Gazelle. Such engines were a major plank on which the modern helicopter industry was based.

Giant Helicopters

BIG LIFTERS

It was inevitable that most early helicopters should be rather small. The 'square/cube law' applies virulently to nearly all rotating-wing aircraft, making their problems increase more rapidly than their growth in size. The stresses that must be borne by large whirling machinery are, in general, even more severe than those of fixed wings. The sheer power needed to fly really large helicopters was, until the turboshaft revolution, extremely difficult to provide. And the mechanical complexity and mass of the necessary gearboxes posed some of the worst problems of all, because what designers had to do was similar to installing the reduction gears of a large ship but for about one-tenth of the bulk and weight. Nevertheless, the capabilities of the giant helicopter proved tantalizing. Many designers longed to build helicopter airliners, or craft that could lift really impressive loads, in contrast to the stripped-down Jeeps and baby saloon cars that in the late 1940s were all the helicopter public-relations men had to excite the customers and the public.

The two pioneer giant helicopters funded by the US Air Force in the mid 'fifties, as the XH-16 and XH-17, were not successful. Some of the most difficult snags encountered by Piasecki with the XH-16 concerned the turbines, gearboxes and shafting. In Britain the Westland design staff at Yeovil boldly began to scheme different solutions. This staff had no experience to speak of, because the only Westland helicopter was the WS-51 which had been designed and developed in the United States. Moreover, the WS-51 was a small four-seater. Undeterred, the British designers planned the W.85 and W.90, both enormous by comparison with earlier helicopters and both to be driven by aircraft turbojet engines fixed to the tips of the main rotor blades. Such a scheme promised to provide all the rotor power needed, without the necessity for any gearbox or even an anti-torque tail rotor. The W.85 was to have two Armstrong Siddeley Vipers on each blade-tip; main-rotor diameter was to be 104 ft, gross weight 53,000 lb, and passenger capacity 102. The W.90 was bigger still: the 196-ft rotor was to be driven by an Armstrong Siddeley Sapphire on each blade, lifting a monster double-deck machine weighing 206,000 lb and seating up to 450. In 1951 a civil 450-passenger aircraft of any sort would have been judged unacceptable, so the W.90 brochure said '450 troops'.

It seemed a fantastic leap-forward, but it was not to be. The British designers were only betraying their ignorance of the problems, and the brochures were premature. In fact, there are aerodynamic, structural and 'systems' reasons why no large conventional turbojet can just be hung on the tip of a helicopter rotor blade. This is undoubtedly a blessing, because, had the Westland team gone ahead and tried to build the W.85 or W.90, they would have wasted a lot of money and effort. Much later they did build a large helicopter of wholly sound conception. Called the Westminster, it had a conventional rotor driven through gearboxes by two Napier Eland turboshaft engines. Two Westminsters were flown, the first having an open-lattice space-frame to carry the tail and anti-torque rotor, and the second a proper fuselage. Sadly for Britain, the Westminster matured just at the time the government was having to pay large sums to support the Rotodyne convertiplane; what helped kill it off was the inability of the Eland engines to get within 700 hp of the promised 3500 hp each.

Westland Aircraft built the Westminster entirely with their own money. The reason they were able to tackle the project was that the difficult parts, the gearbox, rotors and shafting, were borrowed from a large American helicopter built by their licence-partner, Sikorsky. This impressive machine was the last really powerful helicopter ever built with piston engines. It was designed as the Sikorsky S-56 in 1951–52, as an assault transport for the US Marine Corps with Service designation HR2S-1. Powered by two 1900-hp Pratt & Whitney R-2800 Double Wasp radials, carried in bulky nacelles on the ends of a stub wing which also housed the retracted twin-wheel main landing gears, the S-56 demanded a great design effort on a new 72-ft rotor with five blades, driven by complicated shafting and gearboxes. Though rather ungainly, it was vastly more capable than any previous helicopter, and could carry 26 troops, 24 stretcher casualties or an assortment of freight or light vehicles loaded through clamshell doors forming the whole nose under the flight deck. Eventually more than 100 were delivered, including US Army versions and a strange radar-picket model for the US Navy with a vast surveillance radar whose scanner filled a grotesquely widened nose.

John Batchelor

Sikorsky S-64 prototype, one of the West's most useful load-carrying helicopters

Sikorsky S-64 Skycrane
The S-64, known as the CH-54 Tarhe by the US Army, is a flying crane with the bare minimum of fuselage. It can lift up to 15,000 lb on its hoist or can be fitted with a pod accommodating 45 troops or 24 stretchers. The data refer to the CH-54B variant
Engines: 2×4800 shp Pratt & Whitney T73-P-700 turboshafts *Max speed:* 127 mph *Weight fully loaded:* 47,000 lb *Range:* 250 miles *Number of seats:* up to 45 in pod

Top: **Twin radial piston-engine installation on S-56** ***Bottom:*** **Twin turboshaft installation on S-64**

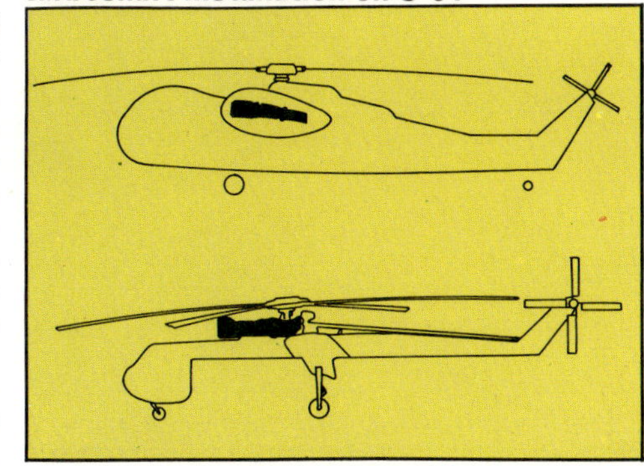

Despite using piston engines one of the HR2S-1 versions set up a world helicopter speed record in 1956, three years after first flight, at 162·7 mph. Another lifted a load of 11,050 lb to 12,000 ft, and 13,250 lb to 7000 ft. (Maximum gross weight was 31,000 lb.) These were all world records in the mid-1950s, but they were soon to be made to look small. Before describing what accomplished this feat it is helpful to note that Sikorsky knew that the excellent dynamic components – gears, shafts and rotors, with the flight control system – of the S-56 were a great achievement which ought in the course of time to be matched with a pair of turboshaft engines to produce a greatly superior helicopter. It took the American engine industry a long time to develop the required engines. Eventually Pratt & Whitney added free power turbines behind the J60 turbojet to yield an attractive turboshaft unit with the un-memorable designation of JFTD12A-1. What it did for the Sikorsky helicopters can be seen in the illustration (right).

Compared with the S-56, the turbine-engined S-64 Skycrane was so much better that comparisons seem pointless. Indeed,

Mil Mi-6s deliver air-portable ASU-57 assault guns during exercise Dnepr. The Soviet Armed Forces maintain complete air-portable divisions of which the big-lift Mi-6 and Mi-10s are an integral part

especially when the rotors are turning, one might be forgiven for failing to see any relationship between the two helicopters. Where the S-56 had bulky engines on stub wings, the S-64 has diminutive engines snuggled up against the main rotor gearbox. Where the S-56 had an ungainly fuselage, the S-64 has merely a slim beam, with a crew compartment at the front and tail rotor at the back. Whereas the S-56 loaded everything through large nose doors, the S-64 straddles its load or slings it from a hook. The Skycrane was just what its name implied: a 'crane helicopter' intended not for long-distance passenger transport but for lifting steeples on to churches, air-conditioning systems to the roofs of skyscrapers, heavy military equipment across rivers and other obstacles, and very large loads of all kinds that no other Western

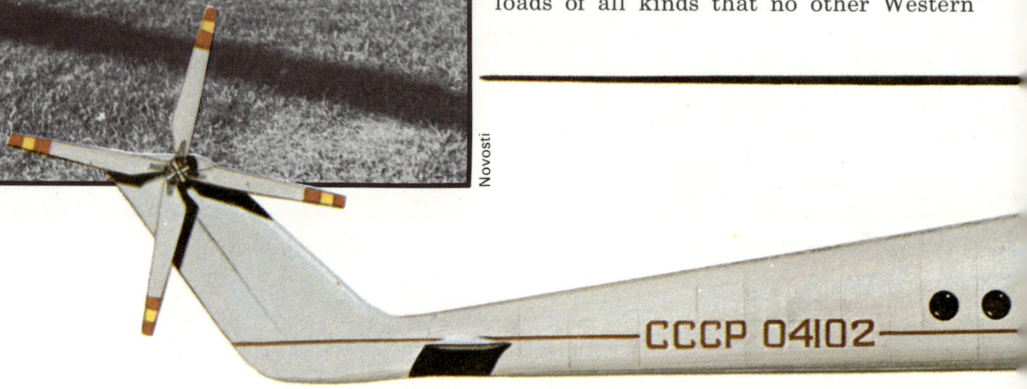

CCCP 04102

Mil Mi-10 (NATO = Harke)
Flying crane development of the Mi-6 and sharing the same powerplant and transmission
Engines: 2×5500 shp Soloviev D-25V turboshafts *Max speed:* 124 mph *Weight fully loaded:* 96,340 lb *Range:* 155 miles

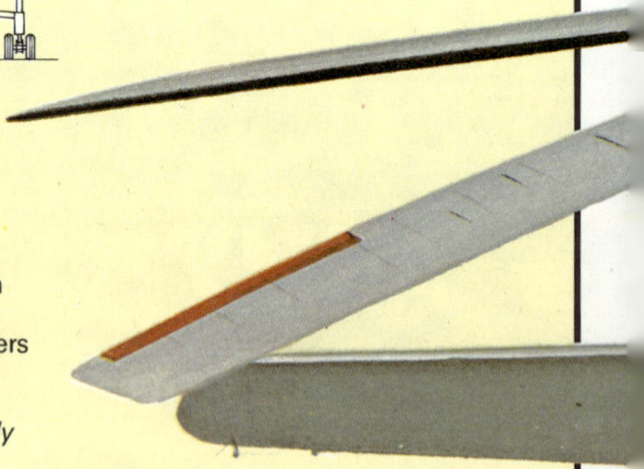

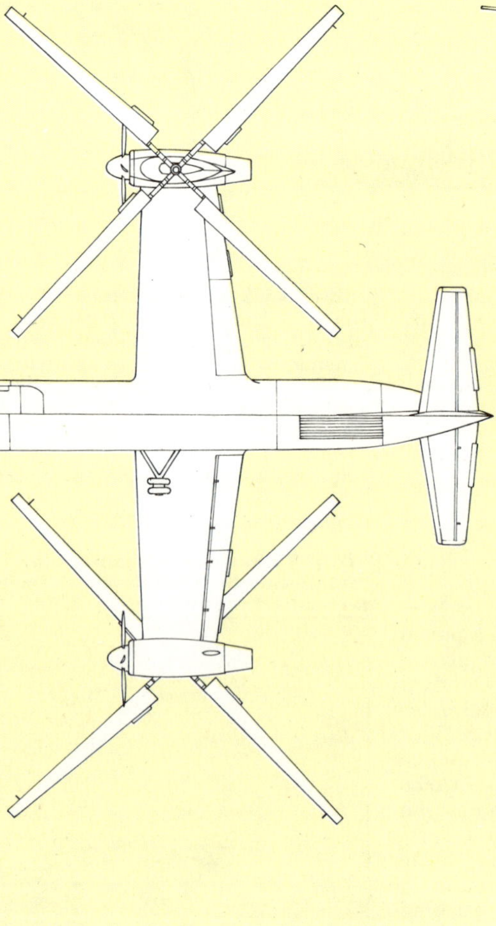

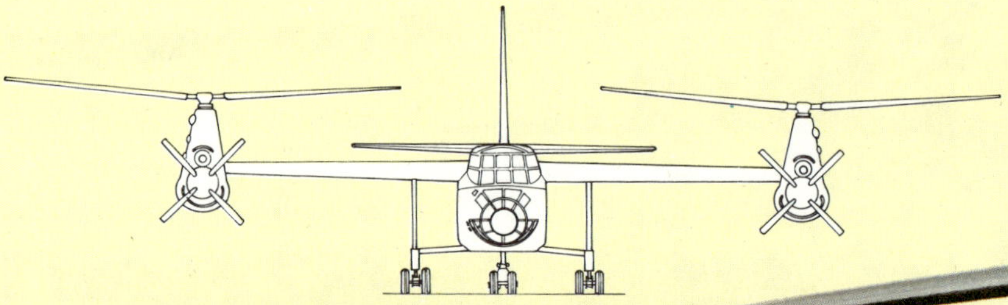

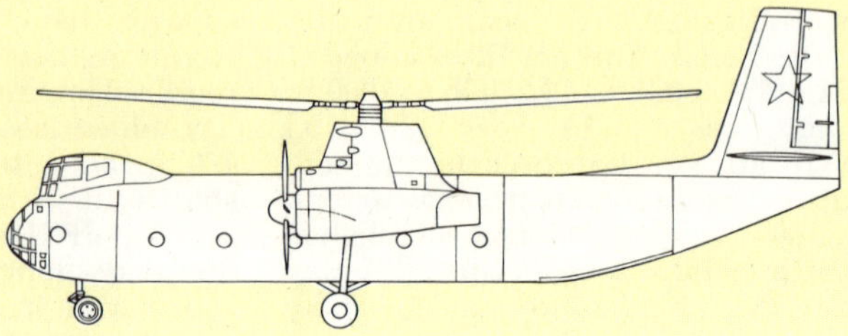

Kamov Ka-22 Vintokryl
Research compound helicopter, first flown in 1961, with two turboshafts powering twin rotors set on stub-wings, and tractor propellers for forward flight
Engines: 2×5500 shp Soloviev D-25V turboshafts *Max speed:* 234 mph *Weight fully loaded:* 74,296 lb

helicopter could attempt. The S-64 first flew in May 1962, with 4050-hp engines. Later the JFTD12A was developed in versions rated at 4500 and then 4800 hp, giving better performance in hot or high-altitude conditions. Whereas the S-56 had carried 24 troops, the military S-64, designated CH-54 Tarhe by the US Army, carries 90. At a gross weight of 47,000 lb the CH-54B carries an external load of 25,000 lb, and many of the 96 Skycranes served in Vietnam where they collected and brought back for re-use more than 380 shot-down aircraft worth $210 million, many times the cost of the helicopters. In 1971 a CH-54 set a helicopter altitude record at 36,122 ft; 31,480 ft was reached with a 4400-lb load, and 10,850 ft with a load of 33,080 lb. In 1972 world helicopter climb records were set at 3000 m (9843 ft) in 1 min 22·2 sec from takeoff, and twice this height in 2 min 58·9 sec. The CH-54 was one of the first helicopters with fully powered flight controls and an autostabilizer both for the helicopter and for the slung load.

Even today this comparatively elderly machine is still the most capable helicopter in the West (save for the prototype YCH-53E mentioned later), but it fades into insignificance beside much older designs developed by Mikhail Mil's bureau in the Soviet Union. Mil did wonders to get his outstanding Mi-4 into production in little over a year in 1952–53. This success prompted the Soviet leaders to issue him with a real challenge: build a helicopter far bigger than any previously available, both for military duties and to help open up the vast undeveloped regions of the Soviet Union where surface transport and even airfields do not exist. He went about the job in the obvious Russian way: he adopted a proven configuration, with conventional turboshaft drive, but just made everything on a gigantic scale. To P A Soloviev fell the responsibility for the engines and gearbox. He too chose a traditional scheme, very conservative and considerably bigger and heavier than it would have been in the West. His engine is the D-25V, but it is commonly known by the Soviet official designation of TV-2BM. Rated at 5500 hp, it is absolutely straightforward and unenterprising. The free turbines of two of these units are coupled to the monster R-7 gearbox, which at 7054 lb weighs even more than the two massive engines. Some idea of what such a gearbox is like can be gained from the R-7's dimensions: 110-in high, 61-in wide and 73-in long, and filled with extremely large gearwheels in high-tensile steel.

This package of two D-25V engines and R-7 gearbox has since proved very useful to the Soviet Union, as will be described. Its first task was to power Mil's Mi-6, first flown in early 1957. The mighty Mi-6, called Hook by NATO, was a remarkably trouble-free machine. The main rotor has five blades and a diameter of 114 ft 10 in, and though blade construction is conventional (old-fashioned by modern standards) the hydraulic power controls and electric blade de-icing called for considerable development effort in the mid-1950s. The fuselage of the standard Mi-6 is again conventional, with a typical Soviet glazed nose for the navigator (a few mount a 14·5-mm gun here) and large clamshell rear doors under the tail boom to admit vehicles and other loads up to a cross section larger than 8 ft by 8 ft. In cruising flight the rotor is off-loaded by a 50 ft 2½ in wing above the cabin just behind the main-rotor axis, which at 150 mph takes over 20% of the weight. A few Mi-6s operated in the crane role have this wing removed, because in hovering and low-speed flight it is dead weight. Other features in-

Mil Mi-6 (NATO = Hook)
Standard heavy transport helicopter of the Soviet Armed Forces, the Mi-6 has been supplied to N Vietnam, Egypt and Indonesia *Engines:* 2×5500 shp Soloviev D-25V turboshafts *Max speed:* 186 mph *Weight fully loaded:* 93,700 lb *Range:* 620 miles

Mil Mi-12 (NATO = Homer)
Currently the world's largest helicopter, the Mi-12 is capable of lifting military loads comparable with the fixed-wing An-22
Engines: 4×6500 Soloviev D-25VF turboshafts *Max speed:* 161 mph *Weight fully loaded:* 231,500 lb *Range:* 310 miles

clude fixed landing gear with twin steerable nosewheels, fuel tanks under the floor supplemented by a tank strapped on each side of the fuselage under the cg, engine cowls which fold down to serve as maintenance platforms, and a variable-incidence trimming tailplane. The interior can be furnished for heavy freight, 65 passengers, 41 stretchers or for many special missions.

Flying Cranes

Several hundred of these impressive machines were built. Though so big, they gained many world records including one for absolute speed at 211·4 mph in 1964. As might be expected, the Mi-6 demolished all previous helicopter load records, lifting payloads of up to 44,350 lb. Gross weight is 93,700 lb. A few were exported to friendly air forces, but most have been used to fight Siberian forest fires, carry heavy gear to remote sites and construction camps, and, above all, support oil drilling in the Tyumen and other Siberian regions. Military examples carry combat teams with such weapons as Frog rockets, ASU-57 mobile artillery, ZSU-23-4 tracked AA guns and many kinds of APC and scout car.

It was logical for Mil to develop a special crane version of the Mi-6, and the resulting Mi-10 (NATO = Harke) flew in 1960. It has the same engines and rotor system, but a slim fuselage with a straight bottom profile. The original Mi-10 has four sets of stalky landing gear for straddling bulky loads up to 66-ft long, 33-ft wide (between the front and rear legs) and 10 ft 2 in high. A later model, the Mi-10K, cuts weight by having a short landing gear and slim tail fin. Instead

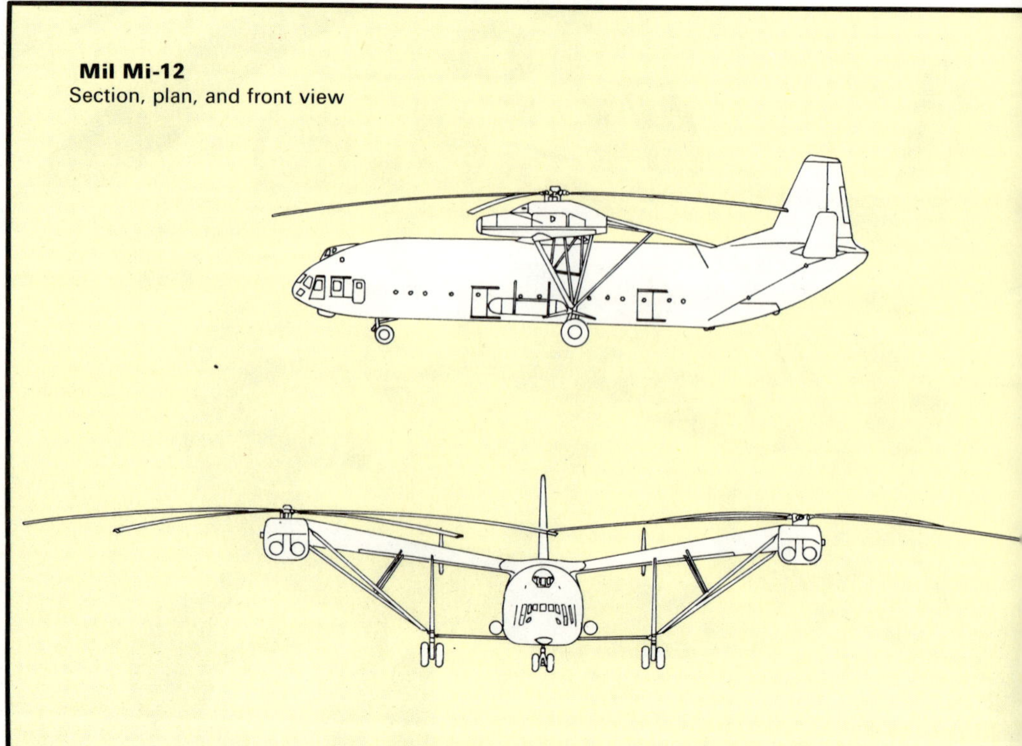
Mil Mi-12
Section, plan, and front view

Novosti

The mighty Mil Mi-12 makes its Western debut at the Paris Air Show, 1971

of straddling the load it hovers over it to pick it up, the operation being accomplished from an aft-facing pilot cockpit under the normal one so that the operator can fly the helicopter whilst watching the load. The Mi-10K weighs only 54,410 lb empty, compared with 60,185 lb for an Mi-10 and 60,055 lb for an Mi-6. With more powerful 6500-hp D-25VF engines it can carry a slung load of 30,865 lb. The maximum payload of a stalky Mi-10 with load platform (not freely slung) is 33,070 lb.

This would have contented most designers, but Mil (who died in January 1970, soon after his 60th birthday) boldly decided to double up the well-proven Mi-6/-10 rotor system to build a gigantic new machine that could combine VTOL with payloads flown in by the big An-22 fixed-wing freighter. The result, flown in 1968 (possibly earlier), is still by far the biggest helicopter in the world. The two sets of engines and rotors are arranged side-by-side, linked by high-speed cross-shafting (steamlined inside inverse-taper 'wings') and with the tips intermeshing, so that the left rotor is fitted with blades of reversed profile and turns in the opposite direction. There is no need for a tail rotor, but the rather troubled flight development eventually led to a tail with three fins, fixed tailplane, rudder and elevators. Mil called the twinned monster Mi-12, the official designation being V-12 and the NATO name Homer. Not many had been built by late 1976, but quantity production for Aeroflot and military use was expected.

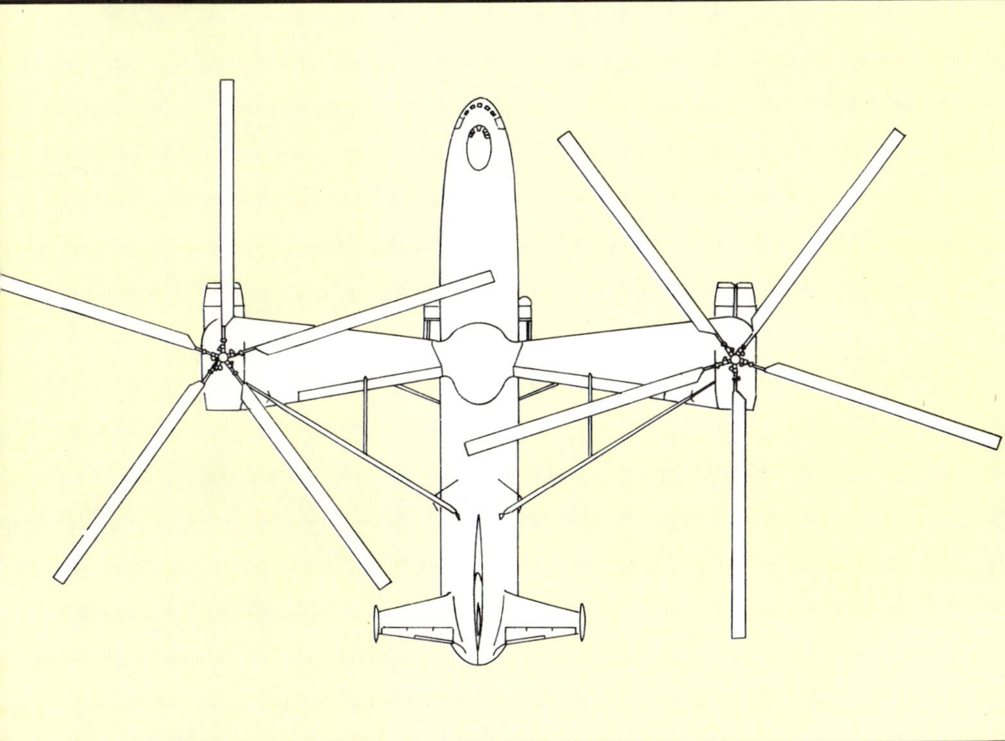

Though only 121 ft 4½ in long (only slightly more than an Mi-6 or Mi-10) the fuselage of the Mi-12 is enormous, with width and height both 14 ft 5 in. In the nose is a flight deck for two pilots, flight engineer and electrical systems operator, while above is a smaller flight deck for navigator and radio operator. Large rear clamshells admit almost any kind of load up to a STOL maximum of 66,000 lb. For record purposes a load of 88,636 lb was lifted to 7400 ft in 1969, in addition to the full crew of six. This is roughly double the *total gross weight* of any Western helicopter. Gross weight of the Mi-12 is normally 231,500 lb, which is unlikely to be surpassed by any other helicopter for a long time to come.

Bell UH-1 Developments

THE HUEY STORY

In a review of all modern rotary-winged aircraft, a single product stands out on its own – the Bell 'Huey' series. Though in no way extraordinary in design, they happen to have been made in more quite different versions than any other rotary-winged machines in history, and in much greater numbers. Indeed, it is probable that more of these helicopters have been made than any other type of aircraft, including fixed-wing aeroplanes, military or civil, since 1945.

It all began in 1955 when Bell Helicopter Company, which had been set up as a separate organization at Fort Worth, Texas, at the start of the 1950s, won a US Army competition for a new utility helicopter suitable for casualty evacuation, instrument training and other tasks. Like most of their rivals, Bell chose to use a turboshaft engine, which considerably increased the price (and in the mid-1950s might have posed a reliability problem) but also improved the flight performance and made it easier to mount the engine close under the rotor hub to leave a completely accessible cockpit and cabin centred around the cg for easy loading. Bell's winning entry was called the Model 204, and the prototype which flew in October 1956 was designated XH-40 by the Army.

Bell chose a completely new free-turbine engine then in early stages of development at Avco Lycoming. A largely ex-German team, led by Dr Anselm Franz, had produced a neat engine with Department of Defense designation T53, rated at about 750 hp. This was ample for the US Army helicopter, and the T53 was expected to be rather cheaper than the rival GE T58 engine in the 1000-hp class, and Bell were also impressed by Lycoming's efforts to make it robust and troublefree even in the extremely harsh operating environment of a battlefield helicopter. Bell tucked it immediately behind the gearbox driving the 44-ft main rotor with a semi-rigid hub and two blades made entirely of aluminium alloy with extruded spars, with the patented Bell stabilizer bar mounted at right angles to the blades right on top of the hub. This tough and efficient rotor, which did not have to fold, was a significant factor in the troublefree development of the XH-40. One of its characteristics

Popperfoto

Hueys fly men and munitions into the vast US base at Khe Sanh, March 1971. Taking off in the background is a CH-47 Chinook.

was 'rotor slap' which has ever since made it possible to hear one of these helicopters rumbling and thumping away several minutes before it comes into view.

After extensive testing by the Army, which led to many minor changes, the Bell went into production in 1959. By this time it had been redesignated HU-1 (Helicopter, Utility 1), which resulted in the enduring name of 'Huey'. To confuse matters, the designation was soon changed yet again, to UH-1A, but by this time 'Huey' had stuck. The UH-1A is a simple six-seater, some of which carried armament or equipment for dual blind instrument training. The T53-L-1 engine was cleared for production at 860 hp, but in the first Huey was derated to 770 hp and thus maintained this power under hot or high conditions. Gross weight was 5800 lb, and a typical cruising speed 115 mph.

Manufacture Worldwide

From the start of the programme Bell subjected the Huey to what Americans call 'product improvement', and in the course of the next 20 years took this process perhaps further than has been possible with any other aircraft. The first improved version, the UH-1B delivered from March 1961, took advantage of uprated engines, starting with the 960-hp T53-L-5 and soon switching to the 1100-hp L-11. This made it possible to increase the weight considerably, first to 8000 and then to 8500 lb, with payload much more than doubled to 3000 lb. Fuji made 89 of this model under licence for the Japan Ground Self-Defense Force. Agusta in Italy made various UH-1B variants including special ASW (Anti-Submarine Warfare) models for the Italian and Spanish navies with dunking sonar, two Mk 44 torpedoes and autostabilization and autohover systems for 'hands off' search low over the ocean. Many Bell and licence-built machines were of the commercial Model 204B type, with the civil T5311 engine or the T58 or Rolls-Royce Gnome. In many parts of the world these were the first capable modern helicopters, and hundreds are still at work.

In 1961 Bell also flew a substantially enlarged machine, the US Army UH-1D or Bell 205. This introduced a cabin roughly 50% longer, and though fuel capacity was greatly increased the fuel cells under the floor were rearranged to provide even more payload space. The T53-L-11 engine was unchanged, but it drove a 48-ft rotor. The result was a payload of 4000 lb, at a gross weight of 9500 lb, with room for a pilot and 12 troops, or six stretcher casualties and an attendant. The Model 205A commercial version, first flown two years after the military UH-1D, seats no fewer than 15, is powered by the 1400-hp T5313A (flat-rated at 1250 hp), and can carry a slung load of 5000 lb, almost the laden weight of the original XH-40!

By 1967 the 1400-hp engine had gone into the military UH-1H and, with the war escalating in Vietnam, Bell was hard pressed to meet the enormous demand. While the UH-1D and UH-1H were built at the rate of two per day for the US Army others were delivered to military customers all over the world, and 352 were made by Dornier for the Luftwaffe and Bundesheer and 118 were licence-built in Taiwan. In Italy, Agusta are still in production in 1976, and total deliveries of the 205/205A now exceed 8000.

This was by no means the end even of the basic Huey development. In April 1965 Bell flew the Model 208 Twin Delta, to explore the use of two engines. A UH-1D re-engined with two Teledyne Continental T72 free-turbine engines, the 208 was encouraging and confirmed that it would be feasible to build a Huey having true engine-out capability and thus 'twin-engine safety' to meet civil overwater and IFR (bad weather) certification requirements. The result was the Model 212 Twin Two-Twelve, powered by a Pratt & Whitney Canada PT6T-3 Twin Pac, which although it is flat-rated at 1250 hp actually incorporates two independent power sections each rated at 900 hp, and flight at gross weight can be sustained after failure of either half. Production of military twin-engined Hueys began with the UH-1N for the US Air Force in 1970 and CH-135 for the Canadian Armed Forces the following year (development of the 212 stemmed from Canadian support). Today many hundreds of these capable helicopters have been sold, a high proportion being civil machines for such duties as oil drilling rig support for which full IFR equipment and twin-engined safety is desirable and usually mandatory. The 212 is no faster than other Hueys, but with allowable weights up to 11,200 lb can carry large payloads despite the burden of full IFR avionics. A fully equipped 212 costs something like $750,000 with spares and technical services.

Even this was not the ultimate development of the basic utility Huey. Further offshoots and developments were numerous, and some have led to a completely new family, the 214 series, with yet further increased capability. One of the oddballs was the RH-2 (research helicopter 2), a much-modified UH-1A used to fly all sorts of experimental flight-control systems, avionics and instruments. The RH-2 has also flown with a high-resolution radar in a large fairing above the cockpit, enabling the crew to avoid obstacles as small as flagpoles and power cables in low-level flight at zero visibility.

Another and even more extensive programme has been undertaken carrying a large Westinghouse surveillance radar. Helicopter-borne surveillance poses great problems, because at such low levels ground clutter – unwanted 'noise' in the radar caused by reflections from everything on the ground – is greatly increased. The Huey-borne radar has a large two-dimensional L-band aerial operating with cunning anti-clutter systems and rotating like a lighthouse at nine rpm. The antenna folds flat between the skids for landing, and special aerials are carried at front and rear of the helicopter to send back the radar 'picture' as a stream of digital pulses.

Experimental Huey-borne radar picket. The large Westinghouse surveillance radar folds down below the skids after takeoff and rotates at 9 rpm

Westinghouse

Another side branch off the main development stream was the HueyTug of 1967–68. This was made possible by Avco Lycoming's decision in the first half of the 1950s to develop a second turbine-engine family with about the same size as the T53 but handling considerably greater airflow, and thus giving more power. The new engine, the T55, at first had no relevance to the Huey because the Bell helicopter did not need more than half as much power. Gradually the inevitable happened. During the 1960s Bell devised a completely new Model 540 main rotor, with a 'door hinge' root and broad blades 27 in across the chord, able to generate far greater lift than the original rotor and also eliminate the rather severe restriction on maximum flight speed of 127 mph imposed on all previous models. This rotor was first flown on the UH-1C of September 1965, built in quantity for the US Army, with considerably greater fuel capacity than earlier models. It was also used in the bulk of the UH-1E assault production for the Marine Corps and all the Navy HH-1K rescue, TH-1L trainer and UH-1L utility versions. With the HueyTug Bell redesigned the whole airframe and dynamic parts to accept the Lycoming T55-L-7 engine rated at 2650 hp. The gearbox and transmission were rated at 2000 hp. The Model 540 rotor was extended to a diameter of 50 ft and the tail boom and tail rotor were enlarged and strengthened. Instead of a rotor stabilizer bar a new stability control and augmentation system was provided. The resulting Tug, planned as a crane helicopter, could hover out of ground effect (without help from the ground being close underneath the rotor) at 4000 ft at a scorching 35°C temperature at a weight of 14,000 lb, and it could also fly at 161 mph.

Big-Bladed Rotors

Rather surprisingly the one-off Tug was just the start of a whole new family of much more powerful Hueys with the T55 engine. To make this possible Bell had to do a lot of further development, part of which was accomplished with the KingCobra described later. One major advance was a way of minimizing inflight vibration by hanging the helicopter from a 'nodalized beam', a springy beam supported at just the points at which, when flexing, it would bend but not move bodily up or down. Bell call this their Noda-Matic system. With the big blades of the 50-ft door-hinge rotor this opened the way to a machine called the Model 214 Huey Plus, powered by the T53-L-702 rated at 1900 hp. But, before selling this machine in quantity, Bell decided that they could do even better with the much more capable T55 engine, which instead of being stretched to give 1900 hp had started life at 2650 hp and by the mid-1960s was offering promise of powers in excess of 4000 hp. So Bell took out the L-702 engine and put in a T55-L-7C rated at 2850 hp, and then sent the Huey Plus, now called the 214A, on a tour of Iran. The result was a gigantic single order from that country for 287 advanced Model 214A helicopters, which today are in service with the further improved LTC4B-8D engine of 2930 hp, flat-rated at 2250 hp to maintain power in hot or high conditions.

The first deliveries to Iran were made in April 1975. The most capable of all military utility Huey versions, the 214A has a normal gross weight of 13,000 lb, can cruise at 150 mph and fly 299 miles with full load of 16 troops. With a slung load it can fly at 15,000 lb. Three days after delivery the first Iranian machine set up world class records for rate of climb and absolute altitude. The 214A is midway in size and capability between such machines as the Lynx and earlier Hueys and the bigger Mi-8. Although less powerful than the important US Army UTTAS machines described later, it can carry considerably more. In civil form, designated Model 214B and powered by the T5508D engine with the same ratings as the military engine, the new Huey can fly at up to 16,000 lb gross weight and carry a slung load of 7000 lb. The 214B introduces further improvements with rotors (main and tail) having raked tips and elastomeric bearings needing no lubrication. Customer options include a fire-fighting version with 800 US gal of water and an agricultural model carrying nearly 8000 lb of chemicals – almost 2200 lb more than the 5800 lb complete laden weight of the first Huey! Probably no other flying machine in history has ever been developed to fly at weights more than 2·75 times the limit for the prototype.

Before completing the Huey story with the Cobra gunships, there was another sidelight, the Bell Model 533. This special high-speed research machine was surprising because instead of having the high-speed Model 540 rotor it retained the old rotor of the YUH-1B (which it originally was). Bell covered the machine with modifications: fairings on the fuselage, a cambered fin to unload the tail rotor, and a tilting main-rotor mast inside a large top fairing. In this form it flew in August 1962. It was then given a small swept wing carrying two 1700-lb thrust J69 jets, and in 1965 at a weight of 8600 lb it reached 254 mph and pulled 2g turns and made 60° banked turns at over 200 mph. In 1968 the 533 was refitted with 3300-lb Pratt & Whitney JT12A jets, and in May 1969 set a level speed of 316 mph that still stands as the all-time high for helicopters or rotorcraft of any kind.

During the escalating conflict in SE Asia in the early 1960s it had become obvious that the unprecedented numbers of troop, logistic, cas-evac and reconnaissance helicopters used by the Americans needed some form of armed escort. The extremely complex AH-56A Cheyenne was started by Lockheed, but Bell found the eventual answer with the Model 209 HueyCobra. In March 1965 the company began to rebuild a UH-1C with Model 540 rotor, and this flew as the first AH-1G HueyCobra in September 1965. It had a new slim fuselage with the gunner in the nose and the pilot above and behind him in a fighter-type cockpit. From the start the Cobra was designed to carry efficient armament. Features included various sighting systems, a variety of turrets, stub wings for offloading the rotor and carrying weapons, and new fixed skids. The whole machine was only 36 in wide, and was well protected against most kinds of ground fire.

Bell UH-1B Iroquois
Universally known in the US Armed Forces as the 'Huey', the UH-1 has been built in many different versions since the first flight in 1956 and was the mainstay of the US helicopter force in Vietnam
Engine: 1100 shp Lycoming T-53-11A turboshaft *Max speed:* 120 mph *Weight fully loaded:* 9500 lb *Range:* 392 miles *Number of seats:* 10

View across an M-60 machine-gun as Aero Rifle Platoon Hueys head out on a mission

US Army

Cas-evac Huey picks up wounded from a Vietnam jungle clearing

Bell

The Cobra story began with the first tactical tests using modified Hueys as armed helicopters. Here a UH-1 fires a 2·75-in rocket salvo at Fort Bragg in January, 1963

US Army

By 1965 the slim shape of the highly specialized HueyCobra had emerged. Bristling with guns and rockets, it was a long way from the first armed Huey lash-ups used in Vietnam

From the start the Cobra was a great success, and it soon became fashionable for US Army 'top brass' to scrounge a ride so that they could experience the thrill of poling a machine round the sky that was virtually a rotary-winged fighter. In fact the Army only got it after winning a long argument with the US Air Force which claimed to have an absolute monopoly of tactical 'combat aircraft'. Deliveries to Vietnam began in the autumn of 1967 and by 1975 the US Army had received 1078, powered by the 1400-hp T53-L-13 derated to a flat 1100 hp. Despite this modest power the basic AH-1G at a weight of 9500 lb can fly on the level at its 'never-exceed' speed of 219 mph, and it is outstandingly manoeuvrable. Although hundreds were lost in Vietnam, the remaining US Army force of over 600 is one of the biggest combat-aircraft forces of one type with one operator in the world. In 1973 the US Army began to receive the first of about 300 which are being converted to AH-1Q TOW/Cobra standard with eight TOW missile containers and a complex helmet sight subsystem. In Vietnam the Q proved unable to carry a full missile load in the harsh environment, so the Army has now converted both the remaining G models and the existing AH-1Q TOW/Cobras into the much improved AH-1S, with the T53-L-700 engine flat-rated at 1400 hp with full sea-level power of 1900 hp.

Recognizing the need for more power the US Marine Corps did not buy a T53-Cobra at all but instead chose the Model 212 twin-engined version, with larger tail boom and tail-rotor blades widened from 8·4 to 11·5 in. The engine is the Pratt & Whitney Canada T400, flat-rated at 1100 hp, with 1250 hp available for 2·5 min, and with either power section of the twin-engine unit able to zip up to 900 hp the moment it receives a signal that the other engine has failed. The Marine aircraft is the Bell AH-1J SeaCobra, and it has different armament and avionics from the Army machines. Some 80 are in use, plus a further 69 on order, the latter being AH-1J (Improved) models with more power and TOW missiles. Iran has bought 202 of the Improved SeaCobras, deliveries of which started in 1974. The Spanish Navy has 20 of the old Army AH-1G version for anti-shipping attack. The USMC is also receiving the AH-1T, incorporating an AH-1J airframe, dynamic components from the Model 214, an uprated engine (a Pratt & Whitney T400-WV-402 twin turbine) and some KingCobra technology. An improved drive system and advanced-design rotor are used and the fire-control system is more accurate than that in the AH-1J. Maximum payload is increased to 5392 lb.

The final Huey to be noted was the King-

Cobra, the Bell Model 309. Company-funded, it transferred to the Cobra family the Model 540 rotor in its final (214B) raked form, with elastomeric bearings, 2000+ hp transmission and a long 49-ft fuselage. The nose was revised to carry different sensors and armament/sight systems, the wings were extended from 10 ft 4 in to 13 ft to carry more weapons, and fuel capacity was increased from 1715 to 2300 lb. Bell built two Kings, one with twin T400 engines and the other with a flat-rated 2050-hp T55 as in the 214A. The King was overtaken by the completely new AAH, for which Bell is competing.

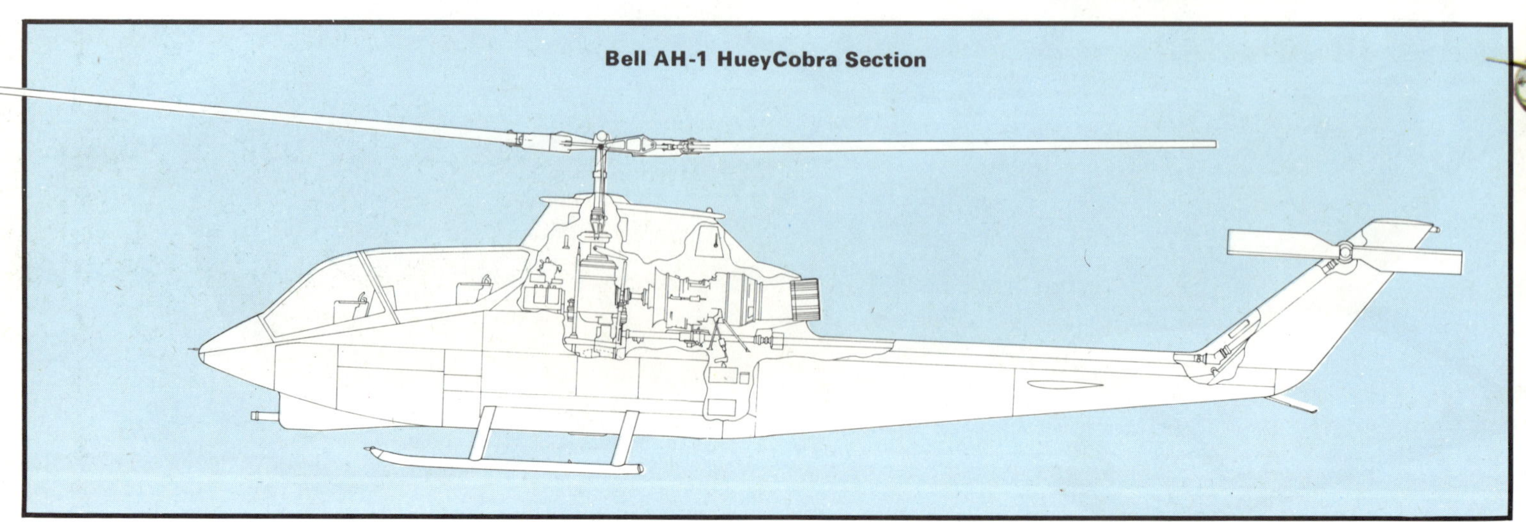

Bell AH-1 HueyCobra Section

US Army

Above: *UH-1D with its side doors removed delivers men of the US 173rd Airborne Brigade to Xuan Loc, Vietnam, 1966. Armament is a single M-60 machine-gun*
Right: *Loading Minigun ammunition and 2·75-in rockets aboard a HueyCobra, Mai Loc, Vietnam, 1969. Using the same dynamic components as the UH-1, the Cobra was literally a flying gun-platform able to carry 4000 Minigun rounds, 300 rounds for the 40-mm grenade launcher and a variety of stores on underwing pylons*

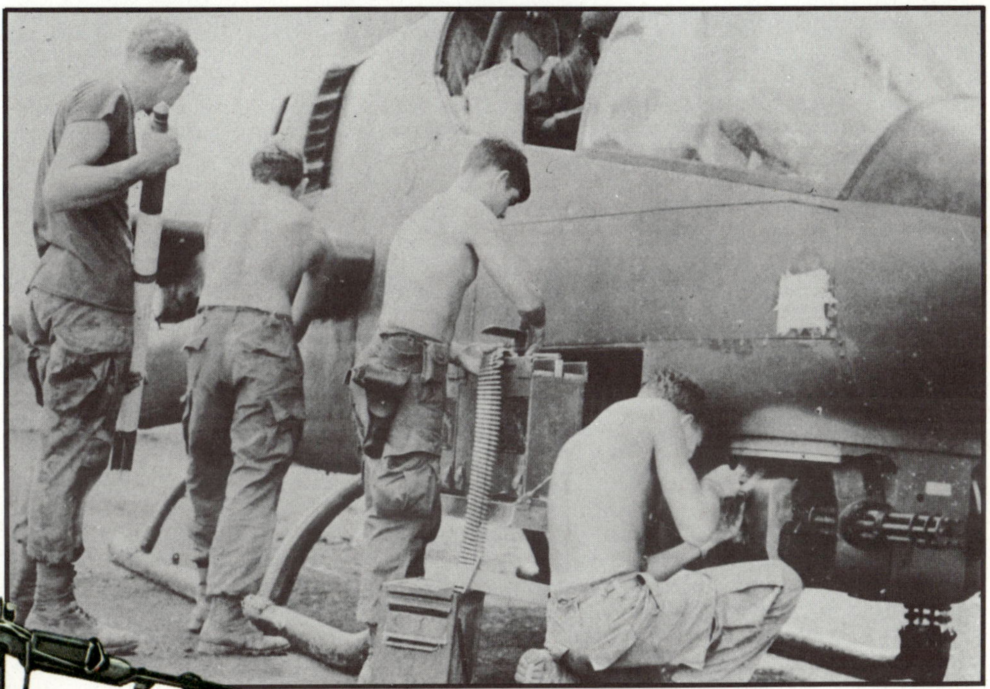

US Army

Bell AH-1G HueyCobra
Engine: 1400 shp Lycoming T53-L-13 turboshaft *Max speed:* 219 mph *Weight fully loaded:* 9500 lb *Armament:* 7·62-mm Minigun, rocket or gun pods

Other US Helicopters

AMERICA'S FRONT LINE

Few would dispute that (Bell with their giant production runs aside) the world helicopter leader remains the Sikorsky Aircraft Division of United Technologies Corporation. No organization has done so much to advance the state of the art of helicopter technology, and none has ever developed so many different families of large and expensive helicopters for the most challenging military and commercial purposes. The one field Sikorsky has not entered is that of light sporting rotorcraft which – most observers agree – come best from small companies and groups with smaller research budgets and lower overheads. Sikorsky is leader of the 'big league' that has to spend many millions of dollars a year simply solving the problems of how to build the helicopters and other rotorcraft of the future. As the final chapter shows, the future may well lie with radically new forms of helicopter, and even with rotorcraft that can fold their rotors and become high-speed fixed-wing machines.

With the S-56, Sikorsky, having spent several millions developing a powerful five-blade 72-ft rotor and drive system, was eventually able to hang under this a modern crane helicopter with turbine engines. It did not need too clever a crystal ball to predict that Sikorsky would see if similar improvements would be possible with its existing smaller dynamic systems, the most urgent example being that of the obsolescent S-55. In Britain, Westland was building a turbine-engined S-55 as the Gnome-Whirlwind, but Sikorsky was more interested in a properly designed machine with the pilot and engine interchanged so that the turbine could lie immediately next to the gearbox and the cockpit occupy the nose. When one looks at the result, the Sikorsky S-62, one wonders that the S-55 ever happened, with its long sloping drive-shaft and lofty cockpit perched on top.

On 14 May 1958 the prototype S-62 ushered in the new era of improved turbine helicopters, though it flew after the rather special Mi-6. Its main advantage lay in the more efficient arrangement of cockpit, cabin and engine, but an extra feature was that the hull was watertight and had a flying boat's planing bottom, and the main wheels retracted into outrigger stabilizing floats. Helicopters do not need to have a stepped planing bottom on such a hull, and can in theory be aerodynamically more efficient than flying boats which have to speed through, or across, the water surface. There are structural penalties in an amphibious hull, but on the other hand there are penalties in the alternative of having large flotation bags able to be swiftly inflated by large stored-gas bottles, as on the Wessex and the Soviet Ka-25. In any case the weight difference is modest, because despite its flying-boat hull and floats the S-62 came out some 160 lb lighter than the original S-55. This was of course entirely due to the switch to turbine power, the single engine being the free-turbine GE T58 or commercial CT58 of 1250 hp but derated to 730 hp to match the dynamic parts and maintain power under the most adverse conditions. The lighter weight and greater power enable the S-62 in all its versions to outperform the S-55 and to carry 12 troops instead of ten, and roughly twice the payload. This trim machine went into production in 1960 and was sold to 26 civil customers, many concerned with offshore work; but the biggest batch comprise 99 for the US Coast Guard designated HH-52A and specially equipped for rescues over or on stormy seas.

Surprisingly, Sikorsky never developed a

March 1959, and the brand-new HSS-2, the US Navy's ASW Sikorsky S-61, taxies on the water under test

HH-3E refuels from a Lockheed HC-130P Hercules tanker over the Mekong Delta

USAF Sikorsky HH-53 (S-65) rescue and transport (foreground) helicopter flying with the smaller HH-3E (S-61R) 'Jolly Green Giant' specialized rescue and recovery helicopter. Plucking NASA space capsules from the ocean or downed aircrew from Vietnam jungle clearings were standard roles for HH-3Es

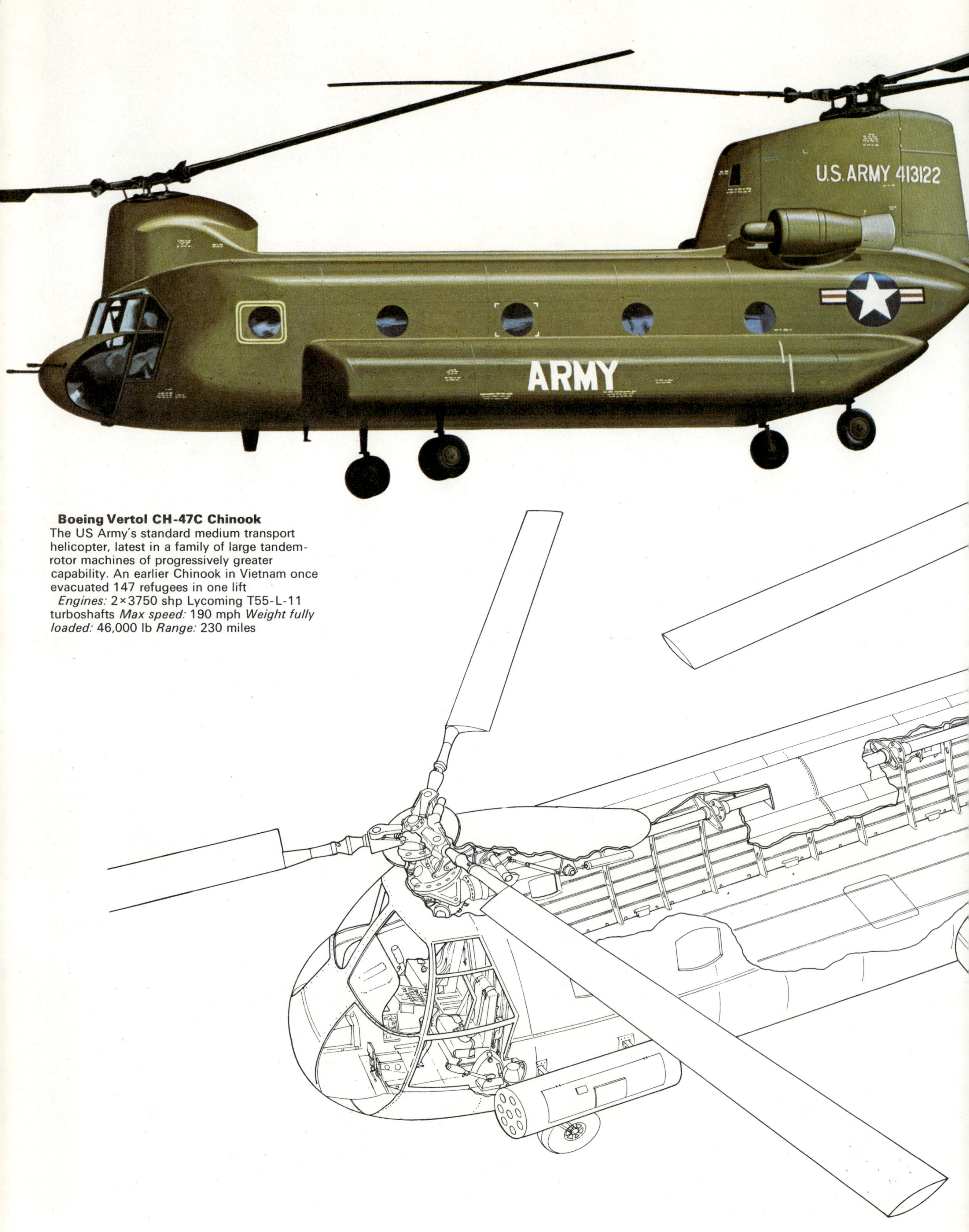

Boeing Vertol CH-47C Chinook
The US Army's standard medium transport helicopter, latest in a family of large tandem-rotor machines of progressively greater capability. An earlier Chinook in Vietnam once evacuated 147 refugees in one lift
Engines: 2×3750 shp Lycoming T55-L-11 turboshafts *Max speed:* 190 mph *Weight fully loaded:* 46,000 lb *Range:* 230 miles

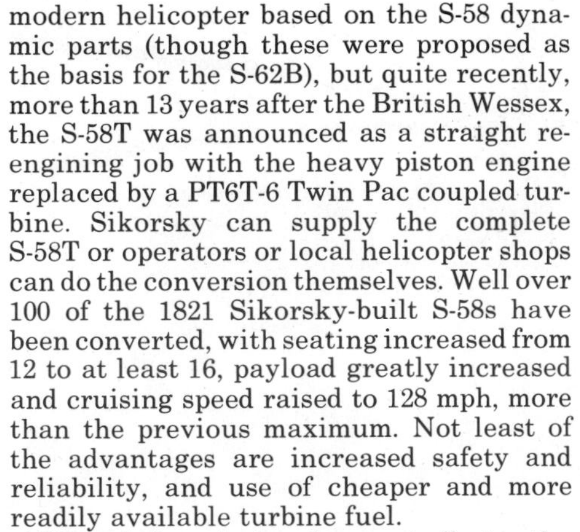

modern helicopter based on the S-58 dynamic parts (though these were proposed as the basis for the S-62B), but quite recently, more than 13 years after the British Wessex, the S-58T was announced as a straight re-engining job with the heavy piston engine replaced by a PT6T-6 Twin Pac coupled turbine. Sikorsky can supply the complete S-58T or operators or local helicopter shops can do the conversion themselves. Well over 100 of the 1821 Sikorsky-built S-58s have been converted, with seating increased from 12 to at least 16, payload greatly increased and cruising speed raised to 128 mph, more than the previous maximum. Not least of the advantages are increased safety and reliability, and use of cheaper and more readily available turbine fuel.

Sikorsky's main development effort in the period 1955–60 concerned a completely new machine midway in size between the S-58 and S-60/64. Designated S-61, this was planned with US Navy funds to meet a need for a better helicopter than the SH-34 for anti-submarine warfare. The first contract was placed in September 1957, and the first S-61, designated XHSS-2, flew on 11 March 1959. Inevitably it was dubbed the 'Hiss', but the official designation eventually became SH-3A Sea King. It had two T58 engines driving a 62-ft five-blade main rotor, an amphibious fuselage with outrigger floats housing twin-wheel main gears, and a fine unobstructed cabin over 6-ft wide and high and nearly 25-ft long. On this basis Sikorsky constructed the helicopter which proved to be market leader for a wealth of military and civil missions, and which remains in production by Sikorsky and by its licensees Westland, Agusta (Italy) and Mitsubishi (Japan). The S-61 family is the only one in the world to rival that of the Huey for diversity, and it has exerted a very great influence on the whole development of the helicopter.

Although it was seen from the start that two T58 engines could, for the first time, make possible an attractive hunter/killer ASW helicopter, able to operate singly in the pursuit of submerged submarines instead of in pairs, the US Navy philosophy in the 1950s was that the helicopter was merely an extension of the all-important surface ship. Even today, of course, ASW helicopters have to operate from surface ships, and this imposes some constraints on their size, design and equipment. The British licensee, Westland, completely redesigned the Sea King to operate independently as a wholly self-contained ASW platform, which was as big an advance as was the original S-61. On the other hand, the basic S-61A weighs 9763 lb while a fully equipped Westland Sea King turns the scales (with no fuel or weapons) at 16,834 lb, which gives a clear indication of the quantity of search and attack equipment needed for this role. SAR (search and rescue) Sea Kings are much lighter, and can carry up to 31 troops or 'rescuees' with a full load of main and auxiliary fuel.

In 1963 Sikorsky flew the first CH-3C, the first of the redesigned S-61R series with a new freight fuselage having watertight rear ramp doors and sponsons instead of floats. Originally developed for missile support and drone-recovery duties, the S-61R has blossomed forth in several major sub-variants including the more powerful CH-3E, the Coast Guard HH-3F Pelican, and the USAF HH-3E Jolly Green Giant with exceptional front-line rescue provisions, retractable flight-refuelling probe, armour and self-sealing tanks and, in many, GE Minigun 7·6-mm turrets on each sponson with over 180° remote-control traverse and 8000 rounds of ammunition for about two minutes' continuous firing. All the S-61R series have retractable tricycle landing gear with twin nosewheels, self-lubricating bearings, and the Sikorsky patented BIM (blade inspection method) in which each main rotor blade is sealed and pumped up with dry nitrogen under pressure, so that even a small fatigue crack will cause loss of pressure and immediate cockpit warning. In 1967 two Jolly Green Giants made the first non-stop rotorcraft crossings of the Atlantic; with nine air-refuellings each, they flew 4270 miles from New York to Paris in 30 hr 45 min – faster than Lindbergh's famous 1927 flight with a fixed-wing machine.

Sikorsky also built a straightforward civil passenger version of the original S-61, and by late 1976 orders (which in the late 1960s had seemed to stop at about 30) were close to 100. Most of the early civil sales were of the S-61L version, in which elimination of the amphibious hull and floats allows 30 passengers to be carried. Los Angeles Airways bought seven, and these today probably have the highest flight-time of any helicopter in history with figures around 25,000 hr each. This L model has fixed twin-wheel main gears of light weight, and like the Mk II version of the amphibious N model has six underfloor cargo/baggage bins. In recent years the upsurge in demand for helicopter support of offshore oil/gas rigs has led to the S-61N becoming the favoured type, with sales to eleven countries. The operator of the biggest fleet is Britain's Bristow Helicopters, which has 19. The British licensee, Westland, has not built civil models. Many of the civil machines, such as the Coast Guard Pelicans and some other military models, have nose radar.

Today the most powerful and capable helicopter outside the Soviet Union is a version of the next Sikorsky 'plateau' of development, the S-65. This began in 1962 as the CH-53A assault transport for the US Marine Corps, and it used dynamic parts closely similar to those of the S-64 but with folding blades in a hub in which aluminium parts were replaced by titanium. Powered by two 2850-hp GE T64-6 engines, the CH-

Boeing Vertol CH-46/107
Under such names as Sea Knight, Labrador and Voyageur, these tandem-rotor helicopters are used as assault transports, ship-supply utility aircraft, rescue and mine-countermeasures aircraft
Engines: 2×1500 shp General Electric T58-GE-5 or Rolls-Royce Gnome turboshafts *Max speed:* 139 mph *Weight fully loaded:* 21,400 lb

Hughes OH-6 Cayuse
Known in the US Army as 'Loach' (LOH)
Engine: 317 shp Allison T63-A-5A turboshaft
Max speed: 152 mph *Weight fully loaded:* 2550 lb
Range: 377 miles

53A Sea Stallion has a watertight amphibious hull with sponsons and retractable tricycle landing gear, and accommodation for 37 troops or 24 stretchers and four attendants. Normal weight available for fuel and payload is some 12,500 lb, but in 1968 an A model flew with a disposable load of 28,000 lb to set new non-Soviet records. Subsequently very many improved versions were delivered with greater power, and often with special gear such as weapons, refuelling probe and terrain-clearance radar. The RH-53D is a multi-mission Navy model with special capability for mine countermeasures and the CH-53E is the first of a powerful new series with a new seven-blade all-titanium rotor, an 11,570-hp transmission and three 4380-hp T64 engines, the third engine being close behind the gearbox on the left.

Outside the Soviet Union the only rival to Sikorsky for large helicopters is the company which was started as Piasecki, became Vertol, and is now the Vertol Division of Boeing. In 1956 Vertol began the design of the Model 107 to match the proven tandem-rotor layout with the new turbine engines becoming available. It had a sealed amphibious fuselage with rear sponsons carrying the main units of the twin-wheel fixed landing gear, but did not have a planing bottom like the S-61. Flown with two 860-hp Lycoming T53 engines in April 1958, the 107 went into production with 1250- or 1400-hp GE T58 or Rolls-Royce Gnome engines for many military and civil customers. Most went to the US Navy and Marines as CH-46 or UH-46 Sea Knight assault, utility and inter-ship transports seating 25 troops or carrying a 6600-lb load with maximum fuel. Heavy freight can be loaded by one man, and the blades can be folded at the touch of a switch. Over 600 were built, including many of versions developed by Kawasaki in Japan.

US Army

Loading the Minigun on an armed OH-6A

Buoyancy Pods

A much larger and more important helicopter, begun at the same time to meet the need for a versatile transport machine for the US Army (to partner the small Huey), is the CH-47 Chinook. In configuration this resembles the Model 107 except that it has long honeycomb-skinned buoyancy pods along each side with four fixed gears, the front units only having twin wheels. The unobstructed cabin has full-section rear ramp/doors and a length exceeding 30 ft, for loads which in the most powerful CH-47C version can reach 23,212 lb. Seating can be provided for up to 44, but in Vietnam an earlier version lifted 147 people to safety in one trip. All Chinooks have been powered by two Lycoming T55 free-turbine engines, with power rising from 2200 hp in early versions to 3750 hp in the C model which has a 7200-hp transmission and new broad-chord cambered blades on the intermeshing three-blade rotors. One Chinook flew in 1969 with 60-ft rotors having glassfibre blades believed to be the largest composite blades ever built. More than 800 Chinooks were built, those for Italy and Iran being made under licence by Elicotteri Meridionali.

Kaman Aircraft pioneered helicopters with servo-flapped intermeshing 'eggbeater' rotors. The last machine with these features was the H-43 Huskie, of which over 200 served at US Air Force bases as the standard crash rescue machine carrying pilot, two firefighters and a 1000-lb pack of chemicals and rescue aids. Powered by an 825-hp T53, this popular machine has a box-like body, long exhaust stack, four fins and four wheel/ski gears, and now serves six foreign air forces supplied under US aid programmes.

Kaman's main product however has been a single-rotor machine for shipboard service, the H-2 Seasprite. Designed as a US Navy utility helicopter with four-blade non-servo-flap rotor driven by a T58 of 1250 hp, the original UH-2A flew in July 1959 and was noteworthy for its neat layout and fully retracting main gears. In 1967 the Navy began to convert all the survivors of the 190 Seasprites to twin-engine configuration, with two 1350-hp T58-8Fs. Some became HH-2C battle rescue machines, with Minigun chin turret, waist guns, armour, and many other changes including twin-wheel gears for a much increased gross weight of 12,840 lb. The most important conversions are the SH-2D and SH-2F LAMPS helicopters discussed later under Helicopters in Sea Warfare.

During the 1960s Hiller, a famous name in light rotorcraft, faded from the scene though many H-23s and a few turbine-engined Fairchild Hiller FH-1100s remain in use. The FH-1100 started as the OH-5, the Hiller entry in the US Army 1961 LOH (Light Observation Helicopter) competition. Over 1000 machines were at stake, and after a long and intense battle the award went to Hughes whose OH-6A Cayuse proved unbeatable. Weighing only just over 1000 lb empty, or 40% less than its rivals, it had a 317-hp Allison T63-5A turbine driving a four-blade rotor of advanced design and only 26 ft 4 in diameter. Yet this tiny rotor lifts six large men, or a variety of armament, and drives the OH-6 at a cruising speed of 150 mph. Eventually Hughes delivered 1424 in four years, plus large numbers of the ongoing Model 500 export version and new 500D which are substantially improved and have more powerful T63 engines. In 1971 Hughes converted an OH-6 to be the quietest helicopter in the world, while other versions have exceeded 200 mph and flown 2213 miles from California to Florida non-stop. Licensees for the Model 500 family include Kawasaki (Japan), RACA (Argentina) and Breda-Nardi (Italy).

Birth of the Gunship

HELICOPTER ARMAMENT

There is little doubt that the first helicopters to carry armament were the Luftwaffe Fa 223 multi-role transports, which from the service-test stage in July 1942 usually carried a flexible MG 15 in the glazed nose. This was mainly because of habit. Not until after the Second World War was it gradually appreciated that helicopters can fly useful offensive missions over a land battle, and fly useful armed missions at sea. In Korea several US Army H-19 (S-55) Chickasaw helicopters carried 14 sets of tandem rocket-launch tubes, and the Army and Marine Corps were also well advanced with fixed and manually aimed machine guns before that war ended in 1953. Even a small OH-13 (Bell 47) blasted off with a Bazooka.

Thereafter progress was slow, as billions of dollars were poured into ballistic missiles and Mach 2 fighters, and it was left to the French to make the running in Indo-China and, especially, Algeria. The prolonged, bitter and cruel war in Algeria was the first in history in which fixed- and rotary-winged aircraft worked together in a concerted way in offensive tactical roles. The chief French helicopters were the S-55 and S-58, Vertol H-21 and Alouette. They carried an assortment of fixed and movable machine guns, 20-mm cannon, SS.10 and SS.11 guided missiles, and several patterns of US and French rocket up to 5-in calibre. The brutal war, partly against the FLN insurgents in the open *Bled* and rugged mountains, and partly against urban guerillas in crowded backstreets, provided a desperate test for

Alouette II of France's ALAT (Aviation Légère de l'Armée de Terre) armed with two SS.11 anti-tank missiles

EC Armées

Helicopter Mission Profile: Guided missile attack against surface target

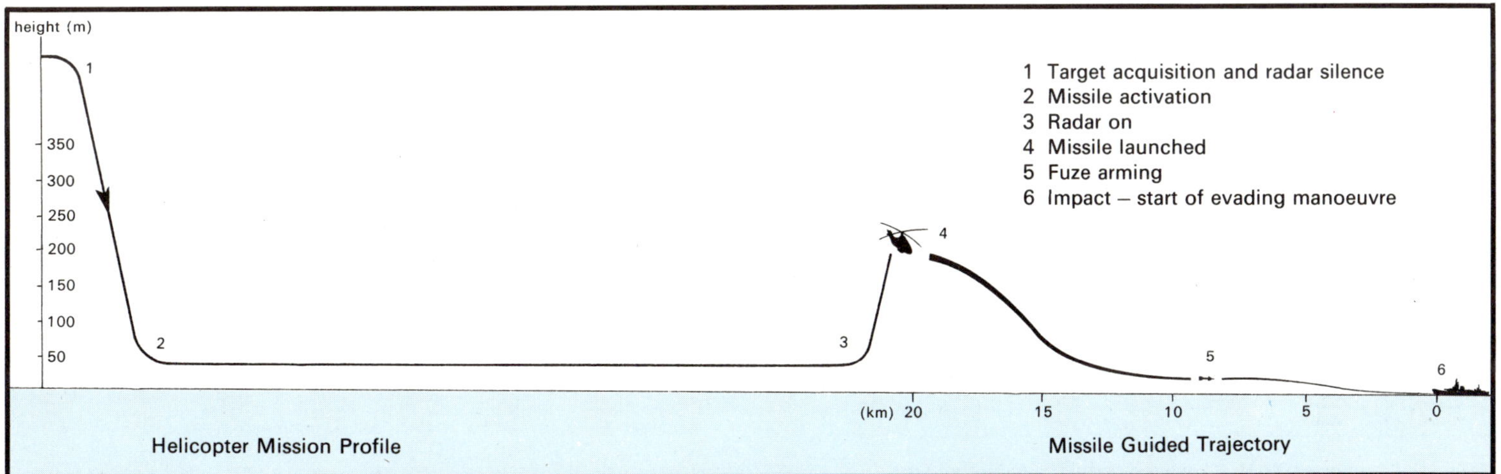

Kaman

Raytheon Sparrow air-to-air missile experimentally installed on a Kaman SH-2F Seasprite

EC Armées

Euromissile HOT wire-guided anti-tank missile launching tubes on a French Army Gazelle. The ALAT plans to operate 110 SA.341 Gazelles armed with four HOTs each by the beginning of 1978

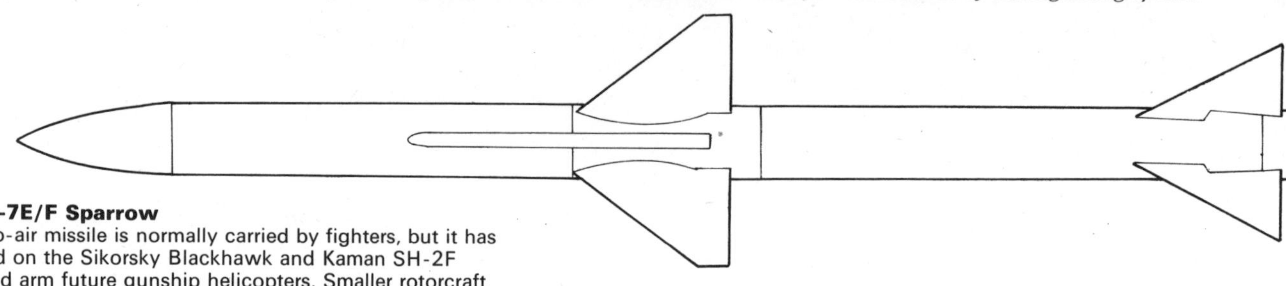

Raytheon AIM-7E/F Sparrow

The Sparrow air-to-air missile is normally carried by fighters, but it has also been mounted on the Sikorsky Blackhawk and Kaman SH-2F Seasprite and could arm future gunship helicopters. Smaller rotorcraft can also be equipped with infra-red homing weapons such as Sidewinder or Magic

Powerplant: Rocketdyne or Hercules solid-propellant rocket *Speed:* Mach 4 *Weight:* 450 lb *Range:* 15 miles *Guidance:* semi-active radar homing *Warhead:* 65 lb high explosive

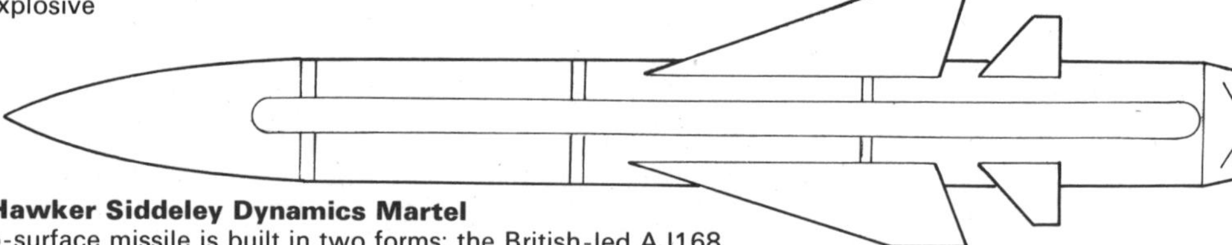

Matra/Hawker Siddeley Dynamics Martel

This air-to-surface missile is built in two forms: the British-led AJ168 television-guided variant and France's AS.37 which homes on to the emissions from enemy radars. The latter version will seek out its target automatically, so long as the radar continues to emit signals but the AJ168 can be steered by an operator on to any target

Powerplant: solid-propellant boost and sustain rocket motors *Speed:* supersonic *Weight:* 1150–1210 lb *Range:* up to 20 miles *Guidance:* television or anti-radiation *Warhead:* 330 lb high explosive

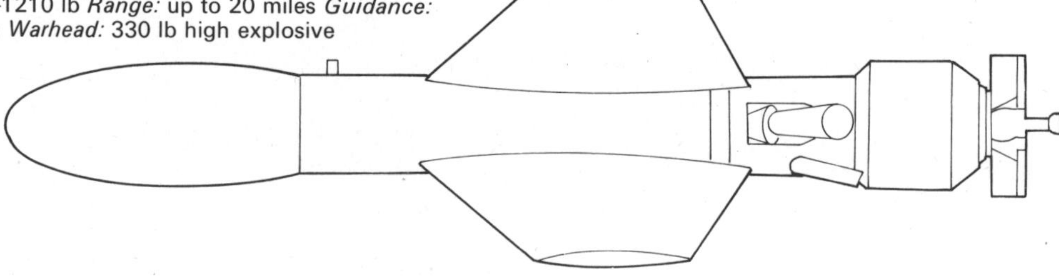

Aérospatiale AS.12

The AS.12 packs as much punch as a 175-mm shell but has no recoil, so it makes a very powerful helicopter weapon. Types equipped include the Alouette III, Wasp and SH-3D Sea King

Powerplant: solid-propellant rocket boost and sustain motors *Speed:* 600 mph *Weight:* 160 lb *Range:* up to 5 miles *Guidance:* wire *Warhead:* 60 lb high explosive

4 TOW		800 — 1200 RDS 30MM		4 TOW
4 TOW	4 TOW	800 — 1200 RDS 30MM	4 TOW	4 TOW
4 TOW	19 2.75" FFAR's	800 — 1200 RDS 30MM	19 2.75" FFAR's	4 TOW
19 2.75" FFAR's	19 2.75" FFAR's	800 — 1200 RDS 30MM	19 2.75" FFAR's	19 2.75" FFAR's
AUX FUEL	AUX FUEL		AUX FUEL	AUX FUEL

Hughes

Ordnance options: YAH-64 Advanced Attack Helicopter

Aérospatiale AM.39 Exocet

Developed from the surface-launched MM.38 variant, AM.39 can confer a long-range anti-ship strike capability on large helicopters such as the Aérospatiale Super Frelon and Westland Sea King. It descends to sea-skimming height following a launch at virtually any altitude

Powerplant: solid-propellant rocket boost and sustain motors *Speed:* Mach 0·95 *Weight:* 1430 lb *Range:* 45 miles *Guidance:* semi-active radar homing *Warhead:* 365 lb high explosive

Major Helicopter Missile Systems

In this table are listed major helicopter missile systems with guided projectiles. Many other missiles have been planned for helicopter use but been abandoned, among them Nord SS.10, Short Hellcat, Aeronutronic Ford Shillelagh and Martin Bullpup.

Aérospatiale AS.11 Wire-guided anti-armour missile *Length:* 47 in *Firing weight:* 66 lb *Cruise speed:* 360 mph *Maximum range:* 9800 ft *Carrier:* S-58, Scout, certain UH-1 built by Agusta, Alouette II, III

Aérospatiale AS.12 Wire-guided missile for use against ships and hard surface targets *Length:* 74 in *Firing weight:* 170 lb *Cruise speed:* 580 mph *Maximum range:* 5 miles *Carrier:* Alouette II, Wasp

Aérospatiale AM.39 Exocet Heavy anti-ship missile with programmed guidance (which is fed before launch with target co-ordinates) plus terminal active homing radar *Length:* 17 ft ¾ in *Firing weight:* 1430 lb *Cruise speed:* Mach 0.93 (sea skimming) *Maximum range from low-flying helicopter:* 32 miles *Carrier:* Super Frelon, Pakistan Sea King

Bofors Bantam Swedish wire-guided anti-armour *Length:* 33.5 in *Firing weight:* 16.5 lb *Cruise speed:* 190 mph *Maximum range:* 6600 ft *Carrier:* Swedish Agusta-Bell 204B

BAC Hawkswing Helicopter version of Swingfire; Lynx planned to carry eight rounds but development unlikely to proceed following choice by British Army of foreign weapon

Rockwell International Hellfire Laser-guided 'fire and forget' missile still under development. Specification not final but launch weight about 50 lb, speed high-subsonic, range several miles *Carrier:* Cobra series, AAH, ASH

Euromissile HOT Franco-German second-generation wire-guided anti-armour missile *Length:* 51.25 in *Firing weight:* 48.5 lb *Cruise speed:* 625 mph *Maximum range:* 13,000 ft *Carrier:* Gazelle, BO105, Alouette III, Lynx

Sistel Marte Italian anti-ship missile with radar altimeter and radio command or radar beam-rider guidance (uses Sea Killer 2 missile) *Length:* 51.25 in *Firing weight:* 660 lb *Maximum speed:* Mach 0.74 *Maximum range:* 15.5+ miles *Carrier:* Agusta-Bell 204AS, Agusta SH-3D, Sea King.

BAC Sea Skua British anti-ship sea skimmer with semi-active radar homing *Length:* 9.2 ft *Firing weight:* 450 lb *Cruise speed:* Mach 0.8 *Maximum range:* 8.7 miles *Carrier:* Lynx (with Seaspray radar)

Raytheon Sparrow US semi-active radar homing air-to-air missile *Length:* 12 ft *Firing weight:* (AIM-7F) 500 lb *Cruise speed:* Mach 3.5 *Maximum range:* 28 miles *Carrier:* Kaman NUH-2C

HSD SRAAM British dogfight missile, planned for possible helicopter use (demonstration only)

AT-2 Swatter Soviet anti-armour missile believed to arm Mi-24, but evidence lacking

Hughes BGM-71A TOW US wire-guided anti-armour *Length:* 46.5 in *Firing weight:* 48 lb *Cruise speed:* Mach 0.9 *Maximum range:* 12,400 ft *Carrier:* AH-1 Cobras, Agusta A109, BO105, Lynx, Gazelle, Alouette

conventional arms. Weapons in plenty were necessary even to rescue a single French soldier among the arid rocks, and by learning the hard way the French forces, especially the ALAT (*Aviation Légère de l'Armée de Terre*), found out a great deal about how to arm helicopters and use them to maximum effect. The work was of a hand-to-mouth nature, research funds being near-zero and most of the many quite sophisticated weapon installations gradually evolving in the field without any approved design or test process.

Radical Idea

With the almost inconceivable (to Frenchmen) withdrawal from Algeria, French morale slumped and the field was left to others. Britain showed a remarkable lack of interest in armed helicopters, except for naval duties, and so did the Soviet Union. It was left to Brig-Gen Carl Hutton of the US Army to push along the concept of a fully-armed helicopter force able to survive over a nuclear battlefield. At his instigation Col Jay D Vanderpool formed the Aerial Combat Reconnaissance Platoon, Provisional (Experimental) in March 1957. The Army clearly did its utmost to suggest that armed helicopters were a radical and almost laughable idea, and Vanderpool had a hard time selling it. In retrospect one wonders why the armed helicopter should have taken so long to mature – many times longer than the armed aeroplane. No formal armed helicopter company was formed as a regular unit of the USAF until July 1962 (at Okinawa). In October that year the pioneer unit was sent to Vietnam, and immediately proved so versatile and useful that its previous critics suddenly changed their tune. The USA's Tactical Mobility Requirements Board, under the man who can be described as the 'father of modern battle aviation', Lt-Gen Hamilton Howze, led to the concept of a complete helicopter assault division. Gradually this threw up the need for helicopters whose sole purpose was to carry armament, as related in the next chapter.

It is one of the puzzles of military aviation that it was well into the 1960s before any attempt was made to build what today is called a gunship. The helicopter designed solely for fighting, rather than the transport of troops and weapons, was being discussed as early as 1942 in Germany and the United States, but nothing was done until Bell Helicopter, on its own initiative, flew the Model 207 Sioux Scout in 1963. This was a streamlined, winged development of the familiar Bell 47, which as the OH-13 Sioux

French Army Alouette III at treetop height armed with AS.11 anti-tank missiles provides a flying ambush for enemy armour

Bell

Forerunner of the HueyCobra, the tandem-seat Bell 207 Sioux Scout made its first flight in 1963 armed with twin ·30 machine-guns in TAT-101 turret

US Army

Loading 20-mm cannon ammunition on UH-1B based at Bien Hoa, Vietnam armed with two XM31 cannon pods

Westland

Door 7·62-mm Minigun on Westland Lynx for the British Army

M21 Helicopter Armament System
2×7·62-mm M134 Miniguns and 2×M158 pods with 7×2·75-in FFAR rockets
The system fires 6 pairs of rockets in 1 second or 4800 rpm Minigun rounds. The minigun has 12° inboard to 70° outboard traverse and +10° to −85° elevation. The system currently equips US and Italian combat helicopters

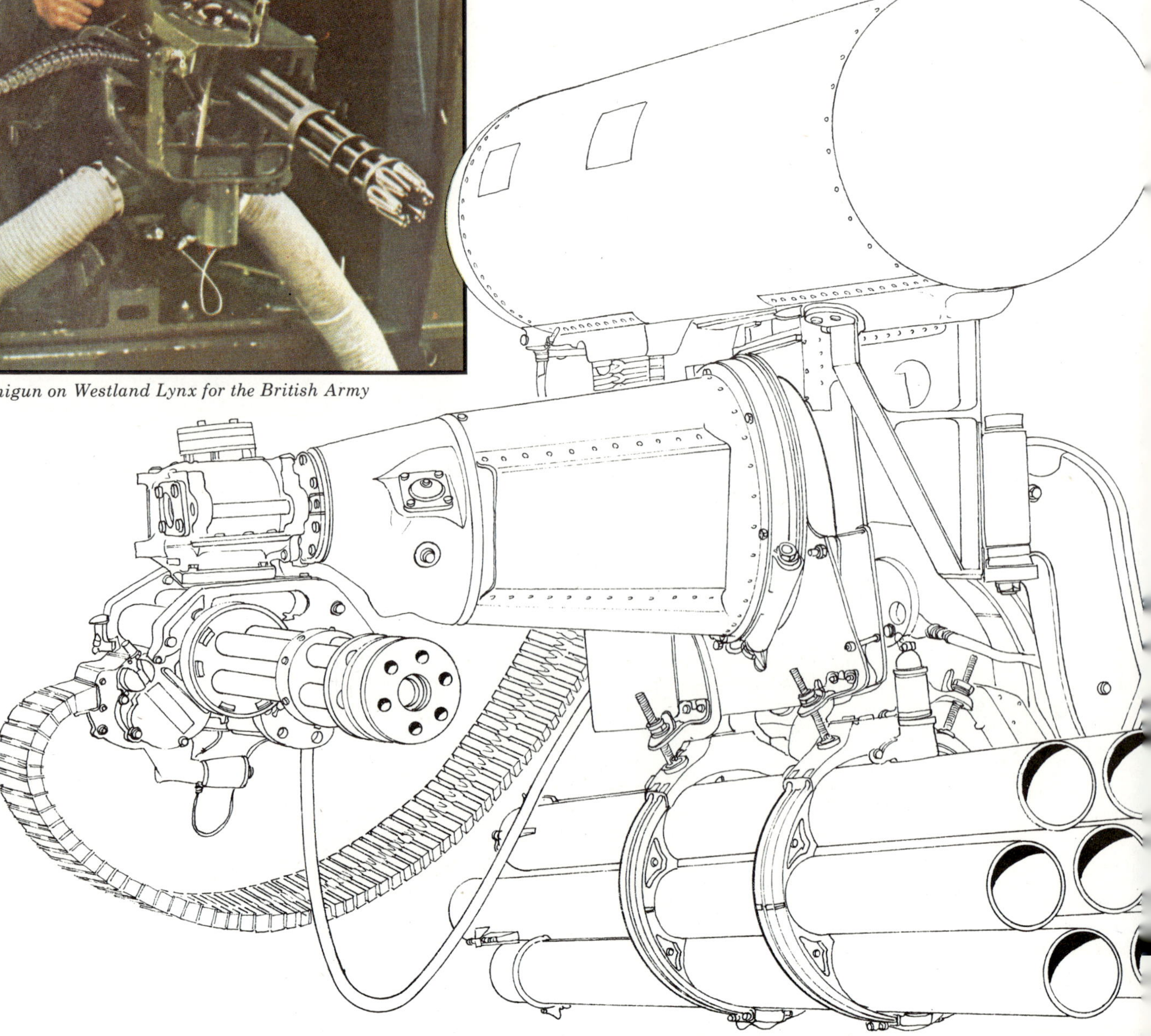

Representative US Helicopter Armament Systems

M5 Ball turret for Bell UH-1B, -1C mounting M75 grenade launcher; system accommodates 150 or 315 grenades, azimuth ±60°, elevation +15° to −60°

XM8 Installation in Hughes OH-6A of XM129 grenade launcher, on left behind pilot; usual capacity 156 grenades, azimuth zero (aim with helicopter rudder pedals), elevation +10° to −24°

M16 Original armament subsystem for UH-1B, -C, comprising two M60C 7·62 mm machine guns and two fixed M158 rocket pods. The guns each have a 3000-round belt fed to the left side, and are remotely trainable from 11° inboard (cutting out the firing circuit if trained further in) to 70° outboard, with elevation limits of +11° to −63°. The rocket pods are fixed to fire dead ahead and are aimed by the pilot manual reflex sight. Activation of the rocket circuits cuts out the guns

XM18 Fixed gun pod for Bell AH-1G HueyCobra, carried as store on weapon sponson; contains M134 gun, with electric drive from pod battery or helicopter AC/DC power, and 1500 rounds linkless feed

M21 Successor to M16 with two M134 7·62 mm Miniguns and two M158 rocket pods. Can fire six pairs of rockets in one second in quick-sequence ripple, or 4800 rounds of 7·62 mm in one minute. Guns remotely aimed over azimuth angle of 82° (12° inboard to 70° out) and elevation limits of +10 to −85°. When either gun reaches 12° inboard traverse it is switched out of circuit and rate of fire of the other is automatically increased to the maximum (4000 rds/min)

M23 Manually aimed gun system for use on both cargo doors of UH-1D. Each door carries one 7·62 mm M60D with 600-round belt, cyclic rate fixed at the lowest (550-600 rds/min). Total weight on each door 209 lb. Aimed with ring sight over 130° azimuth and with elevation limits of +3·5° to −82°

M24 Similar to M23 but incorporates 200-round belt box. Fitted to CH-47 Chinook, one on left forward escape hatch, the other on right forward door

M27 Hughes installation of M134 7·62 mm Minigun on LOH, on left side of forward fuselage. Fired by pilot with cyclic-stick trigger incorporating switch selector for firing rate. Single ammunition container holds 2000 rounds. In OH-6A azimuth 0° (aim with rudder pedals), elevation limits +10° to −24°; in OH-58A azimuth 0°, elevation limits +5½° to −20°

XM28 Standard Cobra chin turret, replaced TAT-102 by same supplier (Emerson). Can be equipped with two M134 7·62 mm Miniguns, each with 4000 rounds, or two XM129 grenade launchers, each with 300 grenades, or one of each with same ammunition capacity. Azimuth limits ±110°; elevation limits +20° to −50°

XM35 Fixed 20 mm multi-barrel cannon installation for AH-1G Cobra. Single XM195 gun attached under left sponson and supplied with approximately 950 rounds link-fed from external tanks on both sides of the fuselage. Total weight with ammunition 1169 lb

M60 Family of 7·62 mm machine guns fed by link belt; rate of fire variable according to model and control setting, within limits of 550 to 2600 rds/min; effective range 3300 ft

M75 Rapid-fire launcher for 40 mm grenades supplied through flexible guide chute. Normal (maximum) rate of fire, 230 rds/min; effective range 5000 ft

M79 Grenade launcher basically to M75 but configured for different installations

XM93 Standardized pintle-mounted gun subsystem for helicopter cargo door (UH-1N and probably UTTAS). Single 7·62 mm GAU-2B/A (Minigun similar to M134) with large ammunition box, feed assemblies and control box weighing in all 1180 lb. Gun can fire with helicopter engine stopped, and can be latched inboard, swung out and fixed to fire ahead under pilot control, or aimed over arc 90° forward to 70° aft, with elevation limits of +5½° to −70°

XM94 Standardized pintle-mounted grenade-launcher subsystem for helicopter cargo door (UH-1N and probably UTTAS). Single XM129 launcher. Interchangeable with XM93 in either left or right door, with same aiming limits

TAT 101 First of Emerson Electric's Tactical Armament Turret (TAT) systems, each normally incorporating one or more guns, ammunition supply, hydraulic gun-charging, gun drive and turret aiming power system, gunner's sight station and system, and circuit and control panels. TAT 101 has two 7·62 mm M60C each firing 600 rds/min from link belt within turret. Azimuth ±115° (with modification ±180°); elevation +15° to −45°

TAT 102 Similar to TAT 101 but equipped with M134 gun. Supplied in several versions, the largest for AH-1G weighing 254 lb without ammunition, with same elevation limits as TAT 101 but slewing faster (80°/sec instead of 45°); elevation limits +25° to −50° (modified, −90°). Maximum ammunition capacity 8000 rounds

XM129 Aeronutronic Ford 40 mm grenade launcher; normal (maximum) rate of fire 400 rds/min

M134 General Electric 7·62 mm six-barrel Minigun. Versatile gun incorporated in many armament systems. Electric drive at speeds of 1600, 2000, 2400 or 4000 rds/min, with linkless feed of NATO 7·62 mm ammunition types M59, M60 or M80

XM140 Aeronutronic Ford lightweight 30 mm gun designed for gunship helicopters, with minimal recoil and directionally controlled blast. Suitable for turret or sponson mounting. Fires up to 3000 rds/min of dual-purpose shaped-charge ammunition

TAT 140 Emerson turret mounting XM140 gun. Overall weight without ammunition 419 lb. Azimuth/elevation limits similar to TAT 102

TAT 141 Emerson turret mounting one M134 gun and one XM129 grenade launcher

XM156 Multipurpose armament mount on UH-1B, -C for XM159C and most other stores up to 540 lb; compatible with M5 subsystem

XM157 XM158 Rocket pod launcher for seven 2·75 in rockets. Rockets have folding fins and either 10 lb or 17 lb heads of HE or HEAT type, effective to 10,000 ft slant range (but poor accuracy)

XM159C Rocket pod launcher for 19 of the same 2·75 in rockets

TAT 161 Emerson turret for GE Vulcan-type cannon, including M61A1, XM188 and XM197. Characteristics basically similar to TAT 101

XM188 General Electric three-barrel lightweight Vulcan-type 20 mm gun firing standard ammunition of M50 series. Rate of fire variable from 30 mm gun firing the XM552 HEDP 30 mm round. Available with hydraulic or electric drive or self-powered, and with link belt or linkless feed. Rate of fire controlled at 500 or 2000 rds/min. Weight 150 lb

XM195 General Electric six-barrel Vulcan-type 20 mm gun, based on M61 but with short 1026 mm length barrels with blast deflectors. Slow rate of fire of 750 rds/min; ammunition link-fed to right side.

XM197 General Electric three-barrel lightweight 20 mm gun using many parts of M61. Rate of fire controllable from 400 to 1500 rds/min of standard M50-type ammunition fed by link or belt or linkless feed. Fitted to AH-1J SeaCobra, with 15-round burst-limiting timer.

XM230 Hughes Helicopters and Ordnance Systems 'Chain Gun', a very simple (fewer than 145 parts) 30 mm single-barrel cannon firing XM552 HEDP ammunition but compatible with aluminium-cased Wecom 30. Externally powered by electric motor adjustable to any speed up to 1000 rds/min but normally 500 or 750. Breech closed by chain-driven rotary bolt allowing simple open-bolt cycle with no chargers, declutching feeders or other devices. Weight 98 lb

Flexible Weapon System General Electric AH-1J SeaCobra turret, interchangeable with XM28, equipped with either XM197 with 750 rounds or XM188 with 500 rounds. Incorporates electrically powered belt booster

5·56 Minigun General Electric multi-barrel self-powered electric or hydraulically powered gun firing 5·56 mm M193 (or M196 tracer) ammunition, the same as the M16 rifle. Each round weighs about half as much as standard 7·62 mm, and rate of fire can be governed from 400 to 10000 rds/min

MiniTAT Emerson turret for 5·56 mm or 7·62 mm Minigun for installation on LOH and other small helicopters. Azimuth ±180°, elevation +10° to −70°

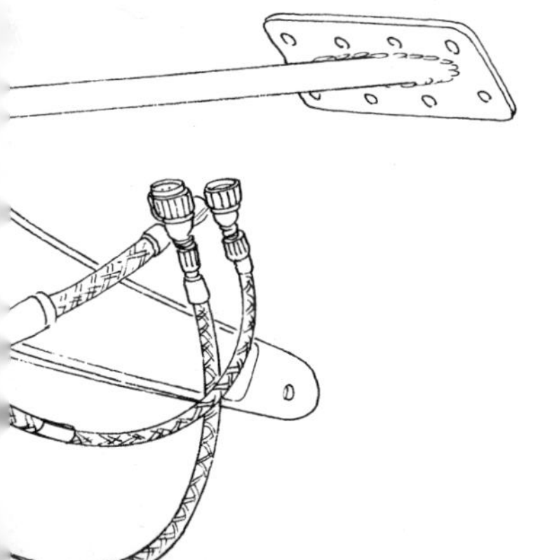

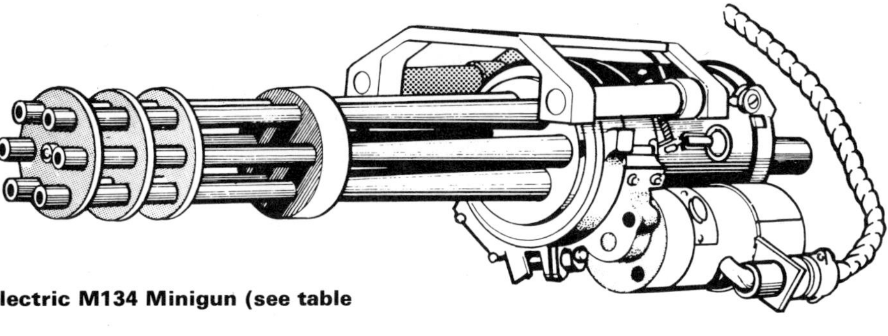

General Electric M134 Minigun (see table above)

had carried fixed machine guns during the Korean war. The Sioux Scout had three seats in an enclosed cabin, weapon racks under its wings and an Emerson TAT-101, the first Tactical Armament Turret, under the nose. It was exciting, but its ancestry imposed crippling limitations on its capability. During 1964 the penny finally dropped: what was needed was a purpose-designed gunship with the engine and dynamic parts of an existing helicopter. The obvious choice for the US Army was the H-1, in UH-1C form with the wide-chord Model 540 rotor to allow violent manoeuvres and higher flight speeds. The result was the Bell 209 HueyCobra, flown on 7 September 1965.

High Rate of Fire

Its original chin turret was the TAT-102A (see table), but this was superseded by the XM28. Both mount a six-barrel Minigun, one of the family of guns developed by GE's Armament Department at Burlington from the original Project Vulcan 20-mm aircraft gun of 1953. Today several of these guns are used in helicopters, among them the M134 or GAU-2B/A, M61A1, XM188, XM195 and XM197. A characteristic of these guns is high rate of fire, which to some degree varies with the number of barrels. Most can be switched by the helicopter pilot or gunner to a low rate of fire, around 1600 rds/min, for searching or registry fire, and to the maximum (4000 to 6000 rds/min for 7·62 and 20 mm, and 10,000 rds/min for 5·56 mm) for attack. These immense firing rates consume vast quantities of ammunition. Great efforts are being made to minimize ammunition weight, both to allow the helicopter to carry more and to ease the inertia problems in the long linked or linkless feed systems when firing starts or stops. Some idea of these problems can be gauged by the fact that full firing rate is attained in 0·1–0·15 sec from rest. These 'Gatling' guns are driven either by an electric or hydraulic motor, or, in some newer models, are self-powered by the propellant gas pressure.

Little need be said of other helicopter guns, though the XM230 Chain Gun offers promise of simpler and cheaper weapons. Virtually nothing appears to have been developed outside the United States in helicopter guns, or in the growing field of rapid-fire launchers for grenades, large-calibre bomblets and other weapons for low-velocity delivery of explosive devices with small installed weapon bulk and minimal recoil. For several reasons the helicopter is an attractive carrier of small rockets and missiles, which have near-zero recoil forces on the helicopter. Following early experiments by the US Army and Marine Corps around 1950, various unguided spin-stabilized rockets became standard on American helicopters, the emphasis gradually swinging in favour of the 2·75-in FFAR (Folding-Fin Aircraft Rocket) originally designed for all-weather jet interceptors. These are 'rippled' against surface targets from cylindrical dispensers, the most common being the XM157 and 159.

France pioneered the use of wire-guided missiles against armour, and though the original production weapon (Nord 5210, SS.10) was tested from fixed-wing aircraft and helicopters it did not see wide use. The major first-generation weapon was the AS. 11, still deployed aboard many Western helicopters despite obsolescence. Likewise the larger AS.12 is still in use, pending availability of faster missiles without wire guidance. Larger helicopters equipped with radar can fly major anti-ship missions using such missiles as the big AM.39 Exocet and purpose-designed Sea Skua. Extensive trials have also confirmed the validity of the helicopter as a platform for anti-aircraft and anti-missile missiles, but no such system has yet gone into service. Methods of use of helicopter armament are discussed in the next two chapters.

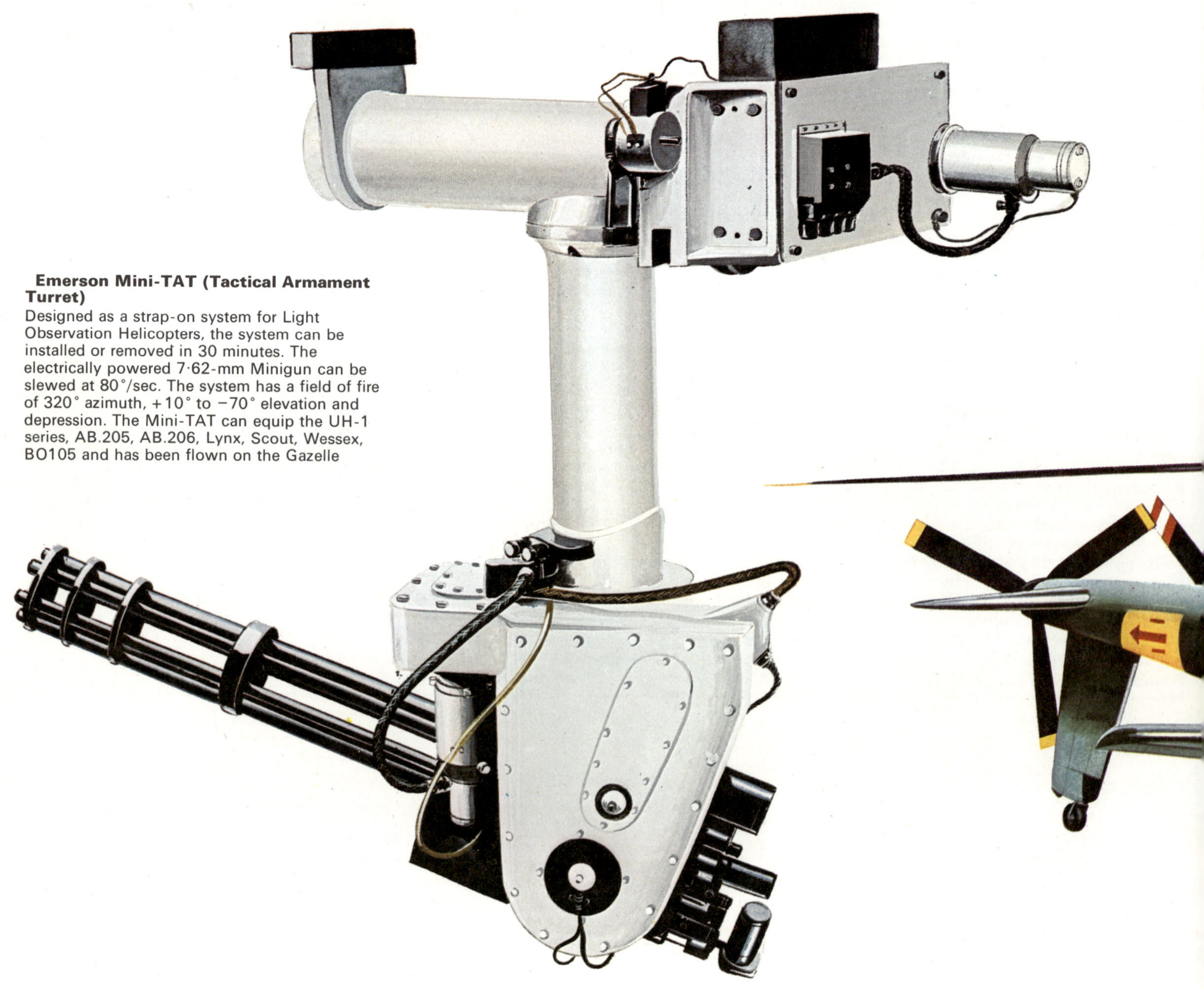

Emerson Mini-TAT (Tactical Armament Turret)
Designed as a strap-on system for Light Observation Helicopters, the system can be installed or removed in 30 minutes. The electrically powered 7·62-mm Minigun can be slewed at 80°/sec. The system has a field of fire of 320° azimuth, +10° to −70° elevation and depression. The Mini-TAT can equip the UH-1 series, AB.205, AB.206, Lynx, Scout, Wessex, BO105 and has been flown on the Gazelle

Helicopters in Land Warfare

THE AERIAL BATTLEFIELD

It is truly remarkable that, while helicopters were quite rapidly developed to carry loads exceeding a ton and were used in large numbers as utility transports in support of land battles, hardly any attempt was made to arm them and use them as combat machines. The many armed helicopters that were flown during the Second World War, Korea (1950–53), the French campaigns in Indo-China (1947–54) and Algeria (1956–62), and Suez (1956) were merely the one-off experiments that proved the rule that nobody knew how to use helicopters as combat weapon platforms. It was not until the early 1960s that the US Army slowly recognized that an armed 'gunship' helicopter might be useful. It could escort troop-carrying and cas-evac helicopters through hostile airspace and reduce their vulnerability to ground fire. It could cut down troop casualties by making the enemy keep their heads down as heli-borne forces were flown in and disembarked. Not least, it could serve as a battlefield weapon platform in its own right, conducting scouting and armed reconnaissance and having the ability to harass or destroy all kinds of enemy land forces.

Performance Like a Fighter

Having nothing else, the US Army began in 1960–61 with simple conversions of the UH-1B and UH-1C with machine guns and, later, with grenade projectors and other weapons. Experience in Vietnam soon showed that even these aircraft were extremely valuable in escorting otherwise almost defenceless H-21 Shawnee and CH-34 Choctaw troop carriers, as well as unarmed Hueys. It became standard practice for each section of three troop helicopters to be accompanied by an armed Huey, which with 7·62-mm machine guns, spin-stabilized rockets and, sometimes, 40-mm grenade launchers, could put down protective fire around the LZ (landing zone).

Front-line troops had to work out 'the hard way' how helicopters should best be used in the presence of known or suspected hostile forces. At all times the problems remained that, compared with most army equipment, helicopters are large, fragile and exceedingly expensive. They are simple to see and impossible to hide when in the air, vulnerable to even rifle-calibre strikes (which might cause no trouble to fixed-wing machines except by sheer bad luck) and lacking the speed and agility that would make them hard to hit.

Bell's research with the rigid-hub rotor and with the broad door-hinge rotor of the UH-1C showed that helicopters could go faster and be more manoeuvrable. Lockheed-California went even further with nimble rigid-rotor machines which were looped and rolled, and then made high-speed tests which reached a world record speed of nearly 303 mph (this was before a Huey reached 316 mph). By 1954 the US Army, the leader with armed helicopters, had decided to fund a full-scale competition for a purpose-designed AAFSS, Advanced Aerial Fire-Support System, to replace the lash-up armed Hueys in Vietnam. After a hotly contested fight the contract went to Lockheed in March 1966. The Army prepared to buy the AH-56A Cheyenne.

This was a staggering leap, from a Huey with a strapped-on machine gun to a helicopter which had performance like a fighter and electronic systems said to be 'more complex than those of a B-52'. The Cheyenne was intended not only for troop escort and protective fire but also armed multi-sensor reconnaissance by day and night and anti-tank missions (by day and, possibly, by night). A big machine, with a 60-ft fuselage and stubby wing housing systems for various kinds of armament, the Cheyenne was powered by a 3925-hp GE T64 driving a rigid rotor specially designed to stand up to hostile fire, with a forged titanium hub and all-metal honeycomb-filled blades joined by 39,000 strands of high-tensile steel. At the back the curious upside-down tail had an anti-torque rotor and also a pusher Hamilton Standard propeller to increase flight speed. The large cockpit seated the pilot above and behind a gunner in a unique stabilized seat that gave him a smooth 'upright' ride during even vicious flight manoeuvres. The whole machine bristled with special devices, including Norden terrain-following radar, Doppler radar and inertial navigation systems, all-weather autopilot, and day/night sensors and weapons including the new XM129 and XM140. Under the wings were to be hung Hughes TOW anti-tank missiles.

Enter the Cobra

In January 1968 the US Army signed for 375 production Cheyennes, but despite impressive test flying the sheer magnitude of the costs and technical problems caused the whole project to be abandoned in 1969. In its place had come already the smaller and cheaper HueyCobra, which had reached SE Asia in late 1967 and had been immediately engaged in escort and offensive roles. It was obvious that the Cobra was far superior to the UH-1 armed conversions, with almost twice the speed, much greater manoeuvrability, much smaller size seen head-on, and completely different armour and armament. By the end of 1968 the US Army helicopter forces in SE Asia had settled down to using

Lockheed AH-56A Cheyenne
Fast and potent attack helicopter, but too complex and expensive even for the US Army
Engine: 3925 shp General Electric T64-GE-16 turboshaft *Max speed:* 244 mph *Weight fully loaded:* 18,300 lb *Armament:* 7·62-mm Minigun/40-mm grenade-launcher, 30-mm barbette-mounted cannon, TOW missiles/70-mm rockets

Bell

Bell's entry in the US Army's Advanced Attack Helicopter competition, the YAH-63, based on their years of experience with the HueyCobra

transport helicopters (often Hueys), armed Hueys, Cobras (called 'Snakes') and Hughes or Bell OH light observation helicopters (called 'Loaches' from LOH). Within the basic Army division there would be formed an Air Cavalry troop, usually with all these types. In general the 1st Platoon of the troop would be the Aero Scouts, the 2nd Platoon the lift (transport), the 3rd the Weapons (Cobra) and the 4th the Aero Rifle (ARP). Aero Scouts, a Cobra or Loach, would investigate the area of a hostile ground force, choose an LZ and mark it, and prepare for the infantry (ARP) coming by Huey. Cobras and Loaches would operate as a hunter/killer team, and over the months and years the business of operating combat helicopters – which was almost unknown in 1967 – grew to a fantastic pitch of professional complexity, refinement and precision. It involved a large number of communications frequencies on UHF, VHF and FM radios, instant marking by coloured smokes, beacons, laser designator and other methods, perfect command of a very wide spectrum of weapons, absolute control of helicopters in what a few months before would have been considered unnatural or dangerous attitudes, and a constant appreciation of position in three dimensions usually close to other helicopters and to the ground. The battle helicopter's role became probably the most full-time job in land warfare.

Snakes and Loaches

Many were surprised that the helicopter could survive at all. In Vietnam more than 600,000 hours were flown by combat Loaches, Cobras and armed Hueys in the face of the enemy, and though casualties were heavy, crews were invariably recovered and on about 60% of occasions so were downed aircraft. Many Loach or Cobra pilots were shot down six times, and Capt Hugh Mills, who flew 3300 hr in 1019 combat missions, was shot down 16 times – almost certainly a record in the history of air warfare.

It was at all times a tough job, in which 'altitude' meant 1500 ft, and most of the actual combat took place well down below the tops of the trees. Navigation was usually the job of one or more front-seat Cobra pilots (who in action became the gunners). Transit to and from action generally took place at 1500 ft, and the let-down to ground level was the most vulnerable period of all, when the helicopters were visible and easy to hit.

The YAH-63 reverses the HueyCobra seating layout. The pilot has the front cockpit for optimum vision in 'nap-of-the-earth' terrain-following flight

Bell

Bell YAH-63
Plan, side and front view

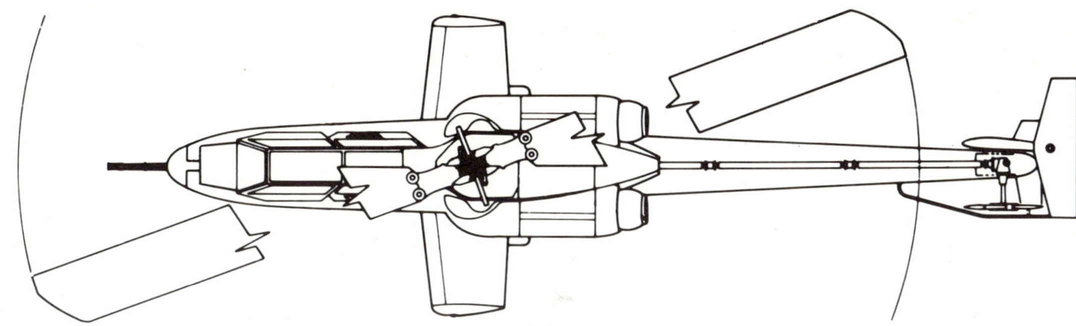

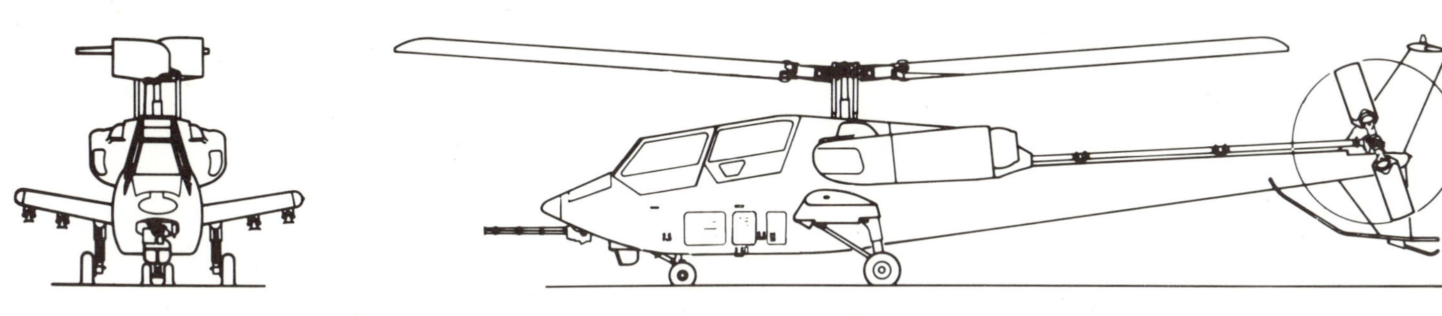

Bell

The YAH-63 is a completely new machine designed for tank-killing on the conventional battlefield, and incorporating a great deal of new technology to survive ground fire and eliminate maintenance

Bell

Loach pilots worked out procedures for minimizing this vulnerability, for example by rolling on their back and pulling through in a half loop, or sliding down in a vicious sideslip (full rudder and opposite cyclic) or a spiral (rudder and cyclic hard over in the same direction) to lose height fast and present a tricky target. It needed great skill to do this, with a hail of hostile fire going past, and recover to hover or level forwards flight at about ten feet altitude. It was usually done over a clear open space, but sometimes into a restricted forest clearing.

Only when hostile strength made it essential would Air Cavalry call in fixed-wing support (A-1 'Sandies', C-130 'King' controllers, and sometimes Air Force jets). An essential support role was flown by Sikorsky HH-3E 'Jolly Green Giant' rescue helicopters of the US Air Force, equipped with retractable FR (Flight Refuelling) probe, heavy armour, self-sealing tanks, Minigun turrets, and 250-ft hoists with Jungle Penetrators for recovering downed aircrew. Recovery of downed aircraft was the job of the CH-54 or 'Pipesmoke' CH-47 force.

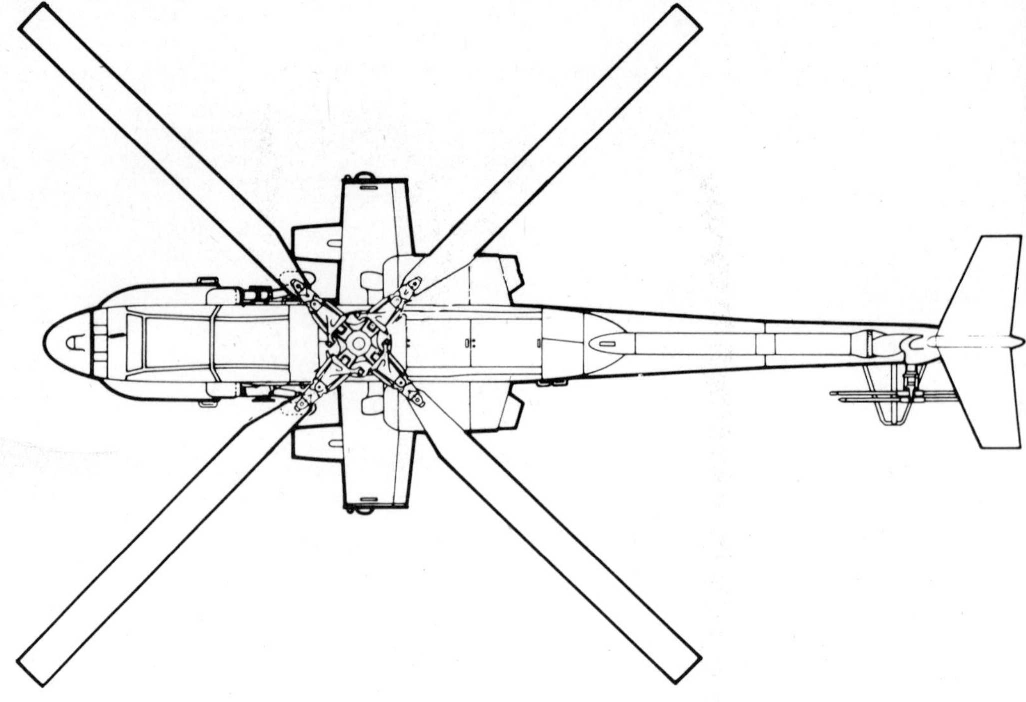

Hughes YAH-64
Plan, side and front view

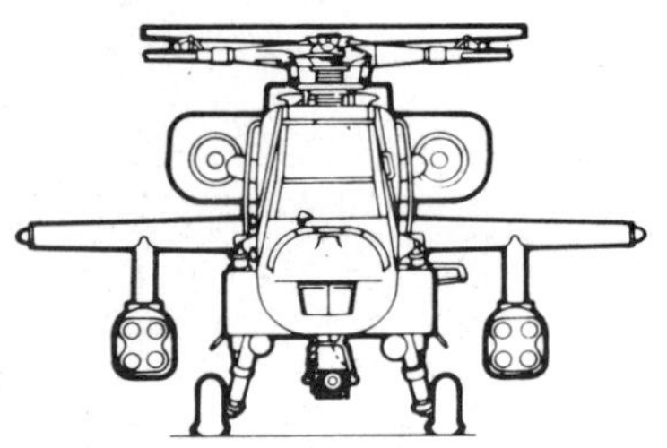

By 1970 the 'Snakes' were in action testing prototype installations of SMASH (SE Asia Multi-sensor Armament System for HueyCobra), comprising nose-mounted passive infra-red sighting system, Emerson APQ-137B radar with high resolution and MTI (Moving-Target Indication, to make even infantry stand out from a clutter of moving grass and leaves) in a pod on the right wing, and interfacing units and displays. This major addition cut into weapon payload but proved extremely valuable, especially when one SMASH Cobra was used with others as a night fire director. Other Snakes continued using Starlight Scopes (image intensifiers), high-intensity Xenon searchlights and batteries of C-130 landing lamps for night operations. The last major addition during the SE Asia fighting was the TOW missile (listed in the weapon table), evaluated in that theatre in the first AH-1Q TOWCobras in June 1972. Vietnam was not primarily a war involving hard-skinned armour, but the report on the early TOW missions claims 39 such hard-skinned point targets knocked out by 62 hits in 77 shots. As a result virtually all the remaining Cobras are being rebuilt as TOW carriers, with designation AH-1Q or AH-1S.

When the Lockheed AAFSS was cancelled in 1969 Sikorsky quickly built an excellent company-financed attack helicopter, the S-67 Blackhawk using dynamic parts of the S-61. The US Army, however, decided the AAH (Advanced Attack Helicopter) was important enough to justify a specially designed machine, and in November 1972 it launched a competition which,

Above: *YAH-64 fires 2·75-in rocket ripple* Below: *YAH-64 with TOW batteries on stub wings. The Hughes Chain Gun and the Hellfire laser-guided missile will make it a potent tank-killer*

Hughes

Hughes YAH-64
Hughes' AAH competitor, the YAH-64, retains the proven gunship seating arrangement of pilot in the rear, and co-pilot/gunner in the front cockpit. The Hughes Chain Gun, a three-barrelled 30-mm weapon designed specifically for the AAH and able to fire at any rate from single shots to 700 rds/min, is turret-mounted under the front fuselage

after elimination of three candidates, resulted in intensive fly-off trials between the Bell YAH-63A and Hughes YAH-64A. Though both carry powerful 30-mm guns for suppression of ground fire, the main role of the AAH will be to stand off (if possible unseen by the enemy) and kill tanks from a distance. For this purpose the expected battery of TOW missiles has been replaced by the deadly Hellfire, which homes on to laser light reflected or diffused from the target. A probable load will be eight Hellfires, with 500 to 800 rounds of 30-mm ammunition. Of course, large loads of other weapons could be substituted.

Both AAH contenders are powered by two of the new 1536-hp GE T700 engines, which are advanced and robust units planned specifically for battlefield helicopters and installed with inlet filters and particle-separators and with cool-air fans discharging into the infra-red screened exhaust plume to minimize vulnerability to heat-seeking missiles. Surface-to-air missiles pose the greatest threat to the battlefield helicopter, because it is not economically practical to protect the helicopter against such devastating warheads. Small-calibre gunfire is less of a threat. The AAH specification called for immunity to rifle-calibre projectiles, immunity to occasional hits up to 12·7-mm calibre, and the ability to fly for 30 minutes after 'hits in critical regions' with 23-mm high-explosive/incendiary shells. The engines are protected and the shafts, bearings and rotors are designed to continue safe operation after severe damage from 23-mm fire. Despite this, everything possible must be done to hide from the enemy, and effective operations at grass-blade height demand perfect pilot view. In contrast the new sensors and Hellfire allow the gunner to work with head-down displays inside the cockpit. Accordingly Bell put the pilot in the front and gunner in the back,

Mil Mi-24 (NATO = Hind)
Soviet Armed Forces combined gunship and assault transport in two versions which differ in the type of auxiliary wing fitted
Engines: 2×1500 shp Isotov TV-2-117A turboshafts *Max speed:* 160 mph *Weight fully loaded:* 25,000 lb *Armament:* 4×55-mm rocket pods, 4×Swatter anti-tank missiles

Westland Commando
Developed from the Sea King anti-submarine and search-and-rescue helicopter, the Commando is designed for troop transport and logistic support. A fixed landing gear replaces the Sea King's units which retract into sponsons. A Mk 2 version is available, with the Rolls-Royce H.1400-1 engine and a six-bladed main rotor
Engines: 2×1500 shp Rolls-Royce Gnome H.1400 turboshafts *Max speed:* 131 mph *Weight fully loaded:* 20,500 lb *Range:* 600 miles *Number of seats:* 30

RAF Westland Wessex HU Mk 5 assault transport, powered by a Rolls-Royce Coupled Gnome with two 1350 shp power sections, delivers equipment during a NATO exercise in Northern Norway

MOD

Aérospatiale SA.321 Super Frelon
SA.321H transport version of France's largest production helicopter for the French Army
Engines: 3×1630 shp Turboméca Turmo IIIC6-70 turboshafts *Max speed:* 149 mph *Weight fully loaded:* 28,660 lb *Range:* 450 miles

Messerschmitt-Bölkow-Blohm BO105
The MBB BO105 has an advanced hingeless rotor which allows it to be looped, rolled and manoeuvred rapidly. This is particularly useful for a military helicopter, and a version armed with Euromissile HOT anti-tank missiles has been ordered for the German *Heeresflieger*
Engines: 2×400 shp Allison 250-C20 turboshafts *Max speed:* 167 mph *Weight fully loaded:* 5000 lb *Range:* 720 miles *Number of seats:* 5

Westland Scout
The Scout is used for spotting and attack by the British Army. It can be armed with Aérospatiale SS.11 anti-tank missiles and is, unlike the naval Wasp, fitted with fixed landing skids
Engine: 685 shp Rolls-Royce Nimbus 101 or 102 turboshaft *Max speed:* 120 mph *Weight fully loaded:* 5500 lb *Range:* 300 miles *Number of seats:* 5/6

while Hughes stuck to Cobra tradition with the gunner in front. Hughes developed a novel and simple gun (XM230, see table p. 29) and their weapon/sensor installation differs markedly from that of Bell. So do their main rotors and landing gears, but both helicopters have tailplanes above and below the high-thrust tail rotors. In both helicopters the weapon wings also carry a significant part of the weight at high forward speeds and assist manoeuvrability (further augmented in the Hughes by camber-changing flaps).

There is no doubt that rival attack helicopters are being urgently planned in the Soviet Union, because the Soviets have never let the West make any advance unchallenged. So far the only battle helicopter in the Warsaw Pact forces is the Mi-24 assault machine, called Hind by NATO, which has a large fuselage able to carry at least eight troops (the Mi-24 is larger than the latest Hueys, which seat 16). The Mi-24 appears to be a mixture between anti-tank and gunship weapon carrier and transporter of assault infantry; all examples so far seen have large wings with multiple weapon stations, but this helicopter is certainly much less survivable – much easier to detect, and easier to destroy – than an AAH.

Though the US Army has by far the most all-round experience of actual helicopter battles in the face of the enemy, it is believed that little of this experience is relevant to a war in Europe or other theatres between forces equipped with modern weapons. The Europeans, led by France and Britain, pioneered the use of wire-guided missiles fired by helicopters against tanks. Today the Gazelle or BO 105, each armed with four or six HOT missiles, and the agile Lynx armed at first with the obsolescent SS.11 and later with a modern weapon such as Hellfire, are regarded as vital weapon platforms in the defence of Western Europe against the threat of the 49,000 tanks of the Soviet Union and its satellites.

In Europe it is essential to keep near the ground, behind cover, avoid exposing the rotor to enemy Doppler radars (which could at once detect the moving blades) and avoid hovering over dusty places. Modern anti-tank missiles have ranges up to five miles, and the ability to see the target at two miles is essential; this calls for all-weather electro-optical systems which give a sharp magnified image by day or night. Yet magnification accentuates the difficulty of holding the sight on-target during wild manoeuvres in a light vibrating helicopter, and so costly stabilized sights are needed which give the missile operator a steady picture no matter which way the helicopter faces or how it vibrates. Ideally tomorrow's anti-tank helicopter needs at least 20 missiles inside it, fed automatically to a quick-fire launcher, a rotor mounted underneath to avoid being seen by hostile radar, and a stabilized sight mounted high on top to see the enemy!

Westland Wisp
Remotely piloted helicopter powered by two small US piston engines and able to carry television cameras or electronic surveillance systems, the Wisp has torque-compensating counter-rotating rotors mounted on an egg-shaped body only 24 inches in diameter. Directional control is achieved by differentially changing the pitch of the Wisp's 5-ft diameter coaxial rotors. Surveillance drones with their low radar, noise and infra-red signatures promise a new dimension in counter-insurgency surveillance and reconnaissance on the conventional battlefield

Helicopters in Sea Warfare

SUBMARINE HUNTERS

MOD

Landing Signals Officer guides the pilot of a Westland Wasp ASW helicopter onto the stern landing platform of the Royal Navy frigate HMS Ashanti

The first true helicopters ever put into operational service were naval. They were the Flettner Fl 282 *Kolibries* of the *Kriegsmarine* (German Navy), boldly flown from small fantail platforms on surface ships in over-the-horizon observation (and sometimes liaison) duties. The Focke-Achgelis Fa 330 rotor-kite (autogyro) fulfilled a similar observation mission for U-Boats. In late 1944 and 1945 Sikorsky R-4 Hoverflies were flown experimentally from US escort carriers. And that is about as far as the victorious Allies got with naval helicopters for the next ten years.

A most unusual, yet successful, helicopter developed solely for the shipboard ASW (Anti-Submarine Warfare) role was the Bell HSL-1. This was the first recognition of the fact that the helicopter combines several qualities that make it eminently suitable for the ASW mission. The importance of ASW had been driven home in both World Wars, and the difficulties were multiplied by the development of the nuclear submarine with its ability to travel at great speed underwater without any restriction on range. By the 1950s the nuclear submarine appeared to pose a completely new and momentous threat, which was then multiplied yet again when such vessels began to be armed with strategic winged or ballistic missiles. This put great urgency into the development of ASW aircraft of all kinds, including helicopters.

The US Navy had conducted experiments with ASW using helicopters in 1944–45. It was then that the helicopter first 'dunked' sonar listening devices into the sea to attempt to pick up sounds from submerged submarines. There are two main groups of these devices, both having as primitive ancestor the Asdic listening system dating from immediately after the First World War (when hydrophones, underwater listening devices, were used). Passive sonar is merely an extremely sensitive underwater listening system able to pick up the noise of a submarine propeller at a distance of many miles. It can also hear the disturbance as the water eddies around the fast-moving hull. As it emits no signals itself, except through the atmosphere to the helicopter or other friendly platform, the target submarine has no knowledge it is being sensed. Active sonar is rather like underwater radar. Powerful sound pulses are radiated through the sea, and if any strike a submarine hull they are diffused and some pulses are reflected back and picked up by receivers. In this case the submarine can itself detect the system searching for it, but active sonar can be used against a submarine lying motionless with its screw(s) stationary.

Two scenes, fifty years apart, and both of VTOL aircraft in the anti-submarine role. The top picture is of an SSZ Class airship, armed with a single Lewis gun, emerging from its hangar on HMS Furious *in 1917. The picture below is of Wessex HAS Mk 3 anti-submarine helicopters bristling with sonar equipment and radar below decks on the anti-submarine cruiser HMS* Blake

Imperial War Museum

MOD

Westland Sea King HAS Mk 1
Licence-built development of the Sikorsky S-61, the Sea King is the principal ASW helicopter of the Royal Navy
Engines: 2×1500 hp Rolls-Royce Gnome H.1400 turboshafts *Max speed:* 155 mph *Weight fully loaded:* 21,000 lb *Range:* 620 miles *Armament:* Up to 4×Mk 44 homing torpedoes, 4×Mk 11 depth charges, A/S missiles

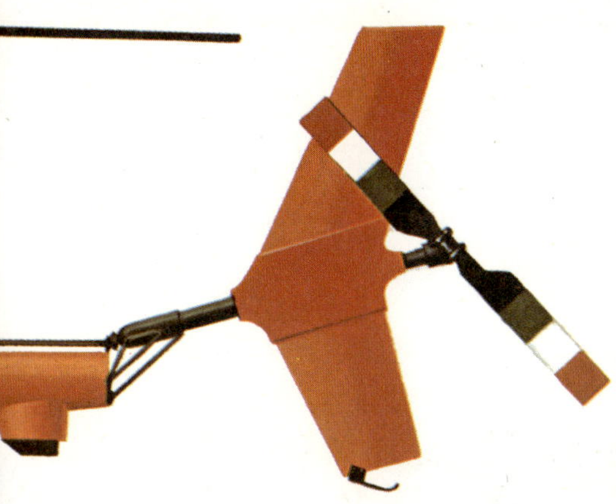

Agusta A.106
Lightweight single-seat helicopter designed for ASW role, the A.106 has served on the Italian Navy's *Impavido* Class destroyers armed with a pair of Mk 44 homing torpedoes
Engine: 354 shp Turboméca-Agusta TM-251 turboshaft *Max speed:* 110 mph *Weight fully loaded:* 3086 lb *Range:* 155 miles

Westland

Westland Sea King, principal SAR helicopter of the German Navy

Both types of equipment are packaged in various ways, the most common being a floating sonobuoy. Aeroplanes have to strew costly sonobuoys which cannot be later gathered up for re-use, but a helicopter need not be so wasteful. Dunking consists of lowering a passive or active sonobuoy into the sea, listening, and then lifting it out and trying in a fresh place.

Dunking with a single sonobuoy is clearly economical. As only a single buoy is used, it can be made large and powerful. More-over, the helicopter, if skilfully flown, can obtain a 'contact' from a hostile submarine, and swiftly pinpoint the enemy by flying in the direction from whence the echoes or noises are coming. As the submarine twists and turns in an effort to escape, so can the even more manoeuvrable helicopter give chase in a way that is impossible with almost any open-sea surface vessel. Displacement ships are too slow, and have insufficient power of manoeuvre. Hydrofoils are good, and so are certain ACVs (air-cushion vehicles, or hovercraft), but the helicopter is the best of all.

Sonics are not the only way of detecting submerged submarines. With diesel boats the 'sniffer' able to detect minute concentrations of diesel exhaust gas in the atmosphere is an economical method able to track down a snorkelling submarine from as far away as 20 miles (but the helicopter has to be down-wind!). Another useful device is the MAD (Magnetic-Anomaly Detector), originally used for geophysical prospecting. The MAD 'bird' is a package towed on a cable just above the sea and able to detect the extremely small disturbance caused to the Earth's magnetic field by the magnetic material of the submerged submarine. Of course, a MAD indication would be given by a sunken wreck, and this would also register with active sonar. Passive sonics, however, gives sure indication of a

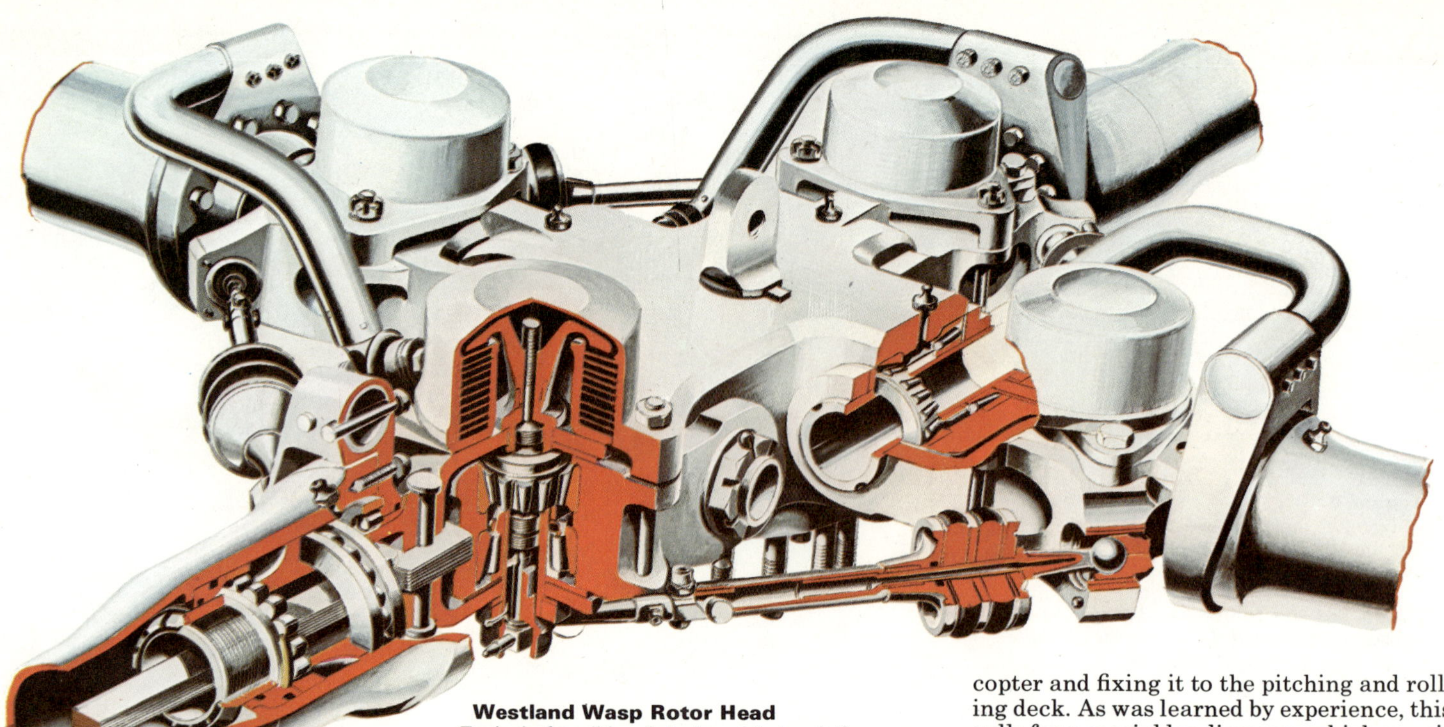

Westland Wasp Rotor Head
Typical of traditional design, this is a fully articulated assembly with the blades held in two sets of pivots and able to rotate in their sockets

submerged submarine proceeding under power. On top of all these are other methods, of which the most used is radar. Radar cannot operate in the depths of the sea, but ASW helicopters need radar to detect tips of snorkels, periscopes, radio or radar masts and other metal parts of a submarine that may show above the surface. It can thus be seen that, to do an ASW job, a helicopter has to be weighed down with a ton or two of equipment merely in order to find the target.

For this reason the immediate post-war era saw aircraft and helicopters having to operate in 'hunter/killer' pairs. One would carry the sensors, to detect and pinpoint the submarine, and the other would carry the weapons. In fact the HSL-1 was intended to try to do both jobs, but was handicapped by its weighty and bulky piston engine and only a few were used. Of course, even today helicopters generally have short range compared with aeroplanes. For mid-ocean submarine hunting they need to be carried into the correct general area by a surface ship, and fortunately the demands of a helicopter for hangar space and an operating platform are very modest compared with most aeroplanes. It is possible to operate a helicopter from quite small surface vessels, as was discovered with the Fl 282 during the Second World War.

All that is needed is a small fantail platform, a hangar, some guideway or track linking the two, and, in most installations, a method of positively retrieving the helicopter and fixing it to the pitching and rolling deck. As was learned by experience, this calls for a special landing gear which can sit firmly on the steel deck without allowing the helicopter to slide or swing as the ship rolls. Several hold-down systems have been developed, most of them involving claws, 'bear-traps' or other grips lowered by a powered cable from the helicopter to a deck anchor, so that the helicopter can winch itself down, balancing the tension in the cable against the rotor lift. Without such a system the pitching deck could come up and crash into the hovering helicopter in a rough sea, and it would be much more difficult to get down safely on to the correct spot.

Shipboard helicopters also need to be capable of folding their main rotor blades. Sometimes the blades are locked by precision-fitted pins of high-tensile steel which deck handling crews can unlock, withdraw and stow, thereafter folding the blades by hand and lashing them with nylon webbing. More sophisticated machines, such as the

Westland Wasp
Designed for use on small frigates, the Wasp relies on the mother ship for submarine detection, but can make the kill with two Mk 44 torpedoes
Engine: 710 shp Rolls-Royce Nimbus
Cruising speed: 100 mph *Weight fully loaded:* 5500 lb *Range:* 305 miles

Sea King, have automatic hydraulic folding controlled from the cockpit, with a safety switch on the landing gear to prohibit folding by error in flight. The Sea King also folds its tail, as could the earlier S-58/ Wessex family, to reduce length. The shipboard 'chopper' must be liberally provided with clearly marked lashing points, handholds and strong fixtures for towing, jacking and manual positioning.

The first shipborne ASW helicopters were simple conversions of the Sikorsky S-58, the HSS-1 Seabat, put into limited service in August 1955. The S-58 was a fine machine for its day, but could not really carry adequate sensors and weapons for the ASW mission, though a few continued in service into the 1960s redesignated SH-34G. Britain aimed much higher with a more advanced tandem-rotor machine derived from the Bristol 173. Eventually by late February 1954 work went ahead on two ASW models, the Bristol 191 for the Royal Navy and Bristol 193 for the RAF, both with ASW sensors and weapons. They were to have begun with Leonides Major piston engines but all were eventually to have had two Napier Gazelle turboshaft engines. Few programmes, however, have been as protracted and unsuccessful as the Bristol tandem helicopters, and though the RAF did eventually receive 26 much-modified general utility Belvederes the naval 191 was replaced by a turbine conversion of the S-58, the Westland Wessex. This was produced very quickly and with a single Napier (later Rolls-Royce) Gazelle carried a much greater sensor and weapon load than the Seabat. The HAS.3 version was dubbed 'the Camel' because it carried search radar in a hump radome behind the main rotor.

Conscious of what could be achieved, Sikorsky and the US Navy jointly schemed the S-61 around two T58 engines, with both sensors and weapons carried on, or in, a flying-boat hull. Redesignated from HSS-2 to SH-3A, these machines did more than any other type to establish the helicopter as a primary ASW platform. Sikorsky built more than 400 ASW versions, and Agusta in Italy is still producing the SH-3D for several customers with APN-195 search radar, APN-182 Doppler radar and a typical range of weapons including AS.12 missiles. These Italian machines retain the US Navy philosophy of using the helicopter merely as extensions of the eyes and ears of the parent ship, which retains complete tactical control. The job of this type of helicopter is to carry sensors and weapons faster and with greater power of manoeuvre than the ship, but not to operate on its own. The ship's radar and underwater sensors direct the helicopter where to search, and the signals from the helicopter's sonic sensors are fed back to the tactical centre in the ship where all decisions are taken.

In Britain, however, a revolution was taking place. The Royal Navy considered that it would be possible and preferable to place the tactical centre in the helicopter, so that the latter could do the whole job, independently of surface ships. The result was the Westland Sea King HAS.1, first flown in 1969. This has two 1400-hp Rolls-Royce Gnome engines and full sensors, displays and weapons for independent all-weather ASW operation. Equipment includes a Newmark flight-control system, radio altimeter, ARI.5955 or AW.391 search radar, Plessey dipping sonar (Bendix for some customers), Marconi-Elliott Doppler radar, and two or four Mk 44 or Mk 46 homing torpedoes, four Mk 11 depth charges or other ASW weapons. Later Sea Kings have the 1590-hp Gnome H.1400-1 engine allowing higher weights to be carried especially in adverse conditions, with transmission uprated from 2300 to 2700 hp and a sixth blade added to the tail rotor.

A Westland Lynx HAS Mk 2 lands on a Royal Navy Type 42 guided missile destroyer, HMS Sheffield, *for the first time – June 1975*

There is no direct rival to the Westland Sea King, in the sense that no other helicopter can fly the ASW search/strike mission independently, but there are many other naval helicopters. The French Aérospatiale group produces the large SA.321G Super Frelon, with three 1550-hp Turmo engines. Using dynamic parts designed and developed by Sikorsky, the Super Frelon can operate at weights up to 28,660 lb, appreciably heavier than a Sea King, and can carry full Sylphe radar, sonar, IFF and other sensors as well as four torpedoes or two AM.39 Exocet missiles. In complete contrast, Agusta in Italy delivered 23 extremely small ASW helicopters which proved to be too limited to be useful. Designated A.106, these neat machines were powered by a 300-hp Turboméca-Agusta TAA230 and incorporated some parts and technology from the Bell JetRanger. Though they could carry sonar, Julie acoustic sensing, all-weather avionics and two Mk 44 torpedoes, these little machines are no longer used aboard Italian destroyers.

Shipborne-Helicopter Training Platform
The platform pitches and rolls to simulate the bucking stern of a ship in the roughest sea

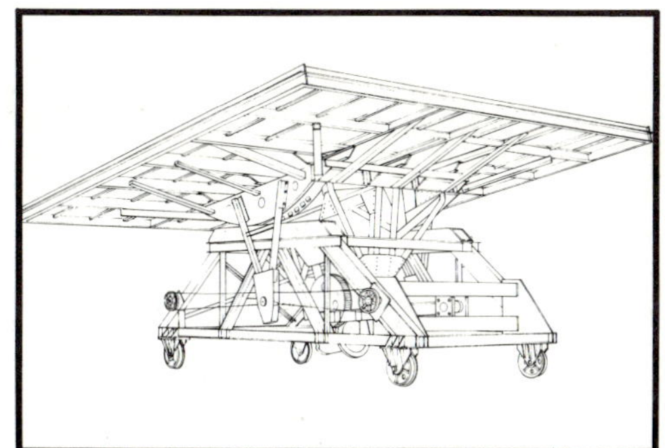

One of the consistently successful producers of shipboard helicopters is the Soviet bureau of Nikolai Kamov, which has adhered to the use of co-axial rotors to achieve a compact shape for naval operations. The AV-MF (Soviet Naval Aviation) used large numbers of piston-engined Ka-10M and Ka-15 machines and today the standard helicopter for Soviet sea deployment is the Ka-25, called Hormone by NATO. This exists in several forms, but all are stumpy and capacious machines powered by two 900-hp Glushenkov GTD-3 engines. Most have a crew of four and carry extensive avionics and sensors including four types of radar, dipping sonar, MAD capsule, electro-optical detector and full all-weather equipment. Weapons include ASW torpedoes and/or nuclear depth charges carried in a long internal bay. The four-leg wheeled gear is fixed, but the wheels can be swivelled to minimize interference with the radar and in some versions are surrounded by quickly inflated buoyancy rings for alighting on the sea – a feature also seen on some types of Wessex.

A much smaller but contemporary Western helicopter is the Westland Wasp, one of the derivatives of the Saunders-Roe P.531 flown in July 1958. Powered by a Rolls-Royce (formerly Blackburn) Nimbus of 710 hp, the Wasp is designed for use from small frigates, destroyers and other surface ships, and has a special four-leg gear with swivelling wheels to prevent rotation on deck. A winch-down system is standard with all naval users. Though carrying no sensors the Wasp flies ASW missions on the direction of the parent ship, with a crew of two and two Mk 44 torpedoes. It is the last helicopter in use as a mere weapon carrier for a surface ship, following the technique first tried with the defunct DASH (Drone Anti-

Kaman SH-2 Seasprite
Standard USN shipborne search and rescue helicopter, the Seasprite force is being modified to meet the USN's LAMPS (Light Airborne Multi-Purpose System) requirements for an ASW and anti-ship missile defence system as the SH-2F
Engines: 2×1350 shp General Electric T58-GE-8F turboshafts *Max speed:* 168 mph *Weight fully loaded:* 12,800 lb

Kaman

Kaman SH-2 Seasprite in rescue and recovery role

Submarine Helicopter) in which ASW surface ships deployed Gyrodyne QH-50C pilotless helicopters carrying torpedoes. Not having to carry a crew meant that these small machines, with co-axial rotors driven by a 300-hp Boeing T50 turbine, could lift two Mk 44 torpedoes and drop them under remote radio guidance. Nearly 400 were built, but they were taken out of service after a short time in 1960–63.

Today the US Navy is searching for the ideal multi-role LAMPS (Light Airborne Multi-Purpose System) helicopter for use from warships. So far the role has been amply filled by advanced conversions of the Kaman H-2 Seasprite already mentioned. Rebuilt with two T58 engines instead of one, these extremely capable little machines are an object-lesson in how to build a better naval helicopter without actually building any new ones. The main current conversions, the SH-2E and SH-2F, carry every required LAMPS sensor including radar, sonar (15 SSQ-47 active or SSQ-41 passive sonobuoys) and MAD 'bird' plus several later sensors and ESM (Electronic Surveillance Measures), together with two Mk 44 or Mk 46 torpedoes. All existing H-2 Seasprites were converted by 1976, and Kaman is a leading contender for the definitive LAMPS for the 1980s.

Novosti

Kamov Ka-25K ASW helicopters on board the Soviet anti-submarine cruiser Moskva. *This machine is carried aboard the large* Kiev *class ships*

European Helicopters

EUROPE KEEPS PACE

MOD

VTOL pair of the RAF. Puma assault transport and Harrier escort fly over the Belize jungle. The Puma is one of the most successful Anglo-French helicopters

Inevitably, European helicopter manufacturers have over the years become concentrated into fewer but larger groups. In Britain, where the process has been deliberate official policy, Bristol, Percival, Fairey, Saunders-Roe, Cierva and all other helicopter companies have ceased to exist, except as portions of Westland Helicopters Ltd. In February 1967 Westland and the French nationalized group Aérospatiale jointly undertook production of two French helicopters and agreed upon joint development and production of a completely new design, as a government-to-government 'package'. This undoubtedly strengthened European helicopter capability, and within the framework of Heli-Europe, a loose association of major manufacturers, future planning is aimed at increasing collaboration and avoiding duplication of effort or head-on collisions.

The point has already been made that, with the exception of the Saunders-Roe P.531, which led to a small production batch of Army Scout and Naval Wasp helicopters, none of Britain's profusion of prototype helicopters of the 1950s achieved any success. During the 1960s the RAF operated 26 tandem-rotor Westland (Bristol) Belvedere utility transports, but these were extremely inconvenient and a travesty of the way turbine engines should be installed (the engines were inside the fuselage, one at each end of the cabin!), and they were scrapped when they reached their pitifully short permitted life of 1600 hours. There could be no greater contrast than the other European twin-turbine military utility helicopter, the Puma.

Designated SA.330, the prototype Puma was developed by Aérospatiale in the days when this powerful national group was called Sud-Aviation, and flew in 1965. In 1967 the Puma was one of the three types named in the Franco-British agreement. It was adopted by the RAF, and Fairey took over manufacture of about 30% of the airframe at Hayes (subsequently switched to Westland at Yeovil), while Rolls-Royce make about the same proportion of the Turmo engines. Early (RAF and French military) versions had two 1328-hp Turmo IIIC4 engines, but later Pumas have 1575-hp Turmo IVCs, arranged in a pair ahead of the main gearbox. The Puma is very neat, with a main cabin about 20-ft long, 5-ft high and 6-ft wide, and twin-wheel landing gears which retract hydraulically to reduce drag. The Puma can carry 16 to 20 troops or 5500 lb of cargo; slung-load limit is 6600 lb. The French ALAT uses 140 of these fast and capable machines, and the RAF has 40. Nine serve the Armée de l'Air, and a further 300 have been exported, showing the kind of business that can be gained by a competitive product. Most current sales are civil SA.-330F or G models, chiefly for oil companies.

The French do not rest on their laurels but wish to compete with the US helicopter builders every inch of the way. During the life of the Puma gross weight has been increased from 14,110 lb to 16,300 lb, speed has been raised and range extended. Originally the increases in weight caused speed to fall, but introduction of new main rotor blades of glassfibre, with continuous variation in section profile and twist, has enabled cruising speed to be increased from 133 to 162 mph, higher than it was at the start. Thus, over a 310-mile sector the payload of the latest Pumas is 5400 lb compared with 3300

EC Armées

French Army Alouette III blasts off an Aérospatiale SS.11B1 wire-guided anti-tank missile

lb of the early machines. Aérospatiale has dramatically extended component-lives and reduced operating costs, and since June 1975 has been looking ahead to the next generation, the Super Puma (which is not a joint programme with Britain). Powered by two of the new 1800 hp Turboméca Makila engines, the Super Puma has a bigger cabin, even more advanced glassfibre rotor and several other new features, one of which is likely to be a *Fenestron* tail. This, an Aérospatiale development that has almost become a trademark, consists of a high-speed multi-blade fan shrouded in a duct forming part of the fin. The *Fenestron* is as efficient as a normal tail rotor, has less drag and is less vulnerable or dangerous to people on the ground. The SA.330Z is flying with such a tail, with a high-mounted tailplane.

Aérospatiale's experience, reputation and worldwide helicopter customers were gained almost entirely with the smaller Alouette series, which were the first successful turbine-engined helicopters in the world. In 1976 HAL in India was still building the Cheetah, the local variant of the Lama utility machine which is also in small-scale production in France. The bigger Alouette III continues in full production, most recent examples being of the SA.319B type with an Astazou engine. And the Astazou is the basic standard engine of the helicopter which inherited the mantle of the Alouette, the SA.341 Gazelle. One of the most attractive five-seat utility helicopters in the world, the Gazelle was also included in the Franco-

Westland/Aérospatiale SA.330E Puma HC Mk I

The largest type built under the Anglo-French agreement of 1967, the Puma combat support helicopter is the standard tactical transport of the RAF and Armée de l'Air

Engines: 2×1320 shp Turboméca Turmo IIIC4 turboshafts *Max speed:* 174 mph *Weight fully loaded:* 14,110 lb *Range:* 390 miles

Aérospatiale SA.316 Alouette III
Highly successful military helicopter with orders for all versions exceeding 1300 by over 40 nations
Engine: 870 shp Turboméca Artouste IIID turboshaft *Max speed:* 130 mph *Weight fully loaded:* 4850 lb *Range:* 335 miles

British agreement of February 1967, just two months before the first flight of the prototype. The dynamic parts owed much to the Alouette III, though the main blades are glassfibre (and, with the hub, rest on exhaustive research by MBB in Germany) and the tail incorporates a *Fenestron*.

By 1976 about 750 Gazelles had been sold, including 310 for the British Army, Navy, Marines and RAF. Army versions carry various sight/weapon fits, while most other military variants are for training and liaison. Many civil variants have been sold, some being ambulance/rescue models. Westland makes 60% of the main production airframes, though ultimately all assembly will probably be at Marignane (Marseilles), Aérospatiale's helicopter centre. Licence production is undertaken in Yugoslavia.

On 2 June 1972 Aérospatiale flew the prototype of a further development in the same class but enlarged to meet the Huey type of market. At the same time Turboméca began designing the 650-hp Arriel engine, and Avco Lycoming the LTS 101 in the same power category. The French prototype was the SA.360 Dauphin, powered by advanced Astazou engines (initially a 980-hp model and later an engine of 1050 hp). Intended to succeed the Alouette III and partner the Gazelle, the Dauphin has a roomy cabin seating 10 to 14. Other features include an advanced *Fenestron* tail, and main blades filled with Nomex honeycomb with skins of carbon fibre (British Grafil) and glassfibre. Twenty years of turbine-helicopter refinement have produced in the Dauphin an outstandingly attractive, easy to fly and smooth machine, with remarkable performance and manoeuvrability (200 knots at 80% engine torque) and a computer-controlled engine. Production began in 1976 of many Dauphins to meet worldwide civil orders, and there is no doubt France will lead off the proposed military variant with several major gun and missile options, sensor and sight systems, and skids instead of spatted landing gear.

Aérospatiale will probably be in production in 1977 with the somewhat different twin-engined version. Though the LTS 101 may be a customer option in the United States, the standard SA.365 Dauphin engine is the Arriel, installed as a neat pair in a streamlined cowl behind the rotor, with free-turbine drive needing no clutch. There are a few aircraft systems and structure changes, with inverted-camber tailplane and the Starflex plastic rotor head and advanced blades. The Starflex, the first to mature of three radical and extremely competitive new forms of rotor hub developed by Aérospatiale, is a dramatic demonstration of the way advanced technology and good engineering can fight inflation. Compared with the Gazelle hub, the Starflex (as fitted to a prototype AS.350, mentioned presently) has 64 parts compared with well over 200, weighs 120 lb compared with 221 lb, and costs roughly half as much. Each blade is held by a fork of reinforced plastics which, via a cone of thin rubber laminates, bears on a hole in a large star plate rigidly attached to the rotor pylon. The blade, fork, bearing and cone can all be removed with simple hand tools and a single blade crutch.

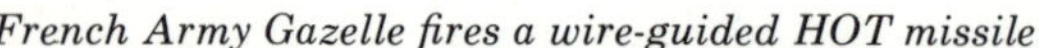

French Army Gazelle fires a wire-guided HOT missile

EC Armées

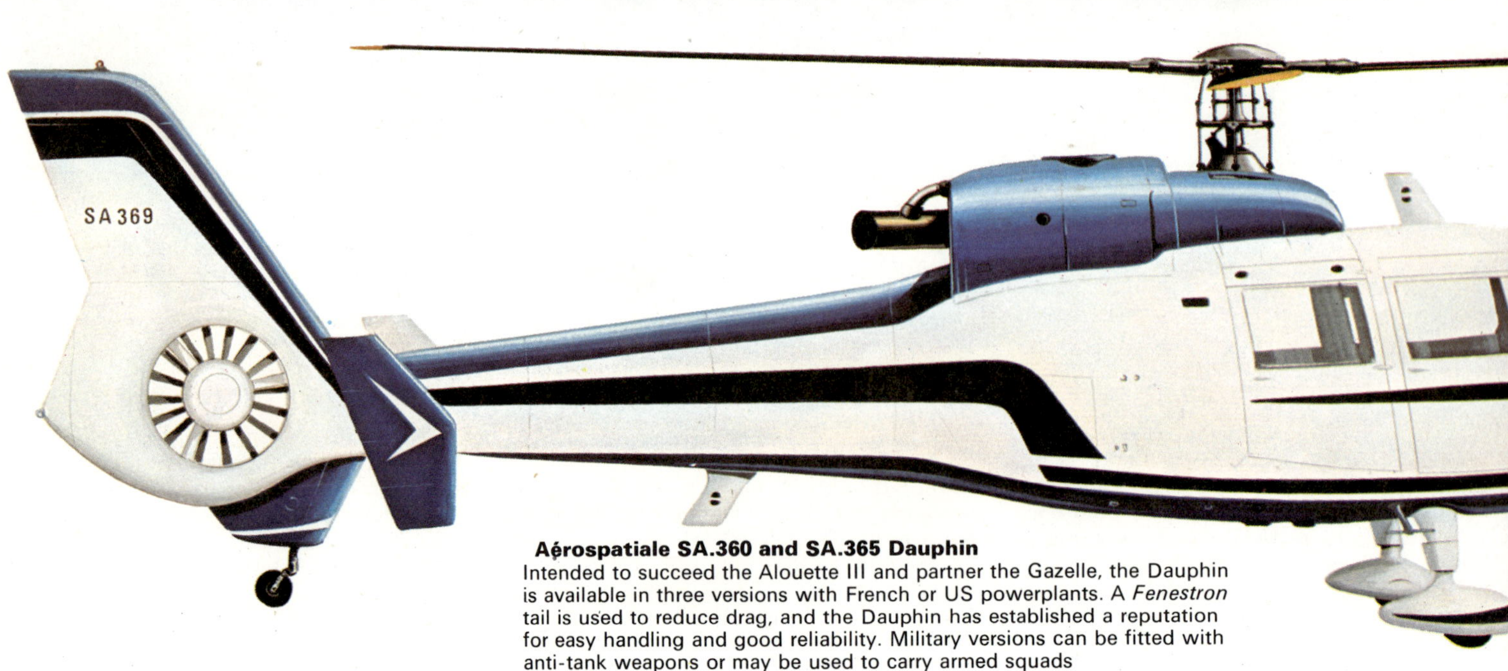

Aérospatiale SA.360 and SA.365 Dauphin
Intended to succeed the Alouette III and partner the Gazelle, the Dauphin is available in three versions with French or US powerplants. A *Fenestron* tail is used to reduce drag, and the Dauphin has established a reputation for easy handling and good reliability. Military versions can be fitted with anti-tank weapons or may be used to carry armed squads
Engines: 1050 shp Turboméca Astazou (SA.360) or 2×650 shp Turboméca Arriel or Avco Lycoming LTS 101 (SA.365) turboshafts *Max speed:* 165 mph *Weight fully loaded:* 6175 lb *Range:* 400 miles

In 1976 Aérospatiale unveiled the AS.350 Ecureuil (Squirrel), a beautiful little five/six-seater powered by a single turbine. The first AS.350 flew in June 1974 with an LTS 101, while the second is fitted with an Arriel. This is discussed in the next chapter.

Federal Germany was perhaps understandably slow to get off the ground with helicopters, though it built several not very successful prototypes as well as the Bell Huey and Sikorsky CH-53 under licence. It was left to the big industrial group MBB to stick to what seemed at first to be very doubtful guns and achieve great world-wide success with the BO105. Outwardly a conventional but somewhat portly five-seater, the 105 is really in a class by itself. Though it is actually slightly smaller in overall dimensions than the JetRanger, it costs much more than twice as much (typically $525,000 compared with $180,000). The main reason is that it has two Allison 250-C20 engines where the JetRanger has just one. As a result it is a fully certificated all-weather IFR machine, capable of doing a remarkable number of demanding missions.

Aérospatiale/Westland SA.341 Gazelle
Lightweight multi-purpose helicopter built in co-operation by Britain and France and proving highly successful in service
Engine: 590 shp Turboméca Astazou III turboshaft *Max speed:* 170 mph *Weight fully loaded:* 3747 lb

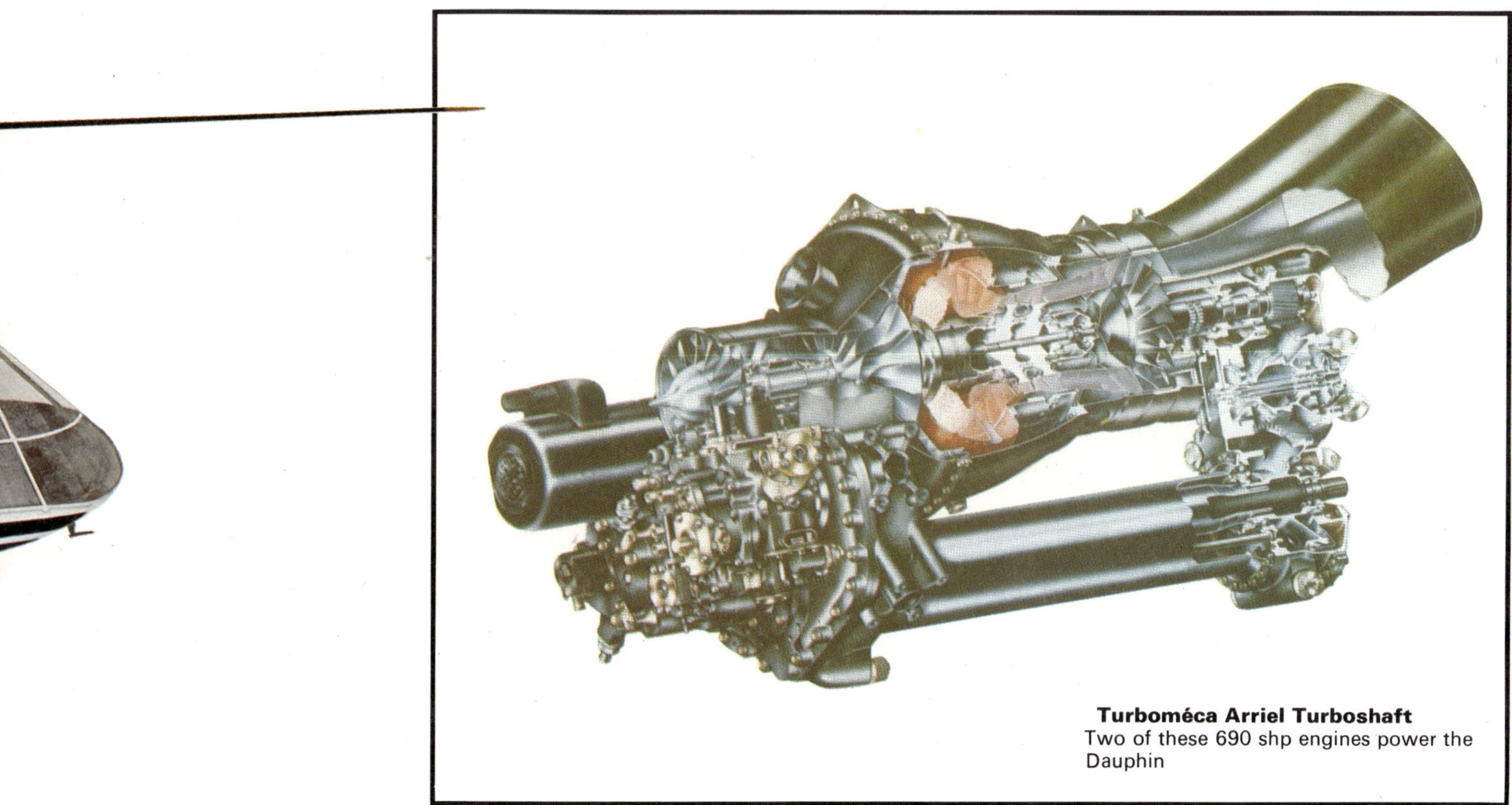

Turboméca Arriel Turboshaft
Two of these 690 shp engines power the Dauphin

Aérospatiale

Aérospatiale AS.350 Ecureuil (Squirrel)
The AS.350 uses Aérospatiale's Starflex rotor, which has only 64 parts compared with more than 200 in the Gazelle's hub. Maximum use is made of existing components and emphasis is placed on simplicity
Engine: 600 shp Avco Lycoming LTS 101 or 640 shp Turboméca Arriel turboshaft *Max speed:* 140 mph *Weight fully loaded:* 4200 lb *Range:* 500 miles *Number of seats:* 5/6

Agusta-Bell 206
Made under licence by Agusta of Italy, this light multi-role helicopter corresponds to the US Army OH-58A Kiowa.
Engine: 400 shp Allison 250-C20 turboshaft *Max speed:* 160 mph *Weight fully loaded:* 3000 lb

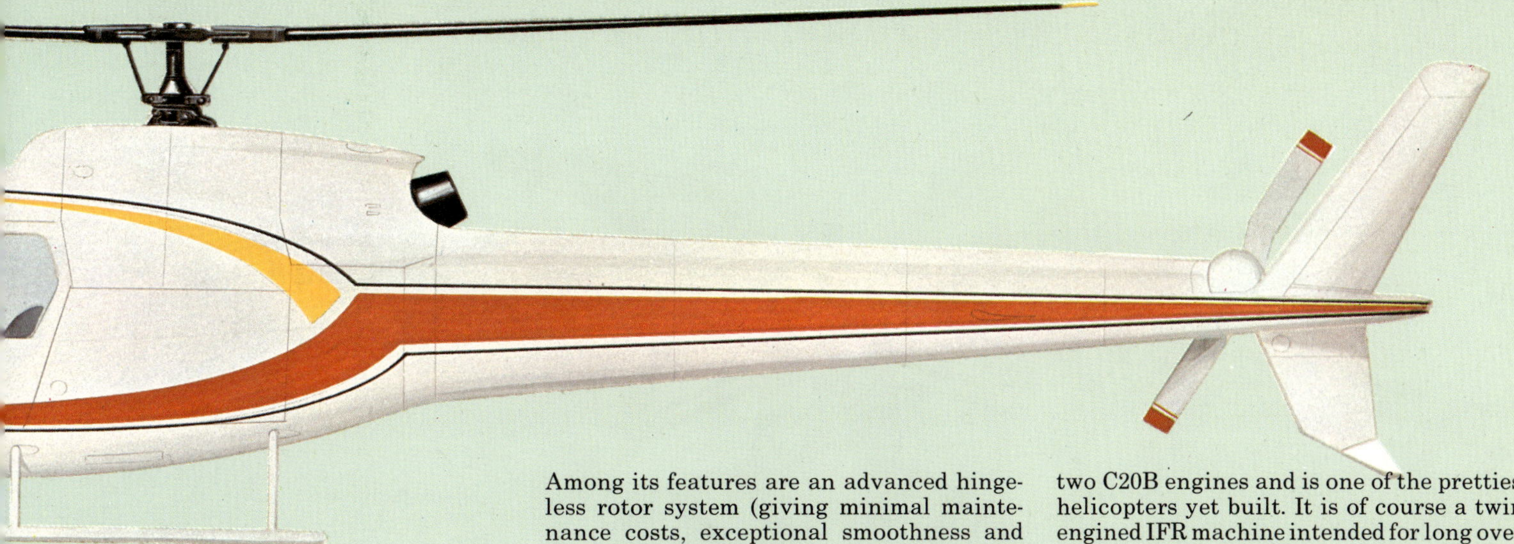

Among its features are an advanced hingeless rotor system (giving minimal maintenance costs, exceptional smoothness and manoeuvrability beating every other helicopter except, perhaps, the Lynx), twin-engine safety, and an all-round capability that is undeniably attractive. The proof of this pudding is commercial success, and by 1976 sales totalled over 400, with about another 300 expected to be ordered by the Germany Army's Air Service (*Heeresflieger*) as an all-weather anti-tank helicopter carrying a stabilized sight and six HOT missiles. MBB have also built or projected several developments, one of which is the winged BO105 HGH high-speed research helicopter which in 1975 reached 251 mph without any auxiliary propulsion.

Somewhat similar in some respects, the Italian Agusta A.109 is likewise powered by two C20B engines and is one of the prettiest helicopters yet built. It is of course a twin-engined IFR machine intended for long over-water missions (such as to oil rigs) where single-engined machines are unlikely to be admissible, and Agusta has also conducted extensive research into military versions including the basic TOW-armed anti-tank variant and the projected A.129 slender gunship. At present the A.109 suffers from having a traditional type of dynamic system with full articulated rotor hubs and a tail/rotor similar to a JetRanger (which the company makes under licence). It is more streamlined than the BO105, and can carry eight people at marginally higher speeds. Both the BO105 and A.109 families are likely to have long lives, with different turboshaft engines (possibly later Allisons) in the 600-hp class.

Starflex Rotor
After several years of study this rotor hub has been selected by Aérospatiale for new production helicopters. Seen on one of the prototype AS. 350 Squirrels, it is made largely of rubber and plastics

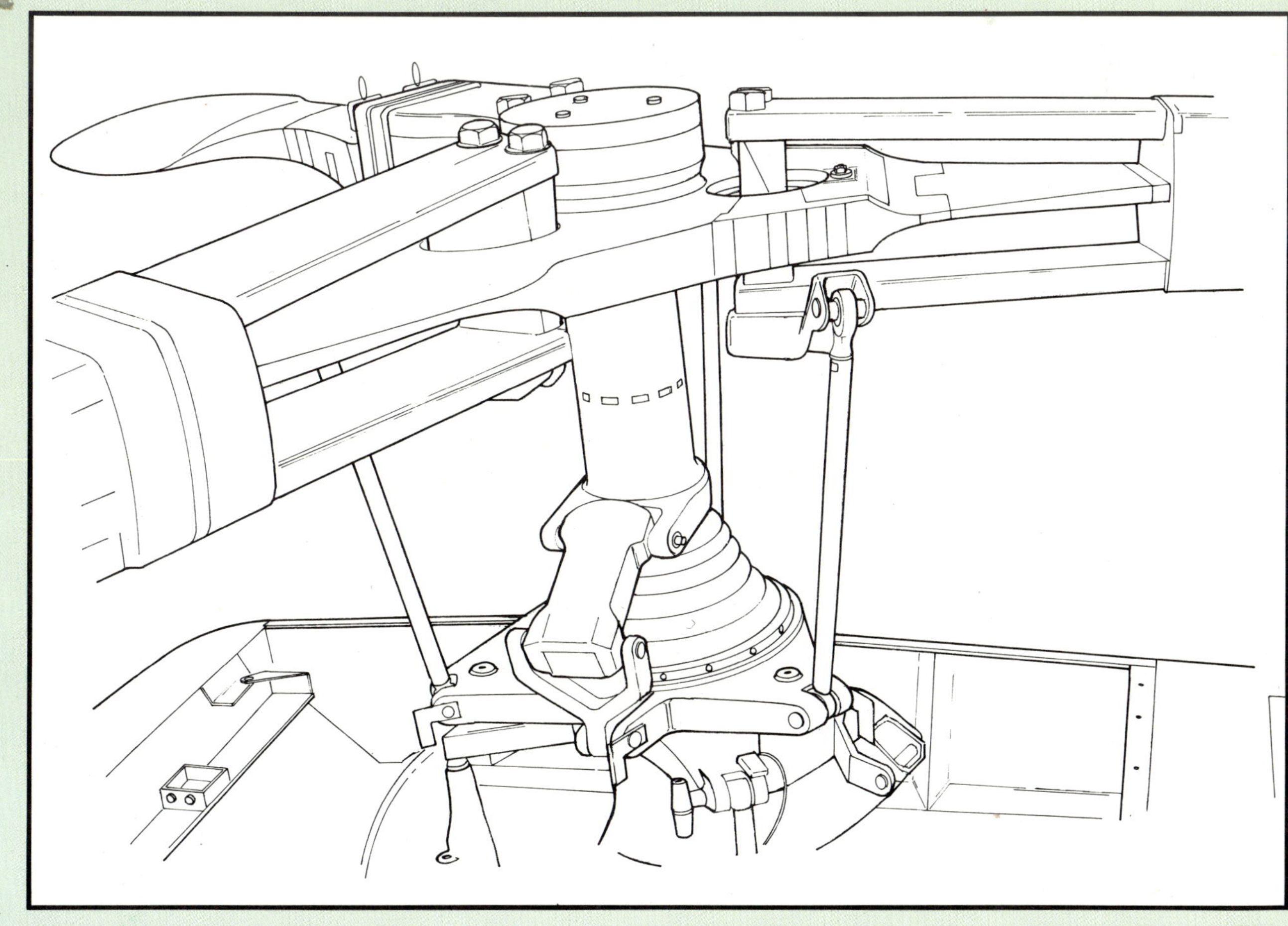

Westland/Aérospatiale WG.13 Lynx

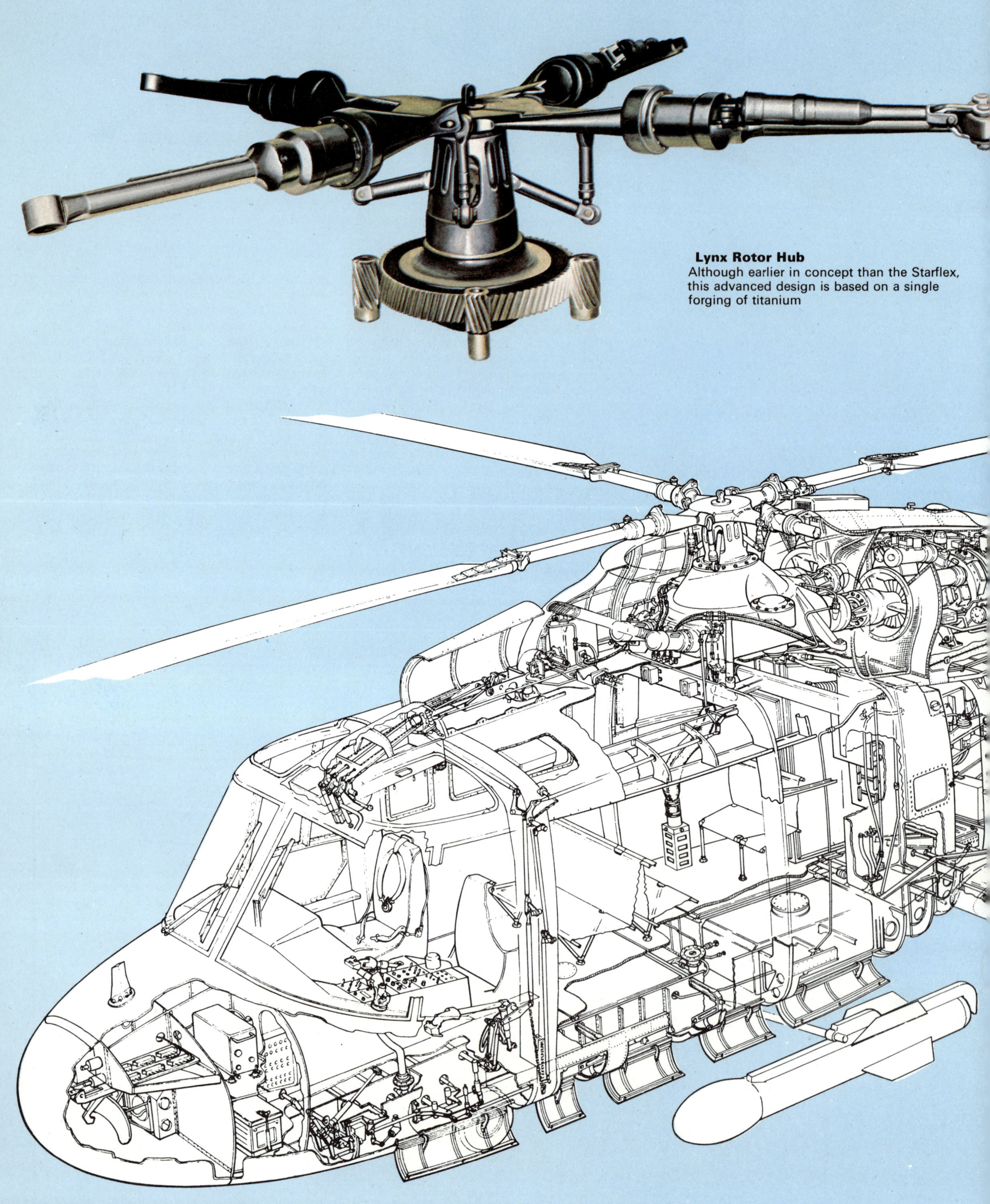

Lynx Rotor Hub
Although earlier in concept than the Starflex, this advanced design is based on a single forging of titanium

Army Lynx demonstrates its agility in a high-speed barrel roll

In Britain there is only one modern helicopter available, and this promises to be an outstandingly successful one. The WG.13 was the third helicopter in the 1967 'package' with the French, and it is the only British-led project in all Britain's 22 collaborative aircraft programmes. Perhaps because of this the partner, France, cancelled its projected gunship version and has ordered only 18 (for the French Navy). Despite this, Westland has never doubted the rightness of the design, and today the Westland/Aérospatiale Lynx, as it is known, has attracted orders from armies and navies in many countries. It is basically a modern machine in the 9500-lb class, powered by two 900-hp Rolls-Royce Gem engines and characterized by an extremely modern semi-rigid rotor, complete automaticity and advanced systems to minimize pilot workload, a large cabin able to carry ten troops, and a quite exceptional response to pilot control demands. At an early date, only two years after the first flight in March 1971 when the engines were giving a mere 700 hp, prototypes had been flown at a world record speed of 200 mph, dived at 230 mph, looped, rolled at more than 100° per second and flown backwards at 80 mph.

In May 1974 the British Ministry of Defence placed a contract for the first 100 Lynxes, covering aircraft for the British Army (AH.1, multi-role, transport, anti-tank, ECM and many other battlefield duties), Royal Navy (HAS.2, ASW classification and strike, anti-ship with Sea Skua missiles, fire support, reconnaissance, transport and many other duties) and French Navy (similar to HAS.2 but with OMERA Heracles radar instead of Ferranti Seaspray). Further Lynxes are on order for the Netherlands and Brazilian navies, an order is expected from the Argentine for aircraft for Type 21 frigates, and with Saudi backing, the Egyptians have since 1974 been considering licence-manufacture of both the Lynx and its advanced three-spool Gem engine. Apart from specialized 'gunship' combat the Lynx can fulfil virtually every tactical battlefield or naval mission requirement, and despite its size it is possibly the most agile helicopter yet built. The Westland 606 civil version is discussed in the next chapter.

Westland/Aérospatiale Lynx cutaway
HAS Mk 2 Royal Navy ASW search and strike version Naval Lynxes have tricycle wheeled landing gear, flotation equipment, deck landing gear and comprehensive ASW electronics and armament

Westland/Aérospatiale Lynx AH Mk 1
General-purpose version of this highly manoeuvrable helicopter for the British Army and RAF
Engine: 2×900 shp Rolls-Royce Mk 10001 Gem turboshafts *Max cruising speed:* 184 mph *Weight fully loaded:* 9500 lb *Range:* 490 miles

Westland/Aérospatiale SA. 330C Pumas of the Abu Dhabi Air Force. This military export version is powered by two Turmo IVB turboshafts

John Batchelor

The 'Biz-Copters'

CIVIL HELICOPTERS

Until the 1960s rotary-winged aircraft had limited commercial appeal. Admittedly large numbers of autogyros were being built for fun, but rotary-winged machines capable of doing a genuine commercial job were few and far between. They were almost restricted to a handful of large airliner-type helicopters, converted from the latest and best military models and used on a very small number of urban routes where conditions were especially favourable, and a small number of other machines operated either in the Communist countries or by large nationalized airlines in the capitalist nations who were content to suffer heavy losses in the interest of either knowledge or prestige.

Today the technical development of the helicopter and of small turbine engines has transformed the picture. Whereas in the past nearly all civil helicopters were small and simple machines used for contract-hire and special purposes, such as pipeline patrol, crop spraying and transport to inaccessible building sites, today many hundreds of helicopters are sold each year for the sheer convenience of passengers. Most are bought by private companies as executive and liaison vehicles, but many join the fleets of helicopter airlines for both scheduled and charter operations. To appreciate the magnitude of the revolution in helicopter marketing one has only to look at the major helicopter programmes. Until well into the 1960s virtually every helicopter was launched and sustained on military orders. Today former military production lines are now delivering mainly civil helicopters, partly because of slashed military budgets (except in the Soviet Union) but mainly because of dramatically increased sales of civil machines. These increased sales have rested on several factors. One is improved safety, reflected in substantially less-crippling insurance premiums (which in the 1950s often accounted for the biggest single item in helicopter operating costs). Another is the greater sales attraction of today's pretty, streamlined, turbine-driven machines, which have load, speed and range comparable with what customers expect from fixed-wing machines. A third, less-obvious, factor is the emergence of twin-engined light helicopters able to comply with full certification requirements for operation in instrument flight conditions at night or in bad weather.

Successful Loser

Even the non-IFR single-engined machines are selling like hot cakes to a vast spectrum of civil customers. The best-seller of all began life as a military prototype, the Bell OH-4A of 1962. When a different helicopter won a big US Army order Bell did not abandon the design but launched it afresh as the civil JetRanger, Model 206, an attractive five-seater powered by the 317-hp Allison 250-C18 engine. Sales began in 1967, and Bell's bold prediction that it would generate the biggest civil demand of any helicopter in history was soon realized. By 1968 output of the JetRanger had reached 20 per month, and Bell signed a five-year contract worth $75 million with Beech for subcontract manufacture of virtually the whole airframe structure. There have been successive follow-on contracts since. Though Bell subsequently won enormous military orders, including 2200 OH-58A Kiowas for the US Army and 74 CH-136s for Canada, the main development effort has been applied to the civil market. It was chiefly for that market that the patented Noda-Matic suspension was developed, in which the helicopter is suspended from the rotor hub via a 'nodalized beam' which minimizes vibration. It was civil product improvement that led to the Model 206B JetRanger II, with greater load and speed made possible by the 400-shp Allison C20 engine, and to the enlarged Model 206L LongRanger powered by the 420-shp C20B engine and with a longer cabin seating seven, and greater fuel capacity to extend range by 45 miles to 370 miles.

To complete the great Bell story, it is almost entirely to meet commercial needs that the company has now developed a light twin-engined helicopter, the Model 222. As attractive as might be expected, this owes nothing directly to any existing design. Two

600-shp Avco Lycoming LTS 101 engines, very neatly installed, drive a 39-ft rotor with extremely broad-chord blades held in a 'dry' (no oil needed) hub with elastomeric bearings, which in turn is nodalized and shock-insulated from the fuselage. Like other new US helicopters the 222 has a biplane tail with horizontal surfaces above and below the traditional-type rotor. Seating from six to ten, it will be marketed with fully retractable landing gear plus emergency flotation equipment, and cruises at over 150 mph for up to 425 miles. Before completing the engineering design Bell talked to many potential customers, as a result of which several changes were made, including enlarging the cabin to allow more passengers to be carried

Bell Model 206 JetRanger
Originally designated the OH-4A, in which form it lost a US Army competition for a scout helicopter, the Model 206 has achieved great success in the civil field. It has also been supplied to many armed forces, as the OH-58A Kiowa (US Army) ironically, bought in greater numbers than the machine which won over the OH-4A, TH-57A SeaRanger (US Navy) and AB.206 (built under licence by Agusta in Italy). The Commonwealth Aircraft Corporation in Australia has also assembled the OH-58A for the Australian Army
Engine: 400 shp Allison 250-C20 turboshaft *Max speed:* 142 mph *Weight fully loaded:* 3200 lb *Range:* 435 miles *Number of seats:* 5

Bell 222
A new design of light executive helicopter, the Model 222 first flew in August 1976. Twin engines allow overwater flights to be made safely, and emergency flotation equipment is provided. The landing gear retracts fully to reduce drag
Engines: 2×650 shp Avco Lycoming LTS 101 turboshafts *Max speed:* 175 mph *Weight fully loaded:* 6700 lb *Range:* 425 miles *Number of seats:* 10

in the high-density configuration, and increasing the size of the lower flight-deck windows to facilitate roof-top landings.

The principal rivals of the 222 – which seems highly likely to be a smashing sales success – are European. For them life is much harder, because there are more builders chasing a much smaller home market. The three chief civil contenders are the Aérospatiale Gazelle/Dauphin, MBB BO 105, Agusta A.109 and Westland 606. As in the United States the proportion of helicopters built in Europe for military customers has dropped from a level close to 95% to a fairly steady level below 50%, and the indications are that it will fall further.

Certainly the military market has served a vital role in funding the creation of helicopters that would otherwise have been impossible, especially in Europe. But, while the Puma, Gazelle and 606 (Lynx) are military-funded programmes now finding substantial civil markets, the Dauphin, 105 and A.109 have all been developed mainly as civil machines. The fact that, at a late stage in each project when production was already in hand, military customers began to come forward merely shows the revolution that has taken place. Of course, the qualities that appeal to the civil market also make for a good military machine, notably twin-engine safety, full IFR capability, low noise and vibration, high speed and (except for a gunship) a large cabin. Sometimes military requirements cause problems, needing time and expense to solve, that would be absent with a civil machine; for example, Aérospatiale battled against severe dynamic resonance and vibration with the Gazelle due entirely to the carriage of loaded weapon pylons. On the other hand it was the need for high speed, especially with civil Gazelles, that led to protracted flight development with its rigid rotor. These European machines have been discussed in the preceding chapter.

Apart from light Bells and Hillers, the first civil helicopters were 'airliners' based on the largest and most powerful military helicopters then developed. For various reasons this is no longer the case, and there

Kamov Ka-26
With contra-rotating rotors and a twin-boom tailplane, the utility version of the Ka-26 has a removable freight hold. Other uses include geological survey and crop dusting.
Engines: 2×325-hp Vedeneev M-14V-26 radial piston engines *Max speed:* 106 mph *Weight fully loaded:* 7165 lb

Kamov Ka-26 in flight with the removable freight hold in place. Piston-engined helicopters still have a role in the medium weight class

Enstrom 280C Shark
Highly competitive US helicopter aimed at the executive transport market
Engine: 205 shp Lycoming H10-360-E1AD
Max speed: 117 mph *Weight fully loaded:* 2200 lb

has never even been a civil version of the CH-47 Chinook or CH-53 Sea Stallion, the most capable helicopters in the West. There have been many projects, and at the time of writing (1976) Sikorsky is still interested in selling the proposed S-65C inter-city airliner, seating up to 44 passengers and with a cruising speed of 184 mph, but there are many problems and no go-ahead seems imminent. The market for big civil helicopters is limited; there are few airline routes where they can earn their keep, and they seldom appeal to the really big markets among the oil companies and industrial corporations who invariably need not more than ten seats. The 30-seat S-61N has been sold in numbers to support oil rigs, but a better size for this work is the Puma with seating for around 17.

Of course Sikorsky, and several commercial operators, have never ceased to study the prospects for large airline helicopters. The first civil S-65 brochure dates from the year of first flight (1964), and by 1966 several airlines were studying its use in detail. One was BEA (now British Airways European Division), which planned an S-65 network linking London, Brussels, Amsterdam and Paris, and serving the Channel Islands (direct from central London to the island harbours, rather than the fogbound airfields on the hills) and Scottish Highlands and island routes. In 1970 a US Marine Corps CH-53D flew a demonstration 'airline' sector between London (Battersea) and Paris in 82 minutes, as a result of which it was concluded there were no problems on the score of noise or other pollution. Admittedly the direct operating cost of all helicopters is still substantially higher than that of comparable fixed-wing machines (for example, Sikorsky reckon a civil S-65 would have an operating cost of about 7 cents per seat-mile, compared with around 2 cents for a typical twin-jet), but the helicopter is judged much less likely to suffer delays, which exert a large adverse effect on the costs of fixed-wing machines (so much so that a DC-9 or 737 with a departure delay of 45 minutes comes out more expensive than the S-65 for all sectors shorter than 130 miles). Sikorsky were enthusiastic in the 1960–73 period at the prospect of halving direct operating costs by fitting wings, to produce a compound helicopter strongly resembling the Rotodyne of the late 1950s.

Why, then, has the airline helicopter not yet come to pass? One reason is the poor economic climate of the mid-1970s, and another the soaring price of petroleum-based fuels. A further factor is the poor traffic-growth of most of the airlines that might buy a big helicopter, and another the restriction on capital works such as city-centre heliports. The ride comfort and general public acceptability of the big passenger helicopter are not in question, but its overall economics still are; though several buh ish experts have predicted profitable operation at existing airline first-class fares, this remains a large question mark. One area where solutions already exist to potential problems is the vital one of en route navigation and bad-weather approach and landing guidance; thanks to British companies the Decca sea-level area-navigation system and MEL Madge microwave landing system are exactly tailored to all-weather helicopter services. It is likely that by the early 1980s the large passenger helicopter may begin to fulfil the promise it has appeared to offer ever since the first airline helicopter services of 30 years earlier.

In 1976 the biggest civil helicopters in prospect were the modest commercial offshoots of the US Army UTTAS (Utility Tactical Transport Aircraft System) competition, which in August 1972 picked two rivals, Boeing Vertol to build the YUH-61A and Sikorsky the YUH-60A. Both are attractive machines powered by two 1536-hp General Electric T700 engines driving advanced rotors with a hingeless hub on the Boeing and elastomeric bearings on the Sikorsky. Whichever one is picked by the Army, the rival is sure to go ahead as a civil machine. Boeing Vertol's Model 179 has the advantage of a prior firm order: in early 1975 Petroleum Helicopters ordered 28, for delivery from 1978. The Model 179 is a 14/20-seater, capable of crusing at 184 mph and claimed to set new low standards of operating cost, noise and vibration. The Sikorsky S-78-20 is similar in capability, but appears to be slightly later in timing. Sikorsky is hedging its bets with a more radically changed S-78-29 with a much larger fuselage seating up to 29, with fuel sponsons and retractable tricycle landing gear instead of a fixed tailwheel type. Sikorsky is also trying to retain its slim foothold in the corporate and executive market gained by the re-

Wallis WA-116 Autogyro
Fast, quiet and reliable, this series of light autogyros has proved its versatility in a variety of specialized roles and with a series of different engines
Engine: Any of several air-cooled piston engines in the 72-hp class *Max speed:* 130 mph *Weight fully loaded:* 550 lb *Range:* 140 miles

engined S-58T with an 8/12-passenger machine designated S-76. Scheduled to fly in mid-1976, but running somewhat late, the S-76 is closely similar to the British Westland 606 in size and weight, and is thus appreciably heavier than the rival Bell 222. Powered by two 650-shp Allison 250-C30 engines, it is a shapely machine with four swept-tip rotor blades of titanium/glass-fibre construction held in elastomeric bearings, a retractable tricycle landing gear, and lavish furnishing and all-weather avionics. Okanagan Helicopters of Canada was the first customer, ordering 10 for 1978.

With this profusion of luxurious but costly turbine-engined machines becoming available, one must not overlook the fact that most civil helicopters in the past (but perhaps not the future) have been small piston-engined machines. Typical of the modern offering are the Enstrom F-28A, of which 500 have been sold, and the rakish Shark, which are three-seaters in the $58,000 class with skid or inflatable-pontoon landing gear and adequate avionics and furnishings. Other modern piston-engined machines include the mass-produced Hughes 300 and more capable 300C, the Italian Silvercraft SH-4 and the evergreen Bell 47 series still available in several forms from Agusta in Italy. Unfortunately the very long and promising development of the Cierva Twin in Britain, a highly refined design with co-axial rotors driven by twin engines, has been dogged by the near-absence of venture capital in Britain under present circumstances, though the prototype flew in August 1969 and, in the words of its sponsors, 'had no competitor in the world at its price level'.

Smallest rotary-winged aircraft available in large numbers are small autogyros, in which the engine drives a pusher propeller and the rotor autorotates, being driven by the slipstream which (unlike a helicopter) passes through the rotor disc in an oblique upwards direction. By far the leading company in this very large field is Bensen Aircraft, of North Carolina, which has developed a wide range of Gyro-Copters, Gyro-Gliders, Hydro-Copters and related machines, and sold them as ready-to-fly, as kits or as plans for homebuilders. There are many similar machines around the world, but special mention must be made of Wallis Autogyros of Britain, which owes nothing to the Bensen but is a completely original and highly refined development organization which has concentrated not on selling products but on producing small rotorcraft that are ever faster, smoother, safer and more versatile. Many variants have set entirely new standards of stability, control and safety, world records for speed and altitude and have also achieved the amazing feat of flying at a loaded weight of 3·14 times the empty weight.

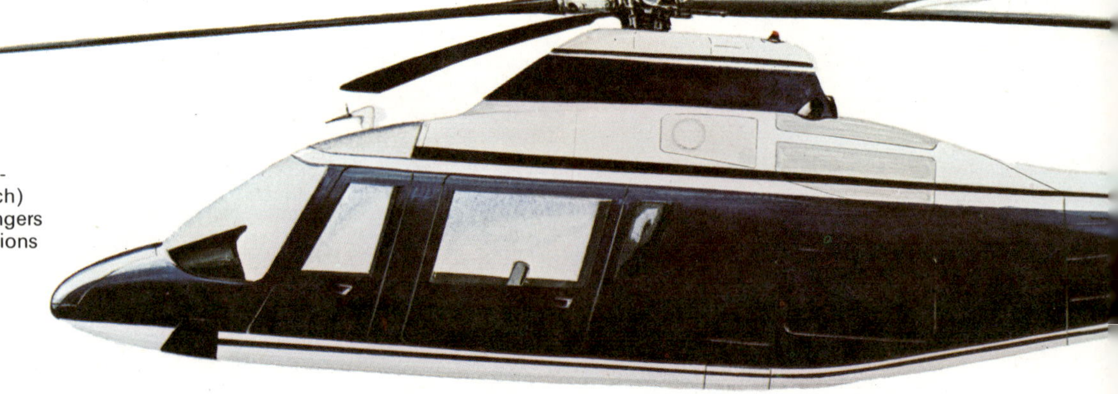

Agusta A.109
One of the prettiest of helicopters, this twin-turbine (Allison C20Bs rated at 420 shp each) machine seats a crew of two and six passengers and cruises at 171 mph. Missile-armed versions have been evaluated

Blueprints for Peace and War

THE FUTURE

Writing about the future of the helicopter is tricky. Anyone who did so in 1944 would have predicted that by the early 1950s they would be almost as common – not only at airfields but in suburbia – as private cars. A forecaster in 1952 would have predicted imminent growth of helicopter scheduled services radiating from every major city, and monster transport helicopters with 200-ft rotors driven by tip jets. During the late 1950s it seemed that nothing could equal the sheer capability and efficiency of the compound helicopter (a combined fixed-wing airliner with helicopter rotor for VTOL), best exemplified by the Rotodyne. During the mid-1960s the large helicopter airliner was again strongly to the fore, but it seemed likely that it would be pipped at the post by the fan-lift V/STOL jetliner (a modern counterpart of the compound helicopter but with a Mach 0·9 airframe and multiple lift fans instead of a rotor) as exemplified by the Hawker Siddeley 141. A little later the sky threatened to shudder with the pounding of vast Mi-12s and Boeing HLH (Heavy-Lift Helicopters) with conventional rotors absorbing tens of thousands of horsepower.

All these things seemed not only certainties but perfectly natural developments. They were much more predictable than the Cobra-type gunship that matches the rotor with the body of a new kind of attack fighter. Yet, while gunships have poured off the production line by the thousand, not one of the other visions has come to pass. Today it is as unwise to predict dramatic growth of airline helicopters as it is to predict V/STOL jetliners. But steady continued growth of the market for both military and civil turbine-engined helicopters is a safe prediction, despite the formidable costs of owning and operating such machines. Year by year such helicopters will become more attractive, partly through general development of helicopter aerodynamics, structures and systems, allied with the essential improvement in worldwide helicopter navigation and blind-landing facilities, and partly through increasing concentration upon features aimed at reducing cost.

In the past the aerospace industry has been more prone to raise costs, by 'improved' technology, than to reduce them by simplification. Today the lesson has been learned. A wonderful start has been made with rotor hubs, which instead of having as many as 680 parts (as was common 20 years ago) may have as few as 18. Not only does the modern rotor have a totally different blade and hub structure but it has improved aerodynamics, better dynamic properties and much longer fatigue-free life without attention. Other cost-cutting philosophy – often seemingly the reverse of traditional aerospace 'progress' – is seen in the increasingly general adoption of standard automotive (car or truck) equipment for civil and even some military helicopters. Typical items include alternators or generators, hydraulic pumps, instruments, radiators and heat exchangers, and a wide range of furnishing accessories. Far from being cheap and nasty, such hardware is often extremely efficient; for example the cheap Citroen radiator now fitted to the AS.350 Squirrel outperforms the specially designed unit originally fitted to the prototype.

Boeing Vertol XCH-62A
The proposed HLH (Heavy-Lift Helicopter) for the US Army was cancelled in July 1975 when the prototype was almost complete. Powered by three 8079 shp Allison T701 turboshafts it would have given the West a much needed VTOL airlift capability

But is the future to hold no more than cost-cutting simplification and retrenchment? What about all the bold technical advances of yesterday, such as the tilting rotor, the circulation-controlled rotor and the folding rotor? Shall the world not see any of the promised rotor-equipped supersonic or other high-speed winged machines? In the short term the answer is negative. In the long term fundamental advances are as predictable as tomorrow's sunrise, but probably none of those listed.

Tilting rotors are almost as old as helicopters. The Baynes Heliplane was a pre-1939 scheme for a high-speed aircraft with two rotors which swivelled through 90° to give lift or thrust. Today, several tilt-rotor research machines are flying, notably the

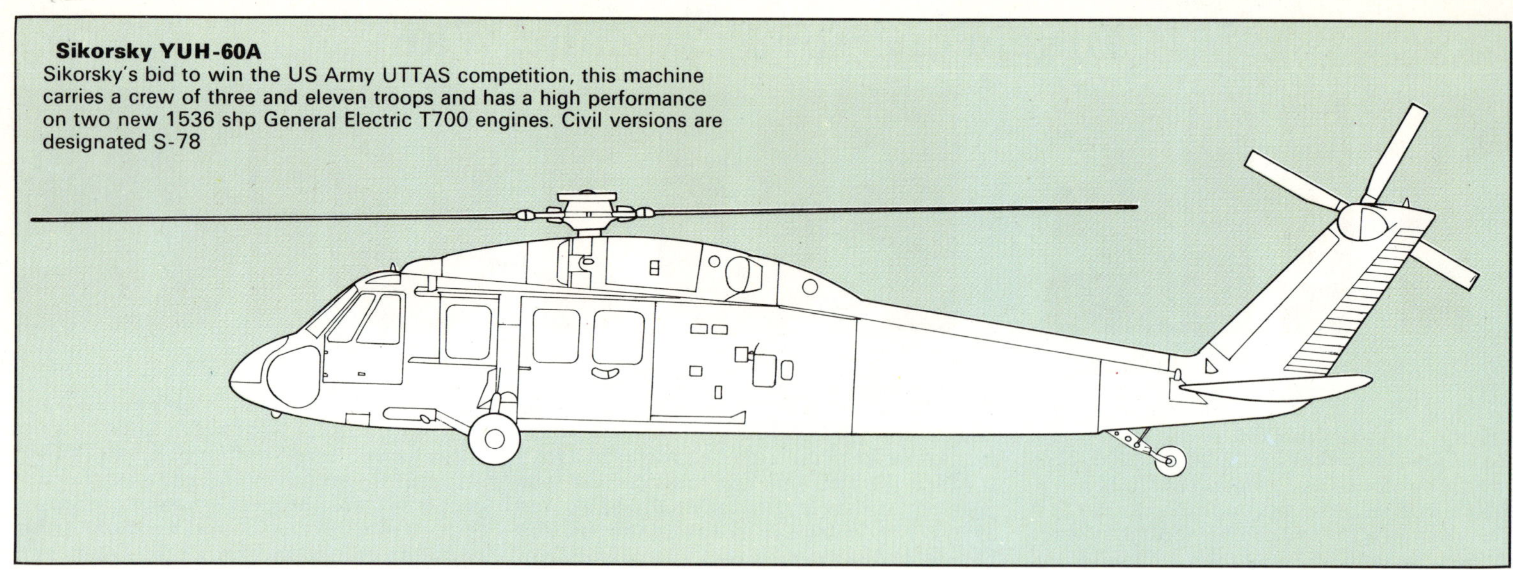

Sikorsky YUH-60A
Sikorsky's bid to win the US Army UTTAS competition, this machine carries a crew of three and eleven troops and has a high performance on two new 1536 shp General Electric T700 engines. Civil versions are designated S-78

Bell Model 301 built for NASA and the US Army as the XV-15. Previously Bell Helicopter Company had built the XV-3 for the Army, with a fuselage engine driving shafting along the wings to rotors swivelling on the tips. Today's XV-15 has two engine/rotor pods which swivel on the tips of the fixed wing. If a use were found for an XV-15, which can reach 415 mph and cruise at 348 mph, it would be as a 12-seater in civil guise or to carry 15 troops – or, possibly, the equivalent weight in weapons. An earlier tilt-rotor machine, the Canadair CL-84 now no longer flying, had its engine/rotor nacelles mounted on a pivoted wing, as did several prototypes of the 1950s. Yet another tilting machine was the grotesque Bell Aerospace (not Bell Helicopter) X-22A, with four engines on a small rear-mounted wing driving four rotors in tilting annular ducts; the surviving example of this nine-ton, 300-mph aircraft has also completed its flight programme.

The circulation-controlled rotor was a natural extrapolation of the circulation-controlled wing. By blowing compressed air through narrow spanwise slits it is possible not only to generate fantastic lift from a small wing but also to use structurally efficient section profiles of flattened oval form. The UK National Gas Turbine Establishment proved the soundness of the concept as applied to a helicopter rotor, but no funds were forthcoming to put it to use. Such a rotor would have been especially suitable for use in a folding-rotor scheme. It will be appreciated that a helicopter rotor is the quietest and most efficient VTOL device, but merely a nuisance in cruising flight in which a wing is far preferable. Many schemes have been tried for devising a winged helicopter whose rotor can be stopped, once a sufficient forward speed has been gained, and folded away inside a high-speed airframe. Around 1959 Sikorsky investigated several schemes, one of them getting as far as having a type number, the S-67 jet fighter with folding rotor. Ten years later the company, with others, was still unable to abandon this tantalizing concept, one scheme having twin folding rotors near the tips of the fixed wing. In parallel with these schemes, Sikorsky has studied a very attractive rotor which folds to 60% of its VTOL span for high-speed flight without suffering excessive rotor-tip Mach numbers.

During the late 1960s Sikorsky, which leads all other world organizations in depth of fundamental helicopter research, studied the advancing-blade concept (ABC) in which two rigid rotors are used co-axially. A way had been found to overcome the basic barriers of the conventional rotor to higher speed: stalling of the retreating blade, which might be moving backwards at a speed hardly any greater than the speed of a fast helicopter through the air, plus compressibility shock-stall at near the speed of sound of the advancing blade (when the two speeds, instead of being subtracted, are added). The key with the ABC rotor is to make extremely slim but stiff blades, to

Boeing Vertol YUH-61A
Rival to the Sikorsky YUH-60A in the UTTAS competition, the YUH-61A has the same engines but a different landing gear and smaller main rotor with hingeless hub and composite blades. A 14–20 passenger civil version is designated Model 179

Howard Levy

On the flight-line at Sikorsky's plant at Stratford are the first S-72 Rotor Systems Research Aircraft and behind the prototype YCH-53E, a greatly up-rated version of the CH-53 Sea Stallion, providing the USMC with an interim big lift helicopter with the cancellation of the HLH programme

achieve high Mach numbers yet avoid up/down flapping (which in the old-fashioned articulated rotor is deliberately allowed). Obviously, close-spaced co-axial rotors have to be stiff to avoid hitting each other, and with the high-speed ABC rotor an extremely advanced structure is used, including not only a great deal of titanium but also, eventually, extensive use of graphite fibre composites to achieve the necessary rigidity. After successful wind-tunnel tests the S-69 was funded by the US Army in 1972. Two have been built, and all the problems seem to have solutions. In particular the S-69s were extremely quiet and smooth in violent manoeuvres. But the US Army no longer wants high speed, and unless Sikorsky can get funds from elsewhere the 350-mph high-speed test programme will be abandoned. This shows how tight the economic situation is today, because here is a certain route to adding about 100 mph to helicopter speeds.

Though it is a more general research tool, Sikorsky has another pointer to the future in the S-72 RSRA (Rotor Systems Research Aircraft) of which two were funded by NASA and the US Army in 1973. These are basically S-61/Blackhawk dynamic systems with special instrument-packed fuselages

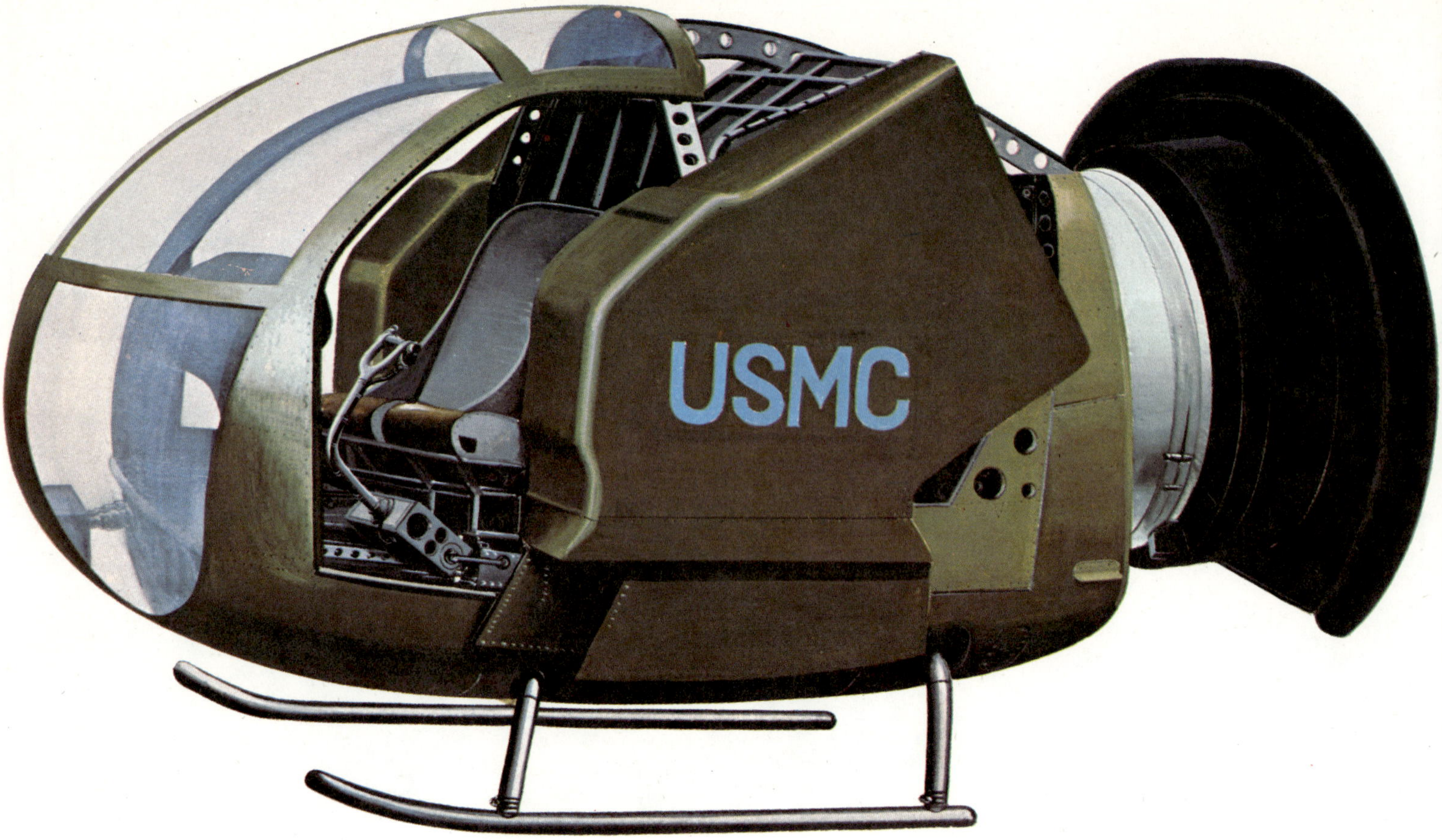

Garrett Stamp
The Small Tactical Aerial Mobility Platform (STAMP) was built for the US Marine Corps to demonstrate the feasibility of a two-man flying Jeep. It used the forward fuselage of a Hughes OH-6A with the rotor system, engine and tailboom removed and a turboshaft engine substituted. The powerplant drives a ducted fan to provide lift and horizontal propulsion

Engine: 475 shp Garrett TSE 231 turboshaft *Max speed:* 75 mph *Weight fully loaded:* 1000 lb *Range:* 30 miles *Number of seats:* 2

with retractable (F-5E) landing gears, and the second S-72 has a 41 ft 10 in wing and attachments for two 9275 lb-thrust GE TF34-400A turbofans for flight at 345 mph. A variety of rotor systems can be tested, and a computer-controlled fly-by-wire flight-control system is fitted. In an emergency the winged machine can fly with its rotor jettisoned. These machines are expected to have a 12-year life, and to explore advanced rotor and blade systems that could not safely be investigated in any other way.

Before rounding off the story with a broad overview of the future it is necessary briefly to look at some of the more unlikely or unconventional VTOL devices that have been proposed or flown. The simplest and yet least versatile is perhaps the Bell Aerosystems Jet Belt, the rocket-elevated strap-on system which enables a man to soar over hangars, trees, rivers and other obstacles. Of all man's dynamic-reaction lift systems the rocket is the least efficient. Bell later produced a gas-turbine Jet Belt, with flight duration lengthened from about two minutes to fifteen, but not even the US military establishment has found a use for it. Jet VTOL is outside the scope of this review, but one may cast a glance at such oddballs as the Nord 500 single-seater with two ducted fans, the WASP (Williams Aerial Systems Platform) and STAMP (Small Tactical Aerial Mobility Platform) with small gas turbines lifting two US Marines and capable of up to 60 mph for 30 minutes. Such things are not yet commercially attractive, but the simple autogyro is the subject of enthusiastic amateur construction all over the world, and in a few places (most have given up, but AISA of Spain continues) there are multi-seat factory-built prototypes.

In general the story of the helicopter reinforces the belief that commercial success follows the engineering refinement of traditional designs, just as it has in the motor car. Dozens of interesting and often exciting radical concepts have been built and flown, often for no better reason than that they had become technically possible, but nearly all have fallen by the wayside. The twin revolutions however in rotor-hubs and turbine power have made possible bold new concepts within the traditional helicopter framework. It is along these lines, with new battlefield and civil roles becoming possible, that helicopter development appears to be travelling.

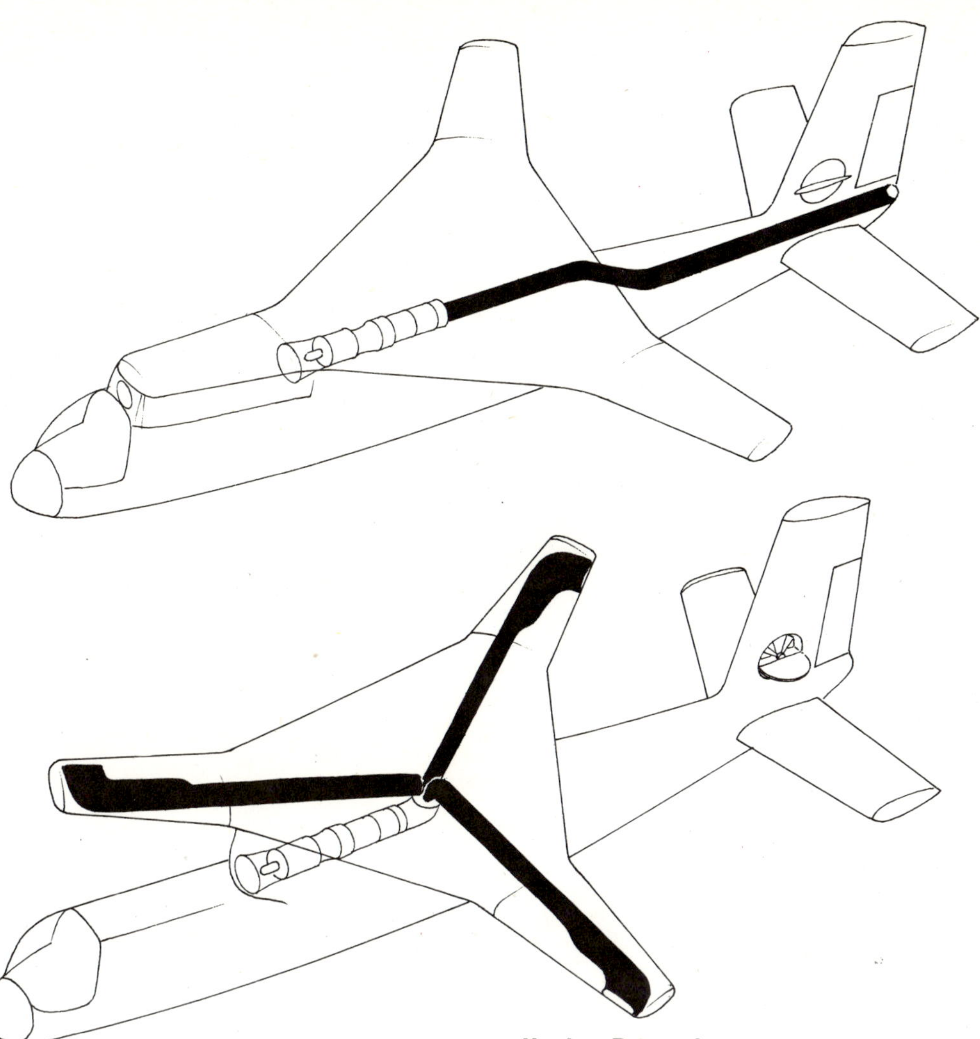

Hughes Rotorwing
One of a wealth of stopped rotor designs (none of which have yet flown), this proposal specified a three-blade rotor with broad blades driven by tip-jets fed from a fuselage compressor.

Piasecki VZ-8P Airgeep
One in a long line of VTOL battlefield mobility experimental flying platforms for the US Army, the Airgeep first flew in 1962. The concept is still under development today with such vehicles as the STAMP and WASP
Engines: 2×530 shp Turboméca Artouste 11C turboshafts *Weight fully loaded:* 4800 lb

Sikorsky S-69 undergoing flight trials, prototype for evaluation of the Advancing Blade Concept

Sikorsky

1
STATES ARMY